The Secret Life of
WILKIE COLLINS

To Faith, the surviving 'Dawson',
and
in memory of Lionel Dawson
and Bobbie West (née Dawson).

The Secret Life of
WILKIE COLLINS

William M. Clarke

ALAN SUTTON PUBLISHING LIMITED

First published in hardback in 1988 by Allison & Busby

Published in paperback in 1989 by W.H. Allen & Co. Plc

First published in paperback in this revised edition in 1996
Alan Sutton Publishing Limited
Phoenix Mill · Far Thrupp · Stroud · Gloucestershire

British Library Cataloguing-in-Publication data

A catalogue record for this book is available from the British
Library

ISBN 0-7509-1208-1

Printed in Great Britain by
The Guernsey Press Company Limited
Guernsey
Channel Islands.

CONTENTS

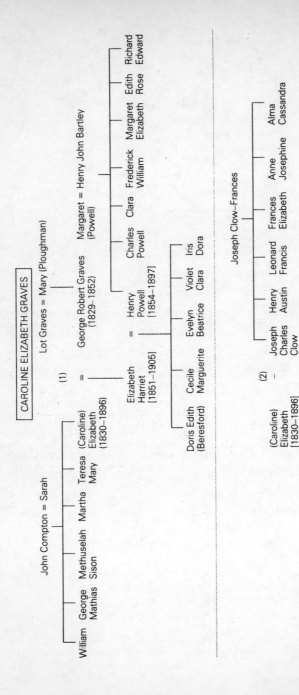

CAROLINE ELIZABETH GRAVES

Lot Graves = Mary (Ploughman)

John Compton = Sarah

William | George Mathias | Methuselah Sison | Martha | Teresa Mary | (Caroline) Elizabeth (1830–1896)

George Robert Graves (1829–1852)

Margaret = Henry John Bartley (Powell)

Charles Powell | Clara | Frederick William | Margaret Elizabeth | Edith Rose | Richard Edward

(1)

=

Elizabeth Harriet [1851–1905]

=

Henry Powell [1854–1897]

Doris Edith (Beresford) | Cecile Marguerite | Evelyn Beatrice | Violet Clara | Iris Dora

(2)

(Caroline) Elizabeth [1830–1896]

–

Joseph Clow–Frances

Joseph Charles Clow | Henry Austin | Leonard Francis | Frances Elizabeth | Anne Josephine | Alma Cassandra

Note: (1) Caroline's first marriage (March 30, 1850)
(2) Caroline's second marriage (October 29, 1868)

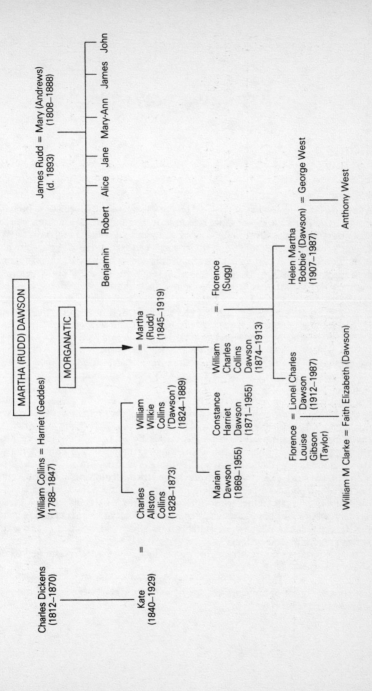

ACKNOWLEDGEMENTS

A large part of this book has been based on the willingness of a dozen or so individuals to cooperate in recalling memories and in providing factual information. The prime supporters were naturally the late 'Bobbie' (Dawson) West and Lionel Dawson, Wilkie Collins's two grandchildren. They understood, better than most, the sensitivities of their two aunts (Wilkie's two daughters), yet they never hesitated in their support and enthusiasm for the project. They saw and approved the early drafts before their untimely deaths last year. It is a personal sadness that they did not live to see the completed work.

Beyond Wilkie's immediate family, I have relied extensively on the descendants of Martha Rudd, Caroline Graves and Henry Bartley (Collins's solicitor), especially Edie Upton in Eastbourne, Rody and Ronald Iredale in Mitcham, Laura and the late Geoffrey Gregson in Maidenhead and Walter Rudd in Winterton. Others deserving my special thanks (mentioned in more detail in the Preface) include Donald Whitton in San Francisco, Bridget Lakin and Emma Hicks in London and Pamela Holding in Naples.

It is perhaps a commentary on the shift in post-war literary archives that while the British Museum has no more than a handful of Collins's letters, easily surpassed in quantity in this country by the Mitchell Library in Glasgow, both are overwhelmed by the hundreds in the possession of the University of Texas, the Pierpont Morgan Library, New York, Princeton University Library, the New York Public Library, the Huntington Library, California, as well as those in libraries in Yale, Harvard, Boston, Stanford, Los Angeles etc. I have acknowledged them all individually in the Appendix but I received particular personal help from the archivists at the University of Texas, the Pierpont Morgan Library, New York and the New York Public Library. I received similar help from the librarian of the Victoria and Albert Museum in London concerning Harriet Collins's diary, short extracts from which are included in the text, and which I gratefully acknowledge.

The numerous drafts were cheerfully typed by Gaye Murdoch, Jasmine Boxall and Sheila Tunnacliffe.

Finally, my wife Faith, Collins's great-granddaughter, not only initiated the quest, but bore the brunt of the research, the travelling and the re-writing. Without her it would not have been written.

INTRODUCTION
TO 1996 EDITION

Interest in Wilkie Collins has been growing since the twenties, when T. S. Eliot took it on himself to heap praise on *The Moonstone* ('the first, the longest and the best of modern English detective novels') and to analyse seriously Collins' contribution to nineteenth-century literature. Since then the tide has continued to move his way, borne up by the obvious attractions of stories well told and plotted, a more serious recognition of his powers of characterisation and an increasing awareness of the deep literary allusions in all his works.

Collins himself never made any pretence of his intentions. The story line – the stronger the better – should be kept to the forefront, he felt, the writer well in the rear. When faced with the accusation that his novels were read 'in every back-kitchen of England', he took it as a compliment and showed no sign of irritation. He was, he said, a simple story teller, his models Walter Scott, Charles Dickens, Alexander Dumas, Honore de Balzac and Fenimore Cooper.

In over forty years of active writing, he managed to complete more than thirty novels and collections of short stories as well as a memoir of his father and a travel book on Cornwall. His last novel, *Blind Love*, already being serialised in the *Illustrated London News* during his final illness, had to be completed for him. His close friend, Walter Besant, found the task easier than expected. Collins' plot, including detailed dialogue at crucial turning points, was already sketched out in full detail. To the end, he instinctively knew what would entice the reader.

Most of Collins' novels are being printed and read to this day, over a century after his death. Thanks to the efforts of Alan Sutton Publishing in this country and the Dover Press in the United States, there are now as many of his novels in print as at any time since the turn of the century. At least eight different editions of *The Woman in White* are available in London. Nor has the stage or television ignored him. In the past decade both *The Haunted Hotel* and *The Frozen*

Deep have joined productions of *The Moonstone* and *The Woman in White* on the London and provincial stage. Foreign interest too has not been far behind over the years, with two American film productions of *The Woman in White*, *The Moonstone* and *Armadale* and a recent half million edition of *The Woman in White* in Moscow.

As for North America, it would not be an exaggeration to say that interest in Collins there has on occasions surpassed that in this country. When the time came for a celebration of the centenary of Collins' death in the autumn of 1989, it was thought just as fitting for scores of enthusiasts and literary experts from Europe and North America to gather on Vancouver Island, as to attend a centenary dinner at the Reform Club in London, a spot he and Dickens often frequented. The Wilkie Collins Society, which publishes regular newsletters and an annual journal, first took root simultaneously in London and California – a place Collins often planned to visit and which is now home to at least one of his family's descendants.

It is a moot point whether North American academic interest in Collins has arisen from the acquisition of hundreds of Collins' letters by American universities and institutions or whether the acquisitions were prompted by growing academic interest. Whatever the reason, it is a fact that while the British Museum has only a handful of Collins' letters, the University of Texas now has some hundreds. It is also significant that Collins' first rejected novel, *Iolani*, which was thought to be lost for ever, is about to be published not in the country of his birth but in the United States. The story of its rediscovery in New York, some 150 years after it was written, is told for the first time in this revised edition.

In revising this edition of *The Secret Life of Wilkie Collins* I must particularly acknowledge the help I have gained from Catherine Peters' *The King of Inventors: A Life of Wilkie Collins*, published in 1991 and from *Wilkie Collins to the Forefront*, edited by Nelson Smith and R. C. Terry, and published in 1995. Both in their different ways reflect the depth and wealth of interest still being shown in one of the nineteenth-century's most prolific writers. The Collins revival will shortly get added support from two other projects. One is the planned production of an illustrated guide and handbook on Collins, combining over 200 photographs with cross-referenced details of Collins life and work, friends, relatives etc. The other is the publication for the first time of his letters, often planned but never published. Both are now scheduled for 1997–8.

WMC
1996

PREFACE

WILKIE COLLINS, the author of *The Woman in White* and *The Moonstone*, has been hailed as 'the father of the detective story'[1] and 'the novelist who invented sensation'. His own life story and its aftermath have a similar mysterious ring about them.

Until forty years ago, there was no Collins biography worth reading, The *Dictionary of National Biography* hinted at 'intimacies' in his life and left it, tantalisingly, at that. His sister-in-law, Charles Dickens's daughter Kate, was the first to speak openly of one of his mistresses, Caroline. A national effort to finance a memorial to him in Westminster Abbey, supported by his literary friends, was quietly dropped after a *Daily Telegraph* leader, as well as the Dean of St Paul's, had hinted at its unsuitability, whatever his literary merits. Collins's own will had probably set the seal on public disapproval, since he divided his estate equally between two mistresses, Caroline Graves and Martha Rudd, and openly acknowledged Martha's three children as his own. Even after his death, the oddities continued, for after Caroline had been buried in the same grave at Kensal Green cemetery, Martha continued to tend it until she left London. It remains in her name even now.

Since then the literary world has done its best to unravel the mystery of Wilkie Collins's private life. An American professor, Clyde K. Hyder, diligently uncovered a few details of Caroline Graves in the years before the Second World War, from the records of Somerset House and from individual London street directories. Kenneth Robinson, in what is probably still the best and fullest biography, added further details in 1951, but finally concluded that the steps Wilkie Collins took 'suggested that he wished the story of his life to remain something of a mystery to all but his closest friends'. And, apart from the indiscretions of Kate Dickens, they never divulged what they knew. To make things more difficult, both of his acknowledged mistresses, and their children, apparently vanished from the London scene. Caroline died in 1895, six years after Wilkie himself, leaving a daughter from an earlier marriage, Elizabeth Harriet, who had married Wilkie's solicitor. Martha Rudd and her three children, Marian, Harriet Constance and William Charles, in the words of Kenneth Robinson, 'soon lost themselves among London's nameless millions'. Professor Robert Ashley, of Ripon College, Wisconsin, hazarded that they might have 'emigrated near the turn of the century'.

Dorothy Sayers also tried her hand at the mystery but, in a posthumously published fragment of her biography now in the hands of the Humanities Research Center, Texas, virtually admitted defeat because of 'the extreme obscurity which surrounds the whole of Collins's private life'[2]. Even as late as 1982 Sue Lonoff, in her excellent literary criticism of Collins's works, *Wilkie Collins and his Victorian Readers*[3], frankly admitted: 'We know little about his relations with the two most important women in his life, Caroline Graves and Martha Rudd,' and went on: 'We do not know what became of his illegitimate children'.

Kenneth Robinson had found out rather more about Wilkie Collins's descendants by the time his biography was revised in 1974, having detected both grandchildren and great-grandchildren (of Wilkie and Martha) living not far from London, but he admitted he did not know exactly where they were[4]. As Sir Charles Snow put it at the time, 'Apparently, they don't wish to be recognised. If I were they I should be proud of such an ancestor, one of the oddest, most gifted and by all accounts most likeable figures of the Victorian Age'[5].

The time had clearly come, therefore, for the offspring of Wilkie's morganatic marriage to rise to such an encouraging bait and to try and fill in some of the gaps. They have at last agreed to do so. This small contribution to the Wilkie Collins saga, therefore, is in part based on the recollections and rather sparse ephemera handed down by his children, grandchildren and great-grandchildren. Two of Wilkie's grandchildren, Lionel Charles Dawson and Helen Martha ('Bobbie') West, were living in Amersham and Harpenden until their deaths last year and they and a great-grandson, Anthony West, have provided me with memories, photographs and lots of their time. The other great-grandchild, Faith Elizabeth (Dawson), my wife, has been a major contributor to the present effort to unravel Wilkie Collins's last, and perhaps best, mystery.

I have gleaned additional clues to his expenditure on Caroline and Martha, and many other details, from his private banking accounts which Coutts & Co. as his bankers, and my wife as a direct descendant, have permitted me to examine in some detail.

I have also leaned heavily in one of the early chapters on a daily diary for the years 1835, 1836 and 1837, written by Wilkie's mother, Harriet, during the family's visit to France and Italy and their stay in Bayswater. I found it in the Victoria and Albert Museum, where it was hardly 'lost', but had been strangely ignored by most previous biographers[6]. It provided the essential clues to the discovery of Wilkie Collins's first headmaster and the address of his first private school. It also enabled me to reconstruct the family's visits to Paris, Nice, Rome, Naples and Sorrento and contains a detailed outline of William Collins's illness in Sorrento, their meeting with Wordsworth in Rome, and even an account of how Charley, Wilkie's brother, broke his arm in a childhood scuffle at the Villa Reale in Naples.

The starting point for these literary inquiries was Martha Rudd's birth certificate, which (along with other bric-a-brac, including a Victorian nursing chair, a davenport, a gold locket commemorating Wilkie's mother's death, and a bill for furniture acquired by Wilkie for Martha, in the name of William Dawson, in the early 1870s) had been handed down to her grandchildren, Lionel Dawson and Bobbie West. It established her age, the names of her parents and, above all, her birthplace, Winterton. It soon led to a visit to Winterton on the Norfolk coast, among the sand dunes and close to the Broads.

The question at the back of my mind was whether any Rudds had survived and would have sufficient memories to fill in Martha's background. The local telephone book quickly proved fruitless – not a Rudd in sight. But the local pub, The Fisherman's Return, and the churchyard provided Rudds living and dead. The landlord pointed the way to Walter Rudd, living in a house beside the church, a former skipper in the Great Yarmouth herring fleet, then in his seventies. He had not heard of Martha but quickly confirmed that her parents, James and Mary Rudd, were his great grandparents, that James had been a shepherd, not a fisherman, and that their grave was literally next door in the churchyard. So were those of Martha's sisters and brothers and other relations. It was the church that Collins's Pre-Raphaelite friends had known well, and not far away, across the fields, was Horsey Mere, the basis for Hurle Mere in *Armadale*. The church records filled in other gaps.

Caroline, Wilkie's other mistress, was at the outset more elusive. Earlier biographies had not fully established who she was, where she came from nor whether she had been married before. But with the help of an expert and enthusiastic genealogist, Bridget Lakin, St Catherine's House soon began to reveal its secrets. Caroline, it became clear, had been married and widowed by an early age and came from the west country. Once again, the wills, birth, marriage and death certificates at St Catherine's House provided the first clues: it was soon established that Caroline's daughter Harriet had had daughters and they in turn had had children. But were they alive and, if so, where were they living? Help was needed from a central source and it came, in an appropriately discreet way, from the Department of Health and Social Security in Newcastle who, having checked on their computer that two descendants of Caroline were still alive, passed on letters seeking further information. Weeks passed and then helpful responses were received from Richmond and Mitcham. And, finally, from a bottom drawer in Mitcham emerged photographs of Wilkie Collins, and even Caroline, and much more.

The jigsaw was beginning to come together. And in the same way, again by courtesy of the Department of Health and Social Security, a lively eighty-year-old niece of Wilkie Collins's solicitor (who had married Caroline's daughter, Harriet) was eventually discovered in Eastbourne. Her mother had often discussed Wilkie and Caroline and she knew what had happened to her Uncle Henry, the solicitor.

All these descendants have given me a great deal of their time and have enabled me to unravel some of Collins's personal relationships. Meanwhile work on Collins himself has gone on apace on both sides of the Atlantic over the past decade and I have benefited greatly from this activity and from many individual experts in universities, colleges, libraries, and other institutions. In London, Peter Caracciolo (at the Royal Holloway College, University of London), Andrew Gasson (secretary of the Wilkie Collins Society), Emma Hicks (Art Researcher, Royal Society of Arts), Jeremy Maas (of the Maas Gallery and author of *Victorian Painters*) and, above all, the indefatigable Bridget Lakin, have been full of encouragement and helpful directions.

In the United States, my wife's long lost cousin, Donald Whitton in San Francisco, who is a direct descendant of one of Wilkie's aunts, was initially re-united through a remarkable coincidence, worthy of a Collins plot, through her London dentist Frank Glass (also a Collins relation). Donald has since not only shared in the quest but made his own contributions in his book, *The Grays of Salisbury*. Other American help has been liberally offered by Kirk Beetz (the president of the Wilkie Collins Society), Robert Ashley (of Ripon College), Verlyn Klinkenberg (Pierpont Morgan Library, New York) and Ellen Dunlap (former Research Librarian, Humanities Research Centre, University of Texas, Austin, Texas). And in Rome and Naples, Pamela Holding diligently resolved so many Italian conundrums, relating to local artists in the 1830s and to the bewildering changes in Roman street names, with enthusiasm.

My aim throughout these inquiries and in the subsequent writing has been simple and straightforward: to throw light, where possible, on Wilkie Collins's private life and to fill the gaps still existing in all earlier biographies. I have not ignored his writings, but in the face of the intense efforts still going on in the literary world to analyse and reassess Collins's contribution to nineteenth-century fiction, it would have been presumptuous of me to join the debate. This is not, therefore, a full, rounded biography covering an assessment of Collins as a writer: rather a simple account of Collins, the man, and the women in his life.

WMC
1989

CHAPTER ONE

The Will

TOWARDS THE end of September 1889, London was already preparing itself for the winter ahead. Snow had fallen in Scotland and cold, wet squalls were sweeping up the Thames. Another mutilated body had been found in Whitechapel.

The London theatre had a lively season ahead of it. *The Yeoman of the Guard* was still running at the Savoy. Marie Tempest was at the Lyric and Henry Irving, Squire Bancroft and Ellen Terry were at the Lyceum. Lillie Langtry was in rehearsal for her first return to the London theatre after three years' absence in the United States.

The sudden turn in the autumn weather proved too much for a frail, bent and prematurely old man, who had known and shared the triumphs of many of those in rehearsal. Wilkie Collins had been battling with the aftermath of a serious stroke since mid-summer. Since his sudden collapse one Sunday morning in June while reading one of his favourite journals, *Reynolds News*[1], both the public and his friends had watched his efforts at recovery with growing anxiety. A month later, in mid-July, *The Times* was again expressing grave fears and Queen Victoria was making discreet inquiries[2]. His literary agent, conscious of Wilkie's latest, and unfinished, novel still running in the *Illustrated London News* was busily unwinding and rearranging contracts with his publishers.

Then for a short time it seemed that Wilkie might shake off the inevitable. In August he was well enough to persuade his old friend Walter Besant to complete what was to be his last novel, *Blind Love*, and perky enough to send a cheery letter round to his closest friends the Lehmanns[3]: 'I have fallen asleep and the doctor forbids the waking of me. Sleep is the cure, he says, and he is really hopeful of me. Don't notice the blots, my dressing gown sleeve is too large, but my hand is still steady. Goodbye for the present dear old friends; we may really hope for healthier days.'

Two weeks later the temperature dropped and Wilkie caught a chest infection. He was in no state to fight off the consequences. Confined to his second floor room overlooking Wimpole Street, he had difficulty in digesting the lightest food. Sitting in a large armchair near the fire draped with blankets, he sensed that the end was near. He was having difficulty getting the only medicine he knew might help. On Saturday September 21st, he scribbled his last, almost indecipherable note to his old friend and doctor, Frank Beard: 'I am dying old friend'. And, on a separate scrap of paper in the same, small envelope: 'I am too muddled to write. They are driving me mad by forbidding the [laudanum]. Come for God's sake'. Frank Beard rarely left him thereafter. And he was with him when he died peacefully the following Monday morning[4].

The journalists quickly filled in the rest, with the *New York Herald* outpacing the local papers on detail. 'He was leaning back with his head buried in the pillow of the chair. From time to time the doctor felt the fluttering pulse, whose throbs were growing weaker and more irregular. Now and then the dying man opened his eyes in a vague, dreamy sense of his condition, but that was all. At half past ten on Monday morning there was a slight convulsive movement and his head sank back. . . .' And it went on, reflecting current sentiment: 'He died alone . . . He had not a relative in the world, save an old aunt, who was far away in Dorsetshire and whom he had not seen for a long time. By his side was only Dr F. Carr Beard, his life-long friend and the old housekeeper, who for thirty years had looked after her master's comfort with the care and devotion of a slave. His valet, George, was not present and it was in the company of a single friend and a servant that the man of so many deaths breathed his last'.

A colourful account and, for all its sentiment, reasonably accurate[5]. But, as so many of his closest friends knew quite well, it was only part of the truth. The old housekeeper, Caroline Graves, had been his mistress and had lived with him, on and off, for over forty years and her daughter, Harriet, had acted as his secretary throughout his literary triumphs. And another mistress, Martha Rudd, the mother of his three illegitimate children, was still not far away in Taunton Place.

He had no family in the ordinary sense. But he hardly died alone. Right to the end he was surrounded by children and grandchildren, both his own in Taunton Place and those of Caroline in Wimpole Street itself. And, occasionally, the twain did meet.

Four days later the blinds of the houses in Wimpole Street were discreetly lowered and by a quarter past eleven a crowd of mourners and sightseers had gathered outside number 82, near the corner of Wigmore Street. Inside Caroline Graves and her daughter Harriet, as housekeeper and secretary, were awaiting the chief mourners, as well as those come to pay respects to a still popular novelist, whose latest novel they were still reading in weekly instalments. They included Collins's doctor, solicitor, publisher and literary agent as well as a few old friends from the worlds of art, literature and the theatre.

Wilkie had specifically asked for a simple funeral. They were to spend no more than twenty-five pounds on it, and he made a point that no-one was to wear 'scarves, hatbands or feathers'. The oak coffin thus bore a brief inscription with his name and the dates of his birth and death on it. But even he could not control the spontaneous outburst of floral tributes. When his coffin was carried out to the glass-pannelled hearse in Wimpole Street, it was completely covered by wreaths and a profusion of flowers of all kinds, some brought personally to the house, which overflowed onto the roof of the funeral coach itself. There was a wreath of scarlet geraniums, Charles Dickens's favourite flower, from his daughter Mamie; lilies and stephanotis from the Society of Authors; tiger lilies from the Baroness de Stern; and a cross of roses and lilies from Blanche Roosevelt, an old theatrical friend.

Standing out among the colourful display was a handsome cross of white chrysanthemums from 'Mrs Dawson and family' – a discreet reminder of his well hidden family. Martha and his three grown-up children could hardly pay their respects at the house, but were probably part of the crowd as the hearse, two mourning coaches and at least seven private carriages (some empty and sent by close friends as tokens of respect) left for Kensal Green cemetery.

The crowds in Wimpole Street, and later at Kensal Green around noon, mingled with well known personalities. Ada Cavendish had played a major part in one of Wilkie's main theatrical triumphs. So had Squire Bancroft (who was appearing on stage again later that week) and Arthur Pinero; and Holman Hunt, Edmund Yates and Hall Caine were friends from the art world and the literary world. Whether people got a glimpse of Oscar Wilde was still in dispute days afterwards. *The Times* said he was at Kensal Green, while Edmund Yates publicly swore that he was 'not within miles of the place'.

The two women who had had the biggest and deepest influence on Wilkie, apart from his mother, remained close to him that week. On the day of the funeral, Caroline and Martha were still playing their appointed roles (one on the inside, one on the outside), the one looking after his domestic affairs, the other caring for his family. And they were in the forefront again, a few days later, when the will was read to them, separately, by Henry Powell Bartley, the husband of Caroline's daughter, Harriet.

Wilkie Collins had planned his will with as much care for detail as he had always given to his most complex plots. He knew exactly what he wanted to achieve and sought the help of his closest advisers, his solicitor (first William Tindall, later Henry Bartley) and his doctor. He had never been a wealthy man; nor had he been deprived of most of life's comforts. His father had left him and his brother (and his mother, while she lived) enough for a modest living, and he himself, at the peak of his earning power, in the ten years following the publication of *The Woman in White*, had sometimes added as much as £5,000 a year to his basic income. Though he had often spent money as fast as he earned it and had hardly made big money from investments, even preferring to take houses on lease rather than buying them outright, he had always been conscious of the potential value of his work.

From the beginning of his writing career to the end, he bickered with his publishers. He knew his worth and was determined to get it. At the outset this drove him into lengthy arguments about slipshod proof-reading in newspaper advertisements for his novels, and into peppering his publishers with detailed suggestions, from the best way to sell his books to the detailed layout of individual papers.

He occasionally overplayed his hand, having his writings turned down or his proposals completely ignored. Later he became infuriated at the ease with which pirate publishers in the United States were able to print his novels, often before their publication in book form in London, while he received nothing. One American publisher informed a friend of his that he had sold one hundred and twenty thousand copies of *The Woman in White*. 'He never sent me a sixpence,' grumbled Collins[6]. He occasionally won a skirmish however, once, to his relief and surprise, with a Dutch publisher, once with an English provincial theatre which had innocently pirated one of his plays.

This continual pressure on the publishing world had one foreseeable result. Towards the end of his life, Wilkie Collins was determined to secure as high a price as he could for his remaining copyrights. He was well aware that, like leaseholds, copyrights had a diminishing value. He was also aware which of them were most saleable and which were less so. And by the early part of 1882 when, to judge by his letters alone, he was rarely free from gout and neuralgic pains of one sort or another, sometimes in the knee, sometimes in the back, invariably in the eyes, his thoughts inevitably turned to his own mortality, his financial affairs and how best to arrange them after his death.

He had two problems on his mind. How could he realise his various assets and ensure that whoever inherited them would have little difficulty in receiving their full benefit? Secondly, to whom should he leave them? His younger brother, Charles, had died before him and, though Wilkie himself had never married, he was hardly bereft of dependants of all kinds. On the face of it the financial problem should have proved the easier to resolve. Yet he quickly made up his mind about the beneficiaries in his will and never changed it, whereas it was only a matter of months before his death, seven years later, that he finally came to an agreement about his copyrights.

His first attempt to quantify the value of the outstanding copyrights was made in 1882. They were set out in handwritten form clearly dictated by Wilkie to his secretary, Harriet Bartley, the daughter of Caroline Graves, and can now be seen in the New York Public Library.

He listed, firstly, the novels of which he still had the copyright. There were nineteen, including both *The Woman in White* and *The Moonstone*. He excluded three novels where the copyright had already been sold to Smith Elder and Co.: *After Dark*, *No Name* and *Armadale*. Then came five plays, or 'dramas' as he liked to call them, and six further plays which had been adapted from his novels. He clearly felt they were not worth much in current conditions. 'In the present disgraceful state of copyright in England, these are not properly speaking property. Any larcenous scoundrel has as much right to dramatise my novels as I have.'

He finally added to the list several short stories 'kept in a drawer of one of the "what-nots" in my study', which had not as then been published in book form. And he preferred a little advice to his chosen executors. Although Chatto and Windus should be consulted first, 'never let it be forgotten that one hundred thousand copies have been sold of Lady Brassey's yachting voyage round the world, issued in a sixpenny pamphlet form, with a few woodcut illustrations[7]. Might not the public be ready for similar cheap editions of *The Woman in White* and *The Moonstone*?'

Six years later he was still wrestling with the value of the remaining copyrights and finally decided to negotiate their sale himself. Early in 1888 he did his sums once more, not on the back of an envelope, but the back of an account statement from Chatto and Windus. He quickly worked out that thirteen of his novels were worth £2,000 (for a seven year extension of their copyright leases), that five more might fetch an additional £250, with *The Woman in White* his most popular novel, whose copyright would run out in 1902, adding further icing to the cake. He could look forward, he thought, to anything between £2,000 and £3,000. He had, alas, either overvalued himself, or not had enough energy to strike the bargain he wanted. By the April of the following year, six months before he died, he had come to a final agreement with Chatto and Windus at a rather lower level. He agreed to take £1,800 for *all* his remaining copyrights and all other interests in twenty-four novels, including *The Moonstone* and *The Woman in White*. The payments were to be spread over six months.

Collins had no such difficulties in deciding on the recipients of his modest wealth. He was always conscious of his responsibilities to his womenfolk and as early as 1870 had decided to leave both Caroline and Martha equal sums in what he called 'ready money' on his death[8]. As soon as Martha provided him with two daughters, he quickly adjusted his will in their favour and, when Martha was pregnant a third time, he made a further change.

He made final adjustments following the marriage of Caroline's daughter, Harriet, to Henry Bartley, a young solicitor, who had replaced William Tindall as his legal adviser. Bartley probably gave little advice on the bequests, confining himself, like Tindall before him, to the intricacies of the legal language, though he was to play a decisive part in the final destruction of most of Wilkie's labours.

In any case Wilkie Collins hardly needed much guidance in the drawing up of wills. He had been called to the bar in his youth, though he had never practised. At least eight of his novels had lawyers as prominent characters and wills had been the crucial factor in several of his main works. A complex will was central to the plot of *The Woman in White* and he had already faced the issue of illegitimacy in a will in *No Name*. Now he had to face the problem of his own illegitimate children, the son and two daughters of Martha Rudd.

In his final will, he made several small bequests, £50 to a cousin and 19 guineas to two servants, as well as small annuities of £20 to two old aunts, whom he had already been helping in a small way for some years. Then came the significant bequests – to the two women in his life.

Caroline Graves was to get his gold studs and cuff-links, some of his furniture, the sum of £200 and half of the income from his estate for life. Martha Rudd, whom he acknowledged for the first time as the mother of his three children, under the name of Mrs Dawson, was to get his gold watch and chain, the sum of £200 and the other half of the income from his estate for life. He then made a clear distinction between Caroline and Martha. While Harriet, Caroline's daughter, would inherit the same income for her lifetime, following her mother's death, once Harriet died, the income would revert to Martha's children. His own illegitimate family were to get the full benefit in the end.

In spite of all Wilkie's reforming zeal in his later novels, it was a typically Victorian will, reflecting a rigid attitude to property and women. Just as in the case of his father's will, under which his mother received income from his father's estate, while subsequently he and his brother Charles received capital sums on her death, Wilkie equally insisted that only his son, William Charles, was to receive his share of the money, when the appropriate time came, as a capital sum. His daughters, Marian and Harriet Constance, following their mother's death, were to receive income for their lifetime.

These plans were made in 1882, at a time when Wilkie's income had settled down to an average of some £2,500 a year, derived from his books and his investments. He was comfortably off, adding slowly to the £5,000 or so capital he had inherited from his mother. But his life-style – his expenditure on drink, food and the good life, the running of two homes, his sailing expeditions from Ramsgate, quite apart from the bringing up of three children and one adopted child – had plainly taken their toll.

On his death, the newspapers quickly hinted that he had left 'a fortune of upwards of £20,000'. A reasonable assumption, considering that Dickens had left £90,000, George Eliot £30,000 and Trollope over £25,000, and only Dickens had commanded the sums Wilkie received from a single book. The truth was otherwise. His estate was valued at £10,831 within a couple of months of his death. And to this was eventually added £1,310 from the sale of his original manuscripts (*The Woman in White* fetching £320, *The Frozen Deep*, £300 and *The Moonstone* only £125), £415 from his pictures and much less from his books. By 1892, three years after his death, the value of his estate was put at £11,414.

If, as he intended, this residue had been invested in Consols or other fixed interest stock, both Caroline and Martha should have been receiving something like £200 to £250 a year, not a princely sum but enough to ward off any pecuniary anxieties and with a trust fund safely behind them. So much for Collins's carefully constructed will. The reality was eventually rather different, for his womenfolk were soon in financial difficulties. Caroline died within five years of Collins, in lodgings in Newman Street, amidst the furniture trade. Harriet, her daughter, was soon dependent on a £200 a year allowance from her mother-in-law, following the death of Henry Powell Bartley. Harriet's four daughters, beautiful and talented though they were, were constantly battling between the glamour of the stage (one became a 'Gaiety girl') and the hazards of earning a regular living, forcing them all, from time to time, on to the reluctant charity of the Bartley family.

And Martha's children were growing up both with the handicap of their birth and the increasing fear of financial insecurity. Following Harriet's death the three of them began to wonder what had happened to the other half of Wilkie's money for it was never passed on to Martha or to them. It was an outcome that for many years soured their memories of Wilkie Collins's whole entourage, although they never tired of praising his many kindnesses and devotion as a father.

How and why Wilkie Collins's last will, which had been so meticulously planned, finally fell apart can now be assessed with reasonable accuracy. Some of the characters in his life were as fallible as those of his imagination. How he managed to surround himself with so many dependants in such unorthodox relationships lies deep in his past. His father, his mother and his brother were all essential ingredients of this deep brew. But Caroline and Martha too, in their different ways, were to bring their own strong flavours. That it all led to financial discord is a sadness that his descendants have had to cope with over the years. It would have been an even greater sadness to Wilkie himself.

CHAPTER TWO

Father

WILKIE COLLINS would have found it as easy to drift into painting as into writing; and without his father's somewhat oppressive personality, and his own independent streak, he might have done so. He had every family encouragement. From birth he was surrounded by painters, rather than writers. Only his paternal grandfather, William Collins, had done any serious writing and even he wrote about painters and was a picture-dealer[1] with one ambition for his son – 'to see poor Bill an R.A.'. Wilkie's father, another William, eventually fulfilled this ambition, becoming a student at the Royal Academy at the age of nineteen, a Royal Academician thirteen years later, and never turning aside from his chosen profession thereafter.

Wilkie's mother, Harriet Geddes, also came from a highly talented family of artists. Their friend, Andrew Geddes (no relation), was one of the best known Scottish painters of the early nineteenth century. Harriet and her four sisters and brother all came under his influence on the estate of Longford Castle, where their parents had leased a farm from Lord Radnor at Alderbury[2], on the outskirts of Salisbury. The farm was only a few miles across the fields from the Castle, which was full of art treasures – Holbein's *Erasmus* and *Ambassadors*, Velazquez's *Juan de Pareja*, Nicholas Hilliard's miniatures as well as works by Franz Hals, Brueghel, Reynolds, Claude Lorraine and Gainsborough.

The Geddes girls shared their friend's enthusiasm and made the most of his visits to them, once he had entered the school of the Royal Academy in London. Two of Harriet's sisters – Margaret (Carpenter) and Catherine (Gray) – spent hours copying the paintings at the Castle. All three sisters must have haunted the place with their sketch-pads and Andrew was on hand to guide them, in the fields or in the Castle. In later life Margaret and Catherine were to become eminent portrait painters.

Not far away across the meadows John Constable, whom William had got to know at the Academy some years earlier and with whom he was to achieve a rather fragile family relationship much later at Hampstead, was also hard at work. Yet Lord Radnor remained oblivious to the artistic endeavours going on on his land. As the present Dowager Countess of Radnor, whose present house, Avonturn, is on the precise spot where the Geddes family lived, now points out, 'my husband used to lament that his ancestor had ignored Constable who must have been working almost under his nose in the Salisbury fields'[3]. And she still sees the Geddes family as an essential part of life at Longford. 'I even believe I know what their dinner service was like, for I still dig up bits of china in my garden.' Whether Harriet or her sisters met Constable on his lonely forays into the Wiltshire countryside remains a mystery.

This was the family William Wilkie Collins was born into on January 8th, 1824. His parents were by then living in New Cavendish Street in Marylebone, an area Wilkie was rarely to leave for any length of time throughout his whole life. They had been married less than eighteen months and were still far from financially secure.

William, it is true, was already a successful painter of landscapes, a member of the Academy with a string of powerful, and rich, patrons. But he was still conscious of how capricious they could be; and he did not need his mother to remind him of the distress they had faced less than ten years earlier, on the death of his father. It was an experience they were unlikely to forget. Every piece of furniture had been removed from their house in Portland Place to pay outstanding debts. They were even forced to have the family evening meal on an old box for a table.

William's early career had often teetered on the edge of similar disasters, and his response to them was to forge the excesses of his religious conviction Wilkie had to endure in his formative years. Sir Thomas Heathcoate had stepped in with a loan to William on his father's death. And further loans were needed in the following years as William continued to grapple with all the insecurity of a developing young painter.

In 1816 William was once again in some despair, summed up in his diary in hardly unfamiliar terms. 'On a dreary, black-looking April day, with one sixpence in my pocket, seven hundred pounds in debt, shabby clothes, a fine house, a large stock of my own handiworks, a certainty (as much, at least, a certainty, as anything short of a bird in the hand can be) of about a couple of hundred, and a determination unshaken, and please God, not to be shook by anything – of becoming a great painter'[4]. His predicament sharpened his mind considerably and he was soon on his way to Hastings to paint the coast, with yet another loan from Sir Thomas in his pocket.

In retrospect it was the shock he needed, for it pointed his talent in a direction which was to become virtually a trade mark of his future work. The first time he had attempted to sketch the sea, as a lively youngster on the beach at Brighton, trying to draw the waves as they rolled to his feet, he had burst into tears of despair.

This time at Hastings, due to financial pressures, domestic responsibilities and utter determination, he spent six intense weeks observing and sketching the seascapes in all their changing characteristics from the glow of the morning sunlight to the gloom of an evening shower. He lodged with a fisherman, existing on fish and tea ('and live *well* too – sometimes to be sure with a chop'), and he came to terms with himself, reawakening and sustaining a moral rectitude, always latent in his inner thoughts and his personal diary, which was rarely to leave him.

He returned to London with enough sketches to prepare pictures for the next Academy Exhibition, and a commission from Sir Thomas Heathcoate, as well as a couple of portraits in reserve. It was enough to keep the family's creditors at bay a little longer. He had also discovered a clear outlet for his talents – an interest in the coast of England which was to continue literally to the end of his life. Pictures in exhibition and in stock, however, were one thing. Regular sales quite another. *Sunrise*, one of his more acclaimed seascapes from this period, and a great success at the Academy Exhibition of 1817, took nearly another year before it was eventually sold. Once again, to make ends meet, he was forced to rely on the generosity of Sir Thomas. And yet, such were his mercurial changes of fortune that within six months, he had sold one of his other seascapes *A Scene on the Coast of Norfolk* to the Prince Regent[5] (after a polite tussle with Lord Liverpool who had secured it a matter of hours before) and other commissions 'began to flow in with unaccustomed prodigality'. William had successfully emerged from a troubling period. But his dependence on patrons had struck deep, on himself and his mother. His income was both lumpy and irregular[6], hardly the circumstances to take on another dependant. His relationship with Harriet Geddes, however, had not stood still. They had first met by accident, at a ball given by a few artists for their girl friends, when William was in his mid-twenties, and they had subsequently run across each other from time to time in London.

William's attraction to the lively girl from Salisbury was finally renewed in 1821, when they discovered, on a chance meeting in London, that neither had become otherwise attached. Their engagement quickly followed, but so did Mrs Collins's objection to an early marriage. After over a year of argument, hopeless persuasion and dithering, however, William finally took the plunge and arranged for their marriage in Edinburgh – a decision as much of Harriet's making as his in the end. Perhaps predictably, his mother acquiesced.

And so, rather less than eighteen months later their first son, William Wilkie, was born. Sir David Wilkie, an old friend of William's student days, who also provided his son with his distinctive Christian name, has provided the closest description we have of his earliest days. In Collins's own words, Sir David 'whose studies of human nature, extended to everything but *infant* human nature, had evidently been refreshing his faculties for the occasion by taxing his boyish recollections of puppies and kittens; for after looking into the child's eyes, as it was held up for inspection, he exclaimed to the father, with serious astonishment and satisfaction, "He sees"'.

It was left to Wilkie's father to provide a more indelible outline – a series of sketches of his first child, pink-faced, almost cherub-like with the now familiar, almost bulbous, forehead[7], completed in coloured chalk over the ensuing months. It is unlikely that George IV was aware of the new arrival in the Collins family, but he chose this particular year to request another picture, thereby ensuring that William spent his summer months at Hastings away from his family – a not unfamiliar habit which Harriet and the boys would gradually grow used to. The outcome was a picture, *Prawn Fishers at Hastings*[8], and, a year later, an audience with the King at Windsor to discuss both the picture and the state of art generally.

This was a particularly active and lucrative period of William's life. They had taken a cottage in Hampstead. Sir David Wilkie was a regular confidant and admirer. 'You have, in "landscape",' he told William, 'the ball at your foot, and in this rich line, an open and unoccupied field before you'. Commissions were becoming more regular. Blake, Coleridge, Linnell, Constable and many other artistic friends became part of the family's daily life.

Sir David, on an extensive visit to Italy, was soon enthusing about the works of Raphael and Michelangelo, placing them above the Dutch, even the Venetian schools, two of William's current enthusiasms, and begging him to bring the family to Italy. 'Here everything is seen clearer than in England – the sky is bluer, the light is brighter, the shadows stronger and colours more vivid than with you. . . . Remember what Wilson and Turner had gained from Italy and Switzerland; and, though as a family man it will require a sacrifice, I think it well worth your deliberate consideration'[9].

Very shortly William's family was enlarged by the birth of a second son – and thoughts of an early family visit to Italy were for the moment put out of mind. Charles Allston Collins was born in Pond Street, Hampstead in January 1828 ('the second house on the way down the hill' as Wilkie later described it[10]) and once again a friendly artist, this time Washington Allston[11] the American historical painter, provided a distinctive Christian name for the new infant. In William's eyes, William Wilkie his first born, forever known to his parents as 'Willy' was now 'a strapping fellow' and his younger brother 'Charlie' was a 'little blue-eyed, red-haired bonny bairn'.

By all accounts, they were a happy family, as the boys grew up in Hampstead and later in Bayswater. William was still moving from the family home to the houses of his patrons, at regular intervals, and Harriet was busy with her domestic chores, her close circle of friends and relations as well as the constant monetary anxieties of a painter's wife.

Their letters to each other, during William's prolonged absences, show all the signs of a devoted young married couple, though William's occasionally have a streak of moralising, even tetchiness, about them. It may have been his particular brand of teasing but in cold print they often read otherwise. He misses her and the boys; he likes to hear from her regularly; he gently chastises her occasional forgetfulness; and, even from a distance, he seeks to keep his growing sons to a strict moral code.

It is hard not to feel a little sorry for Harriet. Stuck at home with two healthy boisterous boys, while her husband, admittedly in their interest, is entertained and clearly often acclaimed in some of the finest houses in the land. And William was perhaps just a little over-impressed by his hosts, even obsequious.

The truth was that William was moving in remarkably exalted circles, considering how close to the breadline he had been only a few years earlier. In the decade and a half since they had sat round the wooden box for dinner in Portland Place, he had cultivated or stayed with Sir Thomas Heathcoate, Sir George Beaumont, Sir Thomas Baring, Lord Liverpool, the Duke of Newcastle, Sir Francis Chantry, Sir Robert Peel and Sir Thomas Lawrence to name a few; had received commissions from the King; and had begun to move freely among the literary and artistic giants of the day, staying with the Wordsworths, Southey, Coleridge, and Walter Scott and regarding David Wilkie, John Constable and John Linnell as some of his closest friends. Throughout this period his letters home paint an impressive picture, though how they were received by Harriet, or his mother before her, can only be conjectured.

'I started for Keswick. Went to Sir George Beaumont's . . . Rode with

Sir George, to Borrowdale and Buttermere, where we dined. . . . Rainy morning painted from Sir George's window. . . . Went to see Southey . . . . Made a sketch for Sara Coleridge's portrait, a drenching day. . . painted, from my window, Grisdale Pike – showery all day. Lord Lowther and Mr Wordsworth at dinner. . . Walked to Ambleside with Wordsworth and his wife – sketched the mill there. . . Rainy morning; Wordsworth read to me; walked out before dinner – took my farewell of the Lakes. . . .'

'. . . almost all my time is spent out of doors – and I think I derive much benefit from the sea air, and the delightful situation of this romantic Castle [Dover Castle]. The view from the living-room is magnificent, and the attentions of my host extremely gratifying. Yesterday I dined at the house of the Archbishop of Canterbury – who has seven daughters, all unmarried – and a very pleasant party we had.'

'. . . We have lately added to our party the Chancellor of the Exchequer, whose conversational powers are so great, that the excitement of our days and nights is much increased; and I am without much inclination to go at all. . . . We have been getting up some capital *Tableaux Vivants*, which has made a great stir. . . . We have found a ready and useful figure, also, in a very pleasant member of our circle, who has just left us – the Solicitor-General. So here, you see, I am in the midst of the Whig Ministry.'

'I cannot help longing for home, although I am so pleasantly spending my time, as pleasantly as the kindest friends, sprightly young ladies, and all the gaieties of this life can make me. I flatter myself that the idle life I am leading will please you, and perhaps make me stronger; and therefore, I am determined to make the most of it.'

Harriet was well aware of the kind of life he must lead, as well as the efforts he must make to keep at the top of his profession. She also knew what it meant to face financial disaster. Her own family prospects had been in jeopardy, not many years earlier, when her father lost a fortune through an unfortunate loan to a close friend in the army. William was certainly insensitive, even priggish, and hardly the most articulate of correspondents. Yet his love for Harriet and his family still managed to shine through his rather awkward letters.

On their tenth wedding anniversary, the first such occasion on which

[14]

they had been separated, his feelings spilled out with a warmth and spontaneity that probably surprised him, if not Harriet. 'This day, as indeed every day since I have left you', he wrote from the Lake District, 'I have drunk after dinner to myself "my own dear Harriet". And now in my own room am writing another love letter to my only Sweetheart . . . I must go to bed without my bride, fare thee well my darling, we are wonderfully well off, you have the darling chicks to comfort you and I know you are happy and so am I'. And again, 'I cannot tell you, when I am alone, how I long for home. Why should we thus be parted I say continually, and my only consolation is that it is not for pleasure alone (although, thank God, I relish the beauties of his creation more than ever), but for the "crumbs" I must take to my "nest". And what a "nest" it is, after all!'[12]

The 'crumbs' were beginning to be quite substantial. He had received £315 for his painting from the King in 1825, a year in which his total income came to four figures for the first time: (£1,114) and he managed to keep it up over the next four years. He not only kept an annual tally of his earnings[13], as well as future painting commissions, but also an interesting assessment of his average earnings at each house he occupied.

While he was living in Pond Street, Hampstead, between 1826 and 1829 (though he also kept his house in New Cavendish Street) his earnings averaged £1,281, actually reaching a peak of £1,378 in 1829[14]. He earned £1,048 in the larger house in Hampstead Square, where he lived for one year and then averaged only £564 over the next five years in Porchester Terrace, Bayswater. The lumpiness in his earnings continued right to the end. By the time he died he had accumulated close on £11,000, enough, as Wilkie put it, for his widow and two sons to live on after his death. 'Not the income of rich people' but 'sufficient for all their wants'.

William was hardly idling among his patrons and their wealthy friends. But one gets the impression that he rather enjoyed this milieu of 'fine folk' as he liked to call them. He remained a devoted husband and father at one remove. He developed an early streak of righteousness, a reflection of the age he was living in, as well as a result of the early trials he had had to endure.

His diary records many of the twists and turns in his conscience over these years, especially during that six week visit to Hastings: 'On Sunday, September 29th, 1816, I made a solemn resolution to abstain from any compliance with desires calculated to weaken my faculties. This resolution was made in St Clement's Church, at Hastings; and, as it has for its end the improvements of my powers as an artist and a man, I shall proceed to adopt a more strict and periodical examination of my conduct, with a view to banish from my constitution those inclinations to indolence, which, by their unobserved agency, might overcome my mental resources'[15].

He drove himself accordingly. His convictions also spilled out into his relations with other people, his family and friends. His letters to Harriet and his two growing boys are filled with pious admonitions. 'Tell the dear children that the only way they can serve their parents is to obey them in all things; let Charlie find out the passages in Scripture where this duty is most strongly insisted on, and write them down for me'[16]. On another occasion, in a separate letter to Willy and Charlie: 'Your mother's account, in her last letter about you both, pleased me much. Go on praying to God, through Jesus Christ, to enable you, by his Holy Spirit, to be blessings to your parents; and then you must be happy'.

Nor did his closest friend escape his occasional censure. The Linnell family were close neighbours both in Hampstead and Bayswater. Their wives and children saw a lot of each other and Linnell and Collins were colleagues at the Academy as well as fellow artists. Linnell had done portraits of several of the Collins family[17]. But John Linnell had become a Dissenter, having concluded that the observance of Sunday as the Sabbath was a simple misinterpretation of the Bible. He chose to ignore it and though a Christian, went about his ordinary work on a Sunday.

One Sunday in spring William happened to see John Linnell nailing his peach and nectarine trees against his northern wall, and was deeply shocked, denouncing him to a visiting Congregational preacher and, some time later, showing a willingness to believe that Linnell had cheated one of his gardeners out of his wages until it was proved otherwise.

When challenged by Linnell about his lack of faith in him, Collins replied 'Of what consequence is it, whether you cheated a man out of his wages or not, when you are constantly doing things ten times worse?'

'I suppose this is a hit at me for nailing up my nectarines on a Sunday afternoon' said Linnell. Collins admitted it was and added 'A man who would break the Sabbath would do any other bad thing'[18].

This religious intolerance was to plague William most of his later life. Crabbe Robinson said that he 'would not shake hands with a Unitarian knowingly'. In the turbulence of the early 1830s when social disturbances were prevalent in several European capitals and the Reform movement was pressing for action at home, William was convinced that both the outbreak of cholera and the Reform Bill riots of 1831 were God's judgment. 'Of the two scourges now afflicting us, I know not which is the worst; but I *do* know that we have fallen into the hands of God in both cases, and not before we deserved it'. He was a dedicated High Church man, a supporter of Dr. Pusey in his spirited defence of the Faith and his letters to Harriet carry repeated denunciations of preachers and academics, as well as comments on the continuing religious debates in the columns of *The Times*[19].

His religious outlook was closely allied to a moral rectitude and a willingness to censure others, a combination which was not guaranteed to endear him to those within range. Benjamin Haydon, who battled with most, found William difficult and Joseph Farrington dubbed him 'presumptuous'[20]. He was said to have met William Blake in the Strand with a pot of porter in his hand and deliberately ignored him. His elevation to the Royal Academy brought further criticisms of his insistence on henceforth being addressed as 'Esquire'. Even a century later Maurice Grant remarked on his 'unattractive goodness'[21].

His behaviour, however, was not always to his discredit. He had a series of squabbles with John Constable, once in a stout defence of his friend Linnell whom Constable had accused of sharp practice over the sale of a picture. William defended Linnell, disproved Constable's charges and gained Linnell's thanks and gratitude. Not long afterwards Constable was again gossiping, on the coach from Hampstead into the City, this time against Collins, repeating a story that he had overcharged Sir Robert Peel for a portrait. Once again the story was disproved.

John Constable was clearly the irritant in both episodes. He was going through a bad patch, selling few pictures, resenting the success of both Collins and Linnell within the Academy, while having to wait far longer for recognition. Constable had had much to put up with. Fame and wealth eluded him, at a time when as a family man it mattered most. While William was commanding four figures annually, John Constable, deliberately eschewing fashionable portraits and 'pretty landscapes', was lucky to get a few hundred pounds. In the year William's income reached over £1,000 for the first time, Constable, the older of the two, was struggling with his now famous *Corn-Field*. 'I am much worn, having worked hard' he complained to a friend, 'and have now the consolation of knowing I must work a great deal harder or go to the workhouse. I have some commissions, and I do hope to sell this picture'.

At a time when patrons were hard to find and even harder to please, Constable remained determined to paint only what he saw, relying solely on nature, and he suffered accordingly. Little wonder that, faced with Collins's current successes at the Academy of 1825, his inner turmoil turned to back-biting and personal quarrels. 'Turner exhibits a large picture of Dieppe . . . Calcotte nothing I hear . . . Collins, a coast scene with fish as usual and a landscape with a large cow turd at least as far as colour and shape is concerned.'

On another occasion Constable wrote to a friend in a particularly hostile mood about William: 'Collins is my neighbour here, but I have made up my mind to rid myself of this unpleasant fellow – at least, if I see him again, it shall not be of my seeking. He is now at war with *some* members of the Academy – and hated by *all*. Many things are said to his disadvantage – and some have even appeared in the newspapers. A meeting of the Academy has been called but they decline interfering between Pickersgill and him who are at daggers drawn. Pickersgill told me (clenching his fist and teeth at the same time) that he would not forgive him till he was in his coffin'[22].

The bitterness, intermittent though it was, was understandable. Constable's time would come. And in spite of these differences, even occasional eruptions, Collins, Linnell and Constable continued to live in close proximity (in Hampstead and central London) and reasonable friendliness. William, at any rate, though regarding Constable as something of an eccentric, with a dry sarcastic humour, paid a warm tribute to his old friend when his biography was being prepared some years later.

William was burdened with an over-developed sense of morality and propriety, yet despite that he remained a loving husband and father, amiable and good-natured. S.C. Hall, the editor of the *Art Journal*, found him 'a truly pleasant companion; pleasant to look at, to sit with, to converse with; a very lovable man, even to those who knew little of him, and greatly so to the domestic circle – wife, children and friends . . . graceful and gracious in manners, considerate and kind to all who approached him'[23].

His close friends grew used to his weaknesses and his amiability and to accept his peculiarities. So clearly did his first born. After Willy and one of the Linnell boys had misbehaved in the garden in Porchester Terrace and brought on their heads the full wrath of John Linnell, Willy later confided to his young friend 'I should not like your father to be mine. Your father is a bull; mine is a cow'.

Willy was already coming to terms with his father's stern exterior and his soft centre. It was a combination Willy learned to live with from an early age, curbing his instinctive reactions when he could and riding the storms when they erupted. And throughout his mother was a natural ally.

CHAPTER THREE

Childhood

WILKIE COLLINS had a happy childhood. 'No one could have had the happiness of possessing kinder or more indulgent parents than myself', he always insisted[1]. 'My father's position as a painter made my early home circumstances easy ones'[2]. By the time he was growing up his father was well-established, earning good commissions from rich patrons and generally running two houses, or at least a summer cottage in Hampstead or Hendon, as well as his studio in New Cavendish Street.

In these early years, their mother was inevitably the major influence. William was often away and Wilkie and Charles (or 'Willy' and 'Charlie' within the family[3]), naturally spent a good deal of their time with their mother, 'a woman', he was later to say, 'of remarkable mental culture, and from her I inherit whatever of poetry and imagination may be in my composition'[4]. The truth of all this was to emerge more fully after William's death, but even in these early days, her influence had full rein.

While William was away Harriet settled down to a comfortable domesticity with her new baby. In the first year of their marriage they had taken a summer cottage in North End, Hampstead, close to the present *Bull and Bush* and to what still exists as Wyldes Farm. Their friends the Linnells had already taken Hope Cottage for the summer and subsequently rented Collins Farm for a couple of months the following year. This was to become the Linnell's summer base for the next few years until ill-health forced them to Bayswater around 1828. William and Harriet adopted a similar lifestyle, maintaining New Cavendish Street as a winter residence and a permanent studio and taking a succession of cottages in Hendon and Hampstead.

Both were tranquil spots in those days, attracting a regular artist community. Constable had had his family with him in Lower Terrace since 1821 moving to other Hampstead houses later, and Linnell, too, with his family, slipped into rural life with enthusiasm, growing fruit, building garden sheds, even becoming something of a local baker. Not far away, at Highgate village, other cronies from the Academy and writer friends gathered together around Coleridge and Blake. A glance at their diaries reveals a succession of regular, lively meetings, sometimes in Hampstead, sometimes in Highgate. Crabbe Robinson[5] spoke of dining at Charles Lamb's and walking back with him to Highgate. 'There we found a large party. Greens, Andersons, Irving, Collins, R.A., Henry Taylor . . . It was a *rich* evening. Coleridge talked his best. Subject: the superiority of the internal evidence of Christianity'. An uplifting evening for William among his closest friends; and there were many others too, as both Blake and Linnell regularly strode the footpaths between Hampstead and Highgate.

It was among such friends that William came back to recover from his travels, to complete his sketches and, hopefully, to start others. Harriet, too, had the Linnells to fall back on and her own sisters, especially Margaret (who had married William Carpenter, later to become Keeper of Prints at the British Museum), as frequent companions. William and Harriet rarely went in for dinner parties of their own and the menfolk inevitably drifted into shop talk. There were cliques too, especially among the R.A.s, and Linnell (before he gained Academy membership) once had the humiliation of being deliberately kept out of a dining room, where he could clearly overhear the voice of William, one of his closest neighbours, declaiming to his hosts.

Willy's early encounter with one of William's close friends left a deep, and lasting, impression. Coleridge often called on the family and on one occasion, in Willy's hearing, confessed to taking opium and to being unable to resist the craving for it, though he had made every effort. 'His grief was excessive', Willy later recalled. 'He even shed tears. At last my mother addressed him, saying "Mr Coleridge, do not cry; if the opium really does you any good, and you *must* have it, why do you not go and get it?" At this the poet ceased to weep, recovered his composure and, turning to my father, said, with an air of much relief and deep conviction: "Collins, your wife is an exceedingly sensible woman!" I suppose that he did not long delay to act upon my mother's suggestion. I was a boy at the time, but the incident made a strong impression on my mind and I could not forget it.' A childish memory perhaps, but one with a long sting in the tail. He had every reason to remember it in later life.

Harriet always rejoiced when William returned and he rarely forgot to bring home some small memento for the two boys. They occasionally heralded a change of routine, from Hampstead (or Hendon) to New Cavendish Street, enabling Harriet to have a different round of activities, different friends, above all different shops (along Oxford Street) and walks (in Regents Park). But behind these changes, Harriet's basic routines continued: dressmaking, visits to the dentist, sewing Willy's first trousers, a new gown for herself, nursing both Willy and Charlie through their first illnesses.

For a time there seemed a chance that William, who was still being pressed by Sir David Wilkie to go off to Italy, might actually go with his young family. But the continued illness of his mother and the semi-dependence of his elder brother Frank were still major hindrances. So short visits to Belgium, Holland and the French coast were the main alternatives.

On one occasion, a proposed visit to Boulogne, William suggested that the whole family should go with him, to the delight of Willy (if not Charlie who was no more than eighteen months old). They crossed the Channel for the first time, spoke their first French and ended up in a charming house in the market place, where from the window William could sketch the local fishermen and farmers as they passed by. But once again the sea-shore pulled him and he was soon exploring the coastline for many miles on each side of Boulogne.

This particular excursion also brought out Willy's early nose for a well-told story. Twenty years later he could still recall the noble tale of one of his father's models, a local fisherman. He had been present at a ship-wreck near Boulogne, 'where all the crew were cast on shore dead, with the exception of a poor negro, who still showed faint signs of life'. Quarantine laws, however, prevented him being taken to a nearby house for help. But the fisherman, 'in defiance of all danger and objection, carried the poor wretch to a straw hut on the beach; and, taking off his own clothes, laid down by him the whole night long, endeavouring to restore the dying negro by the vital warmth of his own body'. All to no avail; by dawn the negro was dead. But the fisherman got double recognition: he was commended by the Boulogne authorities and featured as *The Good Samaritan* in a picture William later sold to Lord Monteagle. He also sharpened a four year old boy's ear for a good plot.

Back in Hampstead, William's plans to build a larger house in order to include both his mother and brother were going painfully slowly and they eventually decided to stay at Ramsgate for a few weeks on their return from Boulogne and invited Frank to join them there. William, however, clearly thought little of the place. In offering Frank a bed for a couple of weeks in Willy's room in their Ramsgate boarding house, while his building plans developed in Hampstead, William painted a gloomy picture of his immediate surroundings. 'I have not yet been to Broadstairs; which has more picturesque beauty, I believe, than any other place in the neighbourhood; there is nothing worth a straw at Ramsgate, except the sea; so I shall have plenty of idle time to go about with you.'

He was probably right. Ramsgate was only just beginning to develop. It lies on two sides of a shallow opening in the cliffs and at that time Nelson Crescent on one shoulder and Wellington Crescent on the other were the only signs of development. They are still there, but in those days open cornfields lay just beyond the row of rather elegant houses facing the sea. Little did young Willy realise that he would learn to swim there, own a large boat there, write several of his novels there, have one mistress in Nelson Crescent and another in Wellington Crescent, with their two families overlapping during the summer months, and that his grand-daughter would eventually be born within a stone's throw of their first boarding house.

In those days coaches could take all of twenty-four hours to make the journey from London to the Kent coast. But Harriet wisely advised Frank to catch the early steam boat from Tower Pier, sailing at 8.00 a.m., which would get him to Ramsgate by 4.15 in the afternoon. He caught the *City of London* and was with them in time for early dinner that evening at Mrs Reed's in Sion Row, alongside Nelson Crescent. The shabbiness noted by William was partly due to the remaining military encampments which lingered in the neighbourhood fifteen years after the Napoleonic wars, and partly to the fact that sea-bathing was in its infancy and the harbour still not fully developed. Sea-bathing – even nude bathing – was not unknown but it needed the commercial introduction of bathing-machines[6] in the late eighteenth century to give it a sufficient boost. But a boost of another kind came the following year when the young Princess Victoria spent a short holiday there – even taking a donkey ride on the sands.

In spite of William's misgivings Harriet and the boys were back again four years later, staying this time on the other Crescent at a small lodging house in Albion Hill. They had a rough start. 'Nothing', as Harriet told Frank later, 'could induce William to sleep there a second night'. So off they set, with the two boys aged five and nine, no doubt enjoying every moment of the adventure, pushing their luggage on a barrow down the cobbled streets of Ramsgate – or at least round the corner to number 4, The Plains of Waterloo, 'the very row of bow-windowed houses' Harriet had had her eye on from the beginning. They were only four houses away from Wellington Crescent. And, in spite of the initial mishap and no doubt William's ruffled pride, it turned out to be a splendid holiday for the boys.

'They are quite wild', Harriet told Frank proudly. 'Willy behaves nobly in the sea.' He had two pennyworths in the bathing machine. Willy also had his eyes opened to other possibilities at Ramsgate, through his father's enthusiasm for the coast. William wanted to know whether he had brought his book on ships, for he might learn 'a good deal while at the sea about vessels'. Whether or not Willy's later passion for sailing really began so early, Ramsgate was where, if anywhere, he was to give it full rein in later life.

Yet behind these happy family pastimes, tragedy was lurking. Shortly after William's arrival in Ramsgate, his brother Frank decided to return to London. Sailing back up river he caught a severe cold, which rapidly developed into typhus. William quickly returned, but before Harriet and the boys could get back to Porchester Terrace, where they were then living, Frank had died. As Willy later put it, William's 'moral system never entirely recovered' from the shock of this bereavement. And he marked each succeeding month in his diary, finding it impossible to start to paint again for some time. Then came the final blow. William's mother died less than three months later. The family were left with their sorrows and William with the melancholy thought that he was the sole survivor on both sides of the family.

Between their visits to Ramsgate, William had at last come to grips with their housing problem. Delays in Hampstead, combined with the continuing persuasion of David Wilkie, eventually led to their buying a house in Porchester Terrace, not only near to their artist friend, but virtually next door to the Linnells, and closer to Harriet's sister Margaret. Bayswater in the early 1830s was still rural, with the odd builder beginning to move in. It was close to the shops of Oxford Street and handy for Kensington Gardens. William may have felt that David Wilkie tipped the scales in their decision; more likely Harriet liked what she saw and leaned heavily on them too.

The Linnells with their four children had moved from Hampstead around 1828[7]. William eventually followed suit two years later moving into 30 Porchester Terrace in the summer of 1830. The Linnells were at number 26 and later moved to number 38 around the time William and Harriet arrived. Soon Harriet was discovering the delights of Kensington Gardens, with the boys, and renewing old friendships.

It was at Porchester Terrace that Willy can be said to have really opened his eyes. Without straining too much most people's early memories seem to emerge around the age of four or five. Earlier ones are not unusual, simply rarer, and Willy seems to have been capable of recalling more events of childhood relating to Porchester Terrace than anywhere else. It was an indelible part of growing up, meeting people, going to school, playing, drawing, having measles. And it all tumbled out in conversation, for the rest of his life. He was still enthralling dinner parties with his wild schoolboy tales forty years later and enjoying every bit of it.

It was also in Porchester Terrace that Willy recalled his first over-whelming calf-love for an older woman. The evidence comes from an early German biography, published during his life-time. Collins, an inde-fatigable corrector of biographical sketches, certainly made no effort to deny the story and the writer Mr E. von Wolzogen[8] was clearly in corre-spondence with him during its preparation.

'The amusing stories of his first love', von Wolzogen wrote, 'demonstrate how his emotional life took its own particular and somewhat unusual direction. At the age of twelve he fell in love with a married woman at least three times his age. His jealousy towards her husband was so intense that he couldn't bear the man's presence and ran away whenever he saw him coming'.

An intriguing confession, if confession it was, from one who managed to cover his later tracks so well for so long. Who could the mysterious lady have been? Since the year concerned is 1836 and since Harriet has provided a daily diary for at least a year, the finger seems to point in one direction only – Anne Linnell. She was the right age, remarkably attractive[9] and would certainly have been in and around the Collins's house enough to be noticed by a growing boy of twelve.

Yearnings of these kinds were not Willy's only memories of this period. Politics had hardly raised much interest except perhaps through his father's stern Toryism, which at hardly any period of his life fitted Willy's temperament. But one repercussion he not only remembered, but with unalloyed pleasure. There was a habit in those days, treasured by the political mobs in most places, of persuading solid citizens to illuminate their houses to celebrate some particular event – a jubilee or a new Act of Parliament; and those disinclined to conform, whatever their basic beliefs, ran the appropriate risks. Let Willy tell his own childhood experience in his own way:

'In the year 1832 when I was eight years old, my poor father was informed that he would have his windows broken if he failed to illuminate in honour of the passing of the First Reform Bill. He was a 'high Tory' and a sincerely religious man – he looked on the Reform Bill and the cholera (then prevalent) as similar judgments of an offended Deity punishing social and political backsliding. And he had to illuminate – and, worse still, he had to see his two boys, mad with delight at being allowed to set up the illuminations. Before we were sent to bed, the tramp of the people was heard in the street. They were marching six abreast (the people were in earnest in those days) provided with stones, and with their officers in command. They broke every pane of glass in an unilluminated house, nearly opposite our house, in less than a minute. I ran out to see the fun, and when the Sovereign people cheered for the Reform Bill I cheered too'[10].

The rest of his immediate childhood was rather more mundane but happy enough. He had the good fortune to be educated in a flexible way by his mother, just like the Linnell children, absorbing everything except the classics in a domestic atmosphere. Charlie had similar treatment though in his case, presumably through a greater tendency to illness which dogged him most of his young life and perhaps a more easily recognisable artistic talent, his domestic tuition was never burdened by school attendance until he entered the Royal Academy school. Both boys loved riding, following their father wherever they could and whenever he could afford it: ponies at first and horses later.

Willy and Charlie thrived on such freedom, naturally sketching when they could, copying from art books, drawing nature and anything within sight, under expert guidance on all sides. Even the Linnells were dragged into the round of providing judgments on the two boys' first oil paintings.

Harriet's influence was great, extending to the books they read, the places they visited and the walks they took together. Her own dairies provide the evidence, especially in the two years before their departure for Italy[11]. They make an enthralling, though terse, account of the Collins family for these limited years. They contain few if any deep thoughts (except under direct stress at the end of their stay in Naples), few personal asides, but a mass of detailed activities.

The flavour of Willy's eleventh year, the year he went to school for the first time, is clear and unequivocal. He had a normal childhood of the time. Harriet's daily extracts speak for themselves.

- Out a little in morning with children
- William in London. With children to buy a gown
- Went to Kensington with boys
- Called on Mrs Linnell. Walked in afternoon in Kensington
- Walked to Oxford Street with Charlie. Very cold. Poorly in the night

- Dear Charlie's birthday. At home with headache. William, Willy at church
- Out in gardens in morning with William and Charlie. Lovely day
- William went to gallery to touch up picture. Dined at Mr and Mrs Linnells' in evening
- Had a dinner party, Wilkies, Landseer, Mr Walters. Mrs Linnell's twins born
- Went to drink tea with Margaret[12]. William came to fetch me
- Willy ill, suspected measles. Poorly all day
- Willy out in the measles. Brought him down to a bed in the little room
- Willy out for the first time
- Charlie sickening for measles
- Charlie's spots came out
- I took Willy in afternoon to have tooth drawn
- Went to town with Willy to get clothes for him
- Went to private view with Wilkie. Very fine exhibition.
- Walked to Kensington with children
- Sat in gardens all morning. Took to Shooters Hill in afternoon. Children in races. Went to grand review at Woolwich. Saw King and Queen. Home to late dinner
- Went to Hampstead, to dinner with Dr Jennings. Walked on the heath
- Charlie very ill with fever
- Letter from William. Willy ill in evening
- Walked to Margaret's in morning with Charlie. Willy better.
- William arrived to tea. Joyful meeting
- Took Willy to have haircut
- Busy with Willy's cloak at home
- Out in Kensington Gardens with Charlie. Finished cloak
- Busy showing new maid her business
- Out with boys sliding.

Willy's schooldays have occasionally been lost in a mystery of his own making. He tended to treat them as an inferior form of education in contrast to learning the ways of the world upon his travels in Italy and France. He was also occasionally inclined to talk of his school at Highbury, omitting his earlier stay at Maida Hill. In fact Harriet's diary, as well as other evidence, including one of the appropriate Censuses, clarifies most of the main points of his education.

He first went to school on Tuesday, January 13th 1835, a few days after his eleventh birthday. 'All up betimes' writes Harriet. 'Dear Willy taken to school first time'. She and William had taken the precaution of calling on his new schoolmaster, the Reverend James Gall, a few evenings before and he in turn had called on them two days later. 'Liked him much' Harriet told her diary. Presumably Willy did too, or at least if he did not there is little evidence of it through Harriet, and he did manage to win first prize in his first year – two volumes of *Southey's Essays*[13].

It was a small preparatory school set back off what is now the Edgware Road and was exactly one mile from Tyburn (near the present Marble Arch) and so well within walking distance from Porchester Terrace. Maida Hill Academy, to give the school its full title, was a boarding and day school, though Willy plainly went home daily[14]. It was actually on Lyon Terrace, on the south side of the Canal and on the east side of the main road. Schools for girls were also in the vicinity.

Several of Wilkie's school stories can be identified with his later school at Highbury (where he was sent on their return from Italy) but one episode at least carries the ring of Maida Hill Academy about it – if only because of the first prize. 'One Christmas time', he wrote partly autobiographically in *The Lazy Tour of Two Idle Apprentices*[15], 'he was stimulated by the evil example of a companion, whom he had always trusted and liked, to be untrue to himself, and to try for a prize at the ensuing half-yearly examination. He did try and he got a prize. No sooner however had the book been placed in his hands than the first troubles of his life began.' The idle boys deserted him as a traitor, the workers regarded him as a rival; and the previous winner gave him a thrashing. 'From that time, the masters made him work and the boys would not let him play. From that time his social position steadily declined, and his life at school became a perpetual burden to him.'

True or false? Probably both, as in so much of Collins' writings based, partly, on his experiences. He often found it difficult to write without experience; and he found it equally difficult not to embellish it. If Harriet is to be believed, Willy did have a 'best friend' at school and he did go through the usual ritual of having him at home occasionally. 'Young Beamish came to tea' she writes. 'Boys went to Beamishes'. And nearer Christmas: 'Drill Sergeant came. Mrs Whishott's boys and Beamishes. Out sliding after.' Then on New Year's Eve: 'Went to Mrs Whishott's to see Willy drilled.' But all this was before he had won the prize. Perhaps retribution of a sort did follow after all. Harriet alas remains silent – or ignorant.

CHAPTER FOUR

Italy

SIR DAVID WILKIE was constantly trying to entice his friend William with the idea of a visit to Italy. He clearly felt it would help William's own efforts, as well as open his eyes to the merits of Raphael, Michelangelo and other Italian artists whom William had not only ignored but positively derided. The only restraint on such an enterprise now was the age of Willy and Charlie (thirteen and nine) and the fact that Willy at least had just started his formal education.

William predictably dithered, in spite of Harriet's quiet acquiescence and Willy's clear enthusiasm and, for a time, there was a plan for William and Harriet to go alone. But not for long. In the face of much friendly advice to the contrary, both Sir David and a friend of the family, Mrs Somerville (well known author of *Physical Geography* and a rather formidable lady) persuaded William that what Willy and Charlie might lose in a formal education they would gain overwhelmingly in the acquisition of foreign languages and in the broadening of the mind which an extended visit to France and Italy would bring.

Soon the family were packing up crates of William's pictures, finished and half-finished, arranging their storage and eventual sale through a friend who agreed to lease their house, amassing such bric-a-brac as an itinerant painter might need for a couple of years abroad (sketch pads, camp stools, colour boxes, canvasses) and poring over Madame Stark's *Handbook to Italy*. To travel so far *en famille* in those days was certainly a challenge and it was one, to her credit, that Harriet rose to magnificently.

William had his contacts, his introductions and his work; the children a simple adventure ahead of them; Harriet had the prospect of existing in foreign lands, with all the backache, stomach complaints and anxieties it then involved and with the knowledge that money, though available, was not in constant supply. She put on a brave face and poured out her

[28]

anxieties into her diary. Even there, there were calm blissful periods on the tortuous way to Rome, Naples and Sorrento.

They left Porchester Terrace, with all their luggage in a fly, at nine o'clock on Monday morning, September 19th, to pick up Henry Rice and his daughter May, a legal friend who was living in Jermyn Street – and whom they were accompanying to Paris. They transferred to the Dover coach, *The Union*, in Piccadilly and apart from noticing Canterbury Cathedral, Harriet found little of interest on the way, arrived at Dover with a headache, disliked the Ship Hotel and had a bad night.

Next day, however, most anxieties had gone. They walked along the pier in the morning sunshine, sailed across to Boulogne around one o'clock and had a remarkably smooth passage. They found Boulogne 'improved' though hardly took to the idea of sharing their evening meal at the *table d'hôte* and turned up their noses at French cooking. It was another four days before they arrived in Paris, William for the second time, Harriet and the boys for the first.

William missed the old trees along the boulevards and felt the place had lost its character. Harriet found the noise and smell insufferable, the streets filthy and 'no shops to be compared to Regent Street'. But there were compensations. The boys were taken to the Tuileries Gardens, got on well with the French boys and were delighted to try the language again. The Louvre too lived up to expectations and William no doubt rejoiced at seeing Sir Robert and Lady Peel there.

Harriet at least had insisted on being taken to the livelier part of Paris around the Palais Royal. The buildings crowded together with their restaurants, trinket shops, ribbon shops and toy shops all on different levels, overlooking three sides of a square, and Harriet was no doubt as interested in the strange people mingling there as in the food they eventually sampled at the Café de Mille Colonnes, clearly the highlight of the visit, rating 'very good' in her little book. Next night was a quieter affair, a dinner *en famille* in their own rooms and once again, alas, the plaintive cry 'tough mutton but glad of anything plain'.

Then came the long haul through France to the Mediterranean, a row with their conductor who was clearly swindling them, switches from the original diligence to a cart, from that to a posting carriage, then on a steam boat and eventually a canal boat. Finally came a scene missed by both William and Harriet in their diaries but recalled in vivid retrospect by the budding author. They had taken refuge for the night beyond Arles, close to the various mouths of the Rhone, in a village built on piles surrounded by water, rather like Venice. Wilkie wrote that the place, Martigue by name, was 'inhabited by a race of people who seemed half-smugglers and half-fishermen and furnished with one small inn, the master of which, never having seen an Englishman before, sat down to dinner with his customers and kept his cap on with edifying independence'.

After this Marseilles was welcome, though not for long. Harriet's burden began to increase as they felt the need to settle down for a little while. The harbour smelled 'in a disgusting manner'. There were 'no gardens, no sea, no country'. Charlie went down with the usual stomach complaints. Harriet had rows with the washerwoman over charges worse than Paris. And very soon she was confiding that 'every day that passes I dislike the place more'.

Meanwhile, William and Willy, partly oblivious to the domestic turmoil, were away sketching. This was virtually the first time that they had had any time together on their own. William took Willy under his wing as a potential art student, as a matter of course. Willy, too, hardly questioned it. But the basic differences between them were already emerging. Subtly at first, more obviously later. Willy found it natural to sketch and join his father, but his interests were also turning to the written word and to the books his temporary tutors were encouraging him to explore. Well-told stories enthralled him and he was soon finding it difficult to replenish the flow of books as they journeyed onward to their Italian goal.

Soon they were through Toulon and Cannes and they reached Nice. Here the Italian frontier beckoned and the mountains and warm November air made them feel that at last they had arrived. While Harriet was busy unpacking, William and the boys were 'sketching in a pretty garden near our church, mountains grouped in the background, orange trees in blossom and a hedge of blooming roses, William drawing figures from recollection'.

It was too good to last. Harriet's stomach rebelled, 'they were almost poisoned with bad mutton chops', the weather turned cold and they suddenly realised that cholera had broken out in Italy. They were stuck only half way to their destination and the stomach infection seemed determined to attack each in turn. And suddenly, to Willy's consternation, they found him a regular tutor.

It was in fact an unsettling time. They had periods of utter bliss, going on donkeys towards Villefranche ('with Charlie in ecstasies'), passing olive groves along the mountain sides, overlooking the sea and passing 'numerous smiling villas surrounded with gardens'. Even in December William was forced to use an umbrella against the fierce sun. At the same time, Harriet was suffering agonies both with her own stomach and with

Charlie who seemed to be growing weak, vomiting constantly and rarely sleeping. Then, to cap it all, William was thrown from his horse hurting his shoulder and probably frightening the family more than himself. It was only a step from this final blow to a decision to go on to Genoa and face the risk of cholera.

The journey to Genoa and by ship to Leghorn was comfortable and indeed restful. They even had a pleasant side trip to see the leaning tower of Pisa, before being greeted by Seymour Kirkups[1], a former student of the Royal Academy, in Florence. They were genuinely astonished at what they saw in the Pitti Palace and had hardly realised what differences there would be between the current copies of the Old Masters they had grown used to in London and the real thing. It was simply a taste of what they were to see in Rome. Their astonishment at what they were seeing in the galleries helped to take their minds off the appalling weather – for after the heat of the south of France, Florence was deep in snow.

Rome, however, was their goal and five days after leaving Florence they drove through the gates of Rome at five in the morning on January 7th. It had taken them three and a half months since leaving Porchester Terrace. They immediately headed for Joseph Severn's house, an associate of the Royal Academy, and an old friend of David Wilkie's. He quickly directed them to the Hotel Spillman, not exactly on the Piazza di Spagna (the centre of the English quarter of Rome) but just two blocks away on the corner of the Corso and the Via della Croce. They needed a rest before looking for permanent lodgings.

Joseph Severn[2] and his wife helped considerably. Harriet's diary still has a list of possible lodging houses pencilled in the front. One along the Via Laurena, another along the Via di Repetia ('second floor is also to be let'), as well as one along the Via Felice. Harriet spent a couple of days, together with Mrs Severn, looking for accommodation, while William sneaked off for his first glimpse of St Peter's. On his return he almost persuaded the family that the old painting quarters of Claude would be ideal, but Harriet disliked the people and they finally settled on a 'nice suite of apartments in the Via Felice[3]' with a charming niche for the Madonna above the door. Fifteen years later Wilkie was reporting back to his brother Charles 'the Virgin is still in the niche – the cabbage stalks and rubbish are strewn about underneath – the very door looks as if it had never been painted since we left it'.

For the first few days William could hardly keep away from St Peter's or the Sistine Chapel. He went alone and he took the boys to hear the music. Then they, or particularly Harriet, discovered the Pincio Hill. It was to prove the equivalent for her of Kensington Gardens, for she was constantly there with the boys while William was away sketching or searching for models. And its impact on Willy's future efforts as a writer was to prove decisive.

Rome intoxicated them, as it can so easily do, in those first few days and weeks. William and Willy went through the Borghese Palace. The whole family went to the horse races. Mr Severn arranged a carriage to take them to the Colosseum by moonlight. They were all taken to the opera including the boys 'who were delighted'. And why not? They saw a comic ballet, the first act of a Bellini opera, a Grand Ball and, as a finale, the first act of another opera. Quite a feast for a fourteen and a ten year old, and close enough to their birthdays to be regarded as an appropriate present from their new found home.

And so the days passed. They were in an agreeable climate, among friends and certainly bumping into new English visitors – either in the Caffe Greco (then as now off the Piazza di Spagna), in the studios, or among the obvious sites. William and Harriet, for example, ran into the Palmers, Linnell's wife's parents, in church one Sunday morning.

The English art community revolved around Gibson[4] and Wyatt, the sculptors, but Severn, Brigstoke, Williams and the indefatigable Miss MacKenzie all stirred the Roman pot nicely for William and Harriet – accompanying them on their visits, negotiating models, making up picnics and smoothing their path generally. Other giants strode the stage from time to time, as the carriages appeared and reassembled in the Piazza di Spagna.

Harriet was startled one evening on the Pincio Hill to be greeted by William Wordsworth and his travelling companion, Henry Crabbe Robinson, an acquaintance of Hampstead days, on their first evening in Rome. Crabbe Robinson got Wordsworth nicely placed in the Caffe Greco while he and Miss MacKenzie (a descendant of the Earl of Seaforth who had become a local resident after a disappointing love affair), planned Wordsworth's next few days.

Miss MacKenzie offered her carriage and William made a number of suggestions about 'some pleasing pictures in an obscure church adjoining the fountain of Trevi'[5]. William had plainly slipped easily into the role of local guide. Wordsworth was quickly put through his paces in his first few days – the Colosseum, Pantheon, St Peter's, the Forum – and Crabbe Robinson's enthusiasm was overwhelming. 'To Wordsworth', he confided to his diary, 'it must have been unparalleled'. Wordsworth himself later had a rather different description for his companion's enthusiasms; 'unbearable'[6]. Harriet and William at least smoothed part of his path and repaid some of his hospitality for William's earlier visits to Grasmere.

It was not long before Willy, too, was introduced to the well-known poet by his father on the Pincio Hill. 'I was a boy then', he reminisced later, 'and was much struck by the remarkable kindliness and mildness of his manners'. Willy was nothing if not observant. 'He seemed as little fitted, as any I ever saw, to bear (much less to *enjoy*) the bustle and constant change of a travelling life – he looked, to use the common phrase, "quite out of his element" in a foreign land, and among foreign people.'

Wordsworth was particularly perturbed at the news of the outbreak of cholera in Naples. 'I remember being quite astonished at the earnestness with which he entreated my father to do as *he* intended to do, and not only abandon all idea of going to Naples, but leave Rome at once for England. My father tried in vain to combat his apprehensions – the very idea of the cholera seemed to fill him with horror – he left Italy, as he had determined to leave it, and we went on, as we had determined'[7].

Before long Easter was upon them and like Protestants before and since, Harriet entered with enthusiasm into the Catholic processions and ceremonies of Holy Week. Her diary was transformed from the usual six terse lines a day to flowing descriptive passages. The excitement got them up early on the Thursday of Holy Week and Harriet's diary began to reflect the atmosphere. She was disappointed that the ears were entranced rather more than the eye by the initial ceremonies, but later she had to confess that she was becoming visually moved.

'We were in the Sistine Chapel soon after half past eight, stayed through a long dull service and then went into the Sala Reggia where we stood to receive the procession of the Pope carrying the host through to the Pauline. This was most splendid and imposing, the cardinals glittering in white and gold robes, the Pope in white and gold and a white and gold veil thrown over a white and gold canopy carried over him. As this glittering cavalcade left the Sistine Chapel a strong gleam of sunshine fell on it and produced the most marvellous effect, while at the other end through the ample folding doors leading to the Pauline Chapel the holy sepulchre was seen dazzling with immeasurable light'.[8]

Even lyricists have to move fast on such occasions and she and the boys had to run 'with all speed' to get to St Peters in time for the washing of the Pilgrims' feet, but, alas, all the best places had been taken and they were soon dashing to the next vantage point at another hall in the Vatican where 'by dint of great pushing and squeezing' she got a tolerable place and saw the Pilgrims come in, each with a bunch of flowers in his hand and draped in white robes and high summer white caps.

Easter day itself was a repeat of such strenuous sight-seeing – at St Peters again by half past eight – in the appointed places (Harriet in the ladies' box and William and the boys in the Loggia of St Andrew), to watch another grand procession go its appointed way. The Swiss guards and the noble guards with their gay uniforms and white plumes excited the boys. The Pope was carried past them in his chair of state of crimson and gold and with a canopy of white and gold, with two immense fans of peacock feathers on each side of him.

'We returned home satisfied,' Harriet noted laconically. 'We had tried our utmost to see everything and considering the crowds and bad weather we succeeded in viewing to the best advantage all the principal ceremonies.' Then followed, as an appropriate finale, a wonderful display of fireworks, set off from the Castle of San Angelo which at one time took on the appearance of a gigantic palace of diamonds, and at another an imitation of the eruption of Vesuvius. Harriet could hardly complain of any lack of visual excitement by the end of the weekend.

These were simply grandiose interruptions to what had become Harriet's routine wanderings through Rome invariably from the Via Felice along what is now the Via Sistina, past the tops of the Spanish steps (the Trinità di Monte) to what was then and possibly still is the best view of Rome: the panorama from the Pincian Hill. An American artist has given us a clear description of it in exactly the year Harriet and the boys frequented it so much.

'When I first saw the place, in 1837, it was a scantily wooded area, ill-kept, and without pretension as to embellishment or order of any kind, although it was, as now the fashionable drive . . . Once more the sun is sinking towards the horizon. The winding ways of the Pincio are crowded, as we see, with equipages of every sort and description . . . People from every clime are driving or promenading to see and to be seen, the greater part of them, that is, but some among them come to watch the sun go down behind St Peter's dome that dwarfs everything near it'.[9]

Not such a far cry from Miss Thackeray's better known description of the Pincio as a 'fashionable halo of sunset and pink parasols'. At any rate Harriet and the boys were there almost daily, between their regular tuition periods (mainly by Harriet, partly by a tutor) and their sketching visits to Monte Mario, the Villa Borghese and the Colosseum.

What Willy thought of the Pincio is not in doubt. Writing ten years later he put it quite simply: 'Who that has been at Rome does not remember with delight the attractions of the Pincian Hill? Who, after toiling through the wonders of the dark, melancholy city has not been revived by a visit to its shady walks, and by breathing its fragrant breezes? . . . From its smooth summit, the city is seen in its utmost majesty, and the surrounding country in its brightest aspect.' It is not hard to see him browsing through the ruins, looking over the parapet at the view, perhaps even brooding over Nero's ghost which was said to pervade the place.

It had a wild history, originally known as the 'Hill of Gardens'[10] where Nero was buried in A.D. 68. His body, Suetonius tells us, was wrapped in white sheetings and deposited there by two of his mistresses. Five hundred years later Belisarius lived in his palace on virtually the same spot. If one looks over the wall of the gardens at the right angle, one can see the so-called Muro-Torto on part of the original Roman wall which has never been fully restored, and which, one likes to think, intrigued Willy enough to ponder and eventually to persuade him to write his first published novel.

If *Antonina* was conceived anywhere, this was the place and this the time. As Willy eventually wrote over ten years later, 'Near the Pincian Gate there is a part of the wall which is rent, the stones having been separated for a long time; and this rent does not only begin from the middle, but goes from the bottom to the top; and makes the wall incline so much, yet without falling, that it seems both to lean out and to be recessed back, owing to the rent and the breach in it'[11]. He was quoting from a contemporary guide. But the break in the wall was one he had noticed himself as a thirteen year old. Like his mother, he was attracted to the visual: he simply began to provide it with a different outlet. And it was on the Pincio Hill and his own forays elsewhere in Italy that the difference may well have been set in motion. The writer had emerged from the artists. Willy could hardly be aware of it himself. To his father the shock that the embryo painter might be tempted to other accomplishments was still to come.

His father's models had clearly intrigued him since his arrival in Rome. The Spanish steps were the main market place, though William had his own contacts too, through Joseph Severn and Thomas Brigstoke. One particular young boy caught Willy's eye – 'a beautiful boy, with features dazzlingly perfect, who had sat to every one for cupids, angels, and whatever else was lovely and refined'. He also caught Willy's developing imagination, for the boy was in private life, 'one of the most consummate rascals in Rome – a gambler, a thief, and a *stiletto* wearer, at twelve years of age'.

Again in the Colosseum one evening, Willy's attention, like William's, was arrested by the sight of a penitent in front of a small altar, accompanied by a peasant woman prostrate in adoration and a Carmelite monk beating his breast. The penitent was covered by a hood with two eye-holes 'looking spectral, as his veiled, motionless form half disappeared in the gathering gloom'. To William it was a visual challenge, which in fact he never finally faced; but in Willy who knows what thoughts the vision was beginning to stir, and did again, in a more acute form, in Naples a few weeks later, where they witnessed the trial of a monk accused of murdering a woman for money.

If Willy himself is to be believed, Rome opened his eyes to more than the characters around him. Little more than a year after his first bout of calf-love in Bayswater, he experienced his 'first love adventure'. Collins recounted the affair to Charles Dickens on his next visit to Rome seventeen years later. Dickens quickly passed on the account to his sister-in-law, Georgina Hogarth[12], adding with relish that the affair had 'proceeded, if I may be allowed the expression, to the utmost extremities'. Dickens spared Georgina any more details, simply stressing that Willy 'came out quite a pagan Jupiter in the business', being all of thirteen years old at the time.

Was Willy as romantically precocious as he claimed or were solid facts being slightly embellished in the telling several years later? Whatever the truth, his sexual awareness was persistently aroused from this time onwards.

Little wonder that Willy was reluctant to move on from Rome. But after a while William began to feel that the time had come to push further south, as a tourist if not an artist. Naples called, even if the shadow of cholera still hung over it. So early one morning saw the family coaching across the Pontine Marshes south of Rome well before the heat of the day, and they were wheeling into the square of the Hotel de la Grande Europe, close to the Villa Reale on the Neapolitan shore-line, by the following evening.

Once again the usual routine followed – an intense week of sight-seeing and, on the part of Harriet, the discovery of another equivalent of Kensington Gardens – somewhere to walk agreeably, read her papers and take the boys while William was away sketching. The Villa Reale might have been made to measure. It was virtually on the seashore where the noisy, smelly Neapolitan traffic now winds around the Villa Communale.

Kathryn Sedgwick[13] preserved its flavour admirably within a year or so of Harriet's visit:

'One of our daily pleasures is a walk in the Villa Reale, a public promenade-garden between the Chiaia – the great streets of Naples – and the bay. The garden is about a mile in length, well planted with trees and flowering shrubs, and abounding in fountains – the very spirit and voice of this land of the South. The brightest flowers are the English children who take their daily recreation in the garden – beautiful scions they are of a noble stock . . . No carriages or beggars are permitted within the garden [which] is embellished with statue casts of our friends in Rome . . . and certain not strikingly modest groups. The unrivalled charm of the Villa Reale is the view of the Bay'.

Little wonder that Harriet made it her base as William and the boys went about their sightseeing. By this time Willy usually accompanied his father and Charlie his mother. William and Willy were soon up to the top of Vesuvius while Charlie had to make do with the Villa Reale. Soon it was Harriet's turn – a full exhausting trip to Pozzuoli, Ischia and back through Procida for lunch, then on to Baiae and to Sybil's cave on donkeys by moonlight; finally by rowing boat and carriage back to the hotel. 'A delightful excursion.' A week later William was off to Capri while Harriet took the boys shopping on the bustling, noisy Strado Toledo. But usually the interludes were back in that familiar oasis – the Villa Reale.

William too soon found its charm – though more likely at the edges where propriety spilled over into the noisy beach scenes he loved to sketch. Frances Trollope had the same experience[14]: 'Upon stretching our wanderings a little beyond the full dressed statue-and-flower-decked precincts of the Villa Reale, we came upon a series of pictures which certainly did not appear to owe their charm to the delicacy of the airs that breathed around them. Where the royal garden ends, in the closest possible juxtaposition to it, being scarcely separated by any fence at all, is a spot sacred to picturesque dirt, historic rags and miscellaneous labour of the most various kinds . . . Here we had Salvators, and Murillos, in life, to a degree of perfection that cannot be conceived without being seen . . . Gangs of men drawing up their boats from the surf . . . while others, at not great distance above them, the tideless waves giving no cause for fear, had their little vessels turned keel upwards, while they repair some threatening leak'.

This was what William had come to Italy to see and experience. But after about a month of the bustle of Naples, they suddenly noticed a strange outcrop of yellow sedan chairs with closed windows moving slowly through the Neopolitan streets; and they quickly learnt they were the victims of cholera being quietly taken to the hospital. Once again William had to make a quick decision and made all haste to move to Sorrento with his family.

It was a wise decision and as it happened, initially, a happy one. The weather was pleasurably hot, the bay full of delights and the plain a mass of orange groves. The short sea journey was not exactly comfortable. 'Not very choice company', as Harriet put it, 'though quiet and civil'. And soon they were in the good hands of their new English friends, Dr Murray, Captain English and Major Thew and their wives.

They quickly found a house to let on a cliff top, overlooking the sea, on the outskirts of Sorrento at what is now the village of S. Agnello. It had many advantages. It was close to their newly-found English friends. It was near the Convento dei Capuccini, where William was able to sketch both the monks and gardens. It was also close to the Cocumella[15], an old Jesuit college with grounds close to the cliff top, from whence William could walk down a tortuous cliff path, through caverns, to the Caves of Ulysses (or Sirens) below.

The Cocumella, (now a hotel) the Capuccine Convent and the cliff path are still there, though the caves are surrounded by hundreds of holidaymakers. In those days it was an idyllic spot, quiet and undisturbed. Harriet found it heavenly walking back in the evening along the cliff top after an enchanting meal with the Englishes. They walked home by moonlight and saw their first firefly. William could go down to the beach any morning for his sketching missions, looking, in Willy's later words, 'one way towards the noble promontory of Massa, the ancient dominion of the Syren Queens, and could see in the other direction, the clear outline of the classic Vesuvius, ever crowned, even on the fairest days, with its thin volcanic cloud of white smoke'. He sketched while Willy bathed.

Their troubles, alas, were about to begin. The weather moved, in Harriet's code, from 'hot' through 'very hot' to 'intensely hot'. William continued to paint outside, finding local models, and even sitting in a boat throughout the midday heat. Willy was found a Latin tutor in the person of Captain English. So June and part of July passed apparently uneventfully. The caves of Ulysses down below their house became more and more attractive both for sketching and bathing. Willy continued to have his almost daily tutorial.

Soon, however, Harriet's diary speaks of being 'quite overcome'; and then, surprisingly, 'Willy very tiresome all day. His father obliged to punish him at dinner time. Made us all miserable'. Next day, as everyone went to the top of the house to see the sunset, and then went out for a walk along the cliffs, Willy thoughtlessly locked Harriet on the roof. The following day William complained of feeling ill and he was soon in bed.

The heat had at last got them down and poor William had had far too much of the sun. It was the beginning of a very worrying August for them all. The trouble was that, as he perked up, as he occasionally did, out he went in the sun again. Finally, he had to give up and took to his bed with rheumatic pains in his back and chest and inflammation in the eyes. Whether the medical treatment helped is a matter of conjecture, for within a matter of days he was treated with leeches, James powder, castor oil, camphor, blue pills, colchium and hot salt water baths. Finally his doctor recommended that he go to take the baths across the water in Ischia. It was a sad sight as all his friends waved him and the family goodbye from the foreshore on his way to what proved to be a reasonable convalescence.

Even there Willy's tantrums continued to erupt. He offended his father soon after arrival and was forbidden to ride his favourite donkey. Next day, Harriet again records 'Willy in disgrace again' and once again he was deprived of his regular ride.

One cannot help feeling that the whole family was nearing the end of its tether, in coping with the heat and with the unnatural surroundings they had chosen for themselves. A few weeks later William had a further accident while out riding, his donkey stumbling and throwing him over its head. He was more frightened than hurt. It hardly helped his recovery, but it hastened their return to Naples.

The weather turned out tranquil and warm throughout November, though both William and Willy managed to catch an irritable (and itchy) fever for a couple of days. (They put it down to the natural results of the baths at Ischia.) The final blow came at the end of the year, and brought Harriet's terse diary into full flood once again on New Year's Eve.

'After a visit to a Palazzo to see a private art gallery we returned home, little before four. Boys in Villa Reale at play. After we came in Mr and Mrs Turner called. While talking with them the boys returned. My poor Charlie with his coat half off. His arm hanging and in broken voice he exclaimed "I have broken my arm". The eldest Iggulden[16] and a strange boy accompanied them and Master Galway[17], whom we afterwards learned was the culprit, who had pushed my poor little victim from the wall of the villa towards the sand. He proposed calling his brother, a surgeon, but Mr Turner over-ruled this and sent off for Mr O'Reilly and Dr Strange. They both came. The arm was set and bound up. My poor child behaving like a hero. His bed was moved into our room and he was put into it. His pain increased all the evening. We got to bed soon after eleven but no sleep. Scarcely all night. Poor Charlie screaming with pain'.

It was a family event that reverberated between them down the years. It was recalled in one of Willy's letters home from school two years later; it cropped up in Wilkie's *Memoirs* of his father; and it crept into one of Charlie's own articles for *Household Words*. Charlie's cries in the night had also penetrated Harriet's soul, for she too poured out all that she had been bottling up for so long on that New Year's Eve.

'Many months of this past year', she wrote that evening, 'have passed in much anxiety and fatigue . . . by the severe affliction of rheumatism suffered by my husband. Many times my patience has failed me. Many times my heart has been oppressed with weariness by reason of sin, a spirit of discord and misery seemed to press upon us that never existed before. Lord remove these burdens that come from the bondage of Satan. The climate of Italy is not favourable to the bodily or mental temperament of my husband. This is a fact of which I am well afraid . . . The chief drawback to the enjoyment of the beauties and advantages of Italy is the dreadful and debasing idolatry they call the Christian religion. Not a trace to be found of the religion revealed in God's word but a few names for instance, Jesu Christo, but how his mother is exalted on every occasion above him.'

There was more to the family discord than religion and the heat of southern Italy. Willy's close proximity to his father for the first time had hardly helped. William's persistence in guiding Willy through his own childhood painting memories and passions had begun to jar, as Willy's interests began to develop in other directions. He was beginning to read avidly and had been stimulated even further by a casual American acquaintance in Sorrento, who lent him further books to read. His eyes had been opened and had already begun to explore other possibilities than painting. And, if he is to be believed, Italy had provided him with a remarkably early sexual experience of a kind his father could hardly have contemplated. Neither Willy nor his father was fully aware of the gulf that was opening up between them. But it was in southern Italy that much of it began.

CHAPTER FIVE

Youth

NAPLES WAS far from the end of the family's Italian journey. But it had reached its climax and they were all, mentally, beginning to return home. William would be returning to the Academy, Willy to a new school, Charlie eventually to art school and Harriet, ultimately, to a life-style she could hardly have contemplated just then.

They had been beaten by the weather. William averred he 'would not venture to live in southern Italy another summer, to be as great as Turner himself'. So they made their leisurely way home, through Rome, Florence (where they met a descendant of Michelangelo), Bologna, Parma, Verona, Padua and Venice. Here they loitered in the melancholy atmosphere, William seeking the odd and strange rather than the grand and obvious, while Willy gathered still more oddities for his growing fund of visual stories (Beppo, Lord Byron's former cook, acting as William's gondolier on condition he did not have to row the boat outside a hotel and William himself holding up traffic on the Grand Canal while he finished a particular canvas, without a murmur from the locals).

So, through Innsbruck, Salzburg and Munich to London and to the problem of where to live and where to send Willy to school. The lease of the Bayswater house had been disposed of and they finally settled on a house at the Regents Park end of Avenue Road – number 20. This in turn suggested a school in North London for Willy, and one run by a fairly well known cleric, the Reverend Henry Cole, at 39 Highbury Place, was finally chosen.

The building is still there overlooking the Green and in those days must have been extremely rural and quiet. The cashier of the Bank of England had lived next door some years earlier. Henry Cole had been running a small, though select, boys' school for some three or four years when Willy's name was put down for the Michaelmas term of 1838; he was also the local Minister at Providence Chapel, on the West side of what is now Upper Street, near the Green.

Henry Cole[1] ran the school with his wife Frances, with the help of a couple of young assistant masters (one French) and four servants. There were normally thirty pupils ranging between the ages of nine and fifteen. Willy's views of the school have come out clearly in his letters home. It was a difficult adjustment for him. He had spent only a year or so at Maida Hill Academy (as a day pupil) before he was whisked away in what must have been the most momentous period of his early life. To return to the discipline of school, to live away from his parents for the first time and to be bursting with 'life abroad' all at the same time, was unlikely to produce the kind of results he achieved so quickly at Maida Hill, nor the friendliness with his school colleagues, nor indeed with the headmaster, that he might have wished for.

His letters home are cheerful enough but the tensions occasionally lurk beneath the banter. To his credit he saw these three scholastic years through with reasonable good humour. His letters home, mainly to Harriet, talk of long walks and sailing home-made boats during the summer and the inevitable sliding on the local ponds during the hard winter months. He was also sketching, asking for his father's opinion of 'a whole host of works of art' he had finished during term-time.

Schoolboys have changed little. He welcomed the delicious figs brought specially by Elizabeth (presumably one of the Linnell girls), found his mother's cake 'delectably luscious', admired his new trousers ('the nicest pair I ever had') and managed to scrape into school after the holidays with five minutes to spare, having had to wait rather longer than he expected for the local connecting omnibus (they still went by way of the Angel, taking close on an hour for the five and a half miles from Avenue Road)[2].

School itself was another matter. Although he had done some Latin privately, before and during his travels, Highbury Place was where he began to take an active dislike to its disciplines. Henry Cole's sermons, which the senior boys had to copy and summarise regularly, were also to remind him rather too vividly of his father's own sermonising. Unfortunately the classics (reflected so painfully in Willy's copper-plate summaries of Virgil's *Aeneid*, under Mr Cole's supervision), and the strict Christian ethic, were the twin hallmarks of this particular private school.

Willy no doubt returned from his Italian adventure something of a travel and art bore. Even on his next trip to Rome with Charles Dickens, fifteen years later, the main complaint about him was his 'continually holding forth about reds and greens and things coming well with other things and lines being wrong and lines being right'. Dickens regarded it as a mild eccentricity. His companions at school plainly reacted more violently and he upset both the senior boys and the headmaster's wife.

In a couple of letters to his mother, written in schoolboy Italian (fluent but with the occasional ungrammatical idiom, with lapses into English)[3], he confessed that he had been given extra 'lines' as a punishment because of a contretemps with 'the beautiful and amiable wife of the master of the prison'. She had told him he could 'tell a *lie* beautifully. She is a bit inclined, poor dear, to anger'. He told his mother he was practising his languages by writing in Italian. More likely it was the only way he could let off steam without Mr Cole or his wife being aware of his views, for he added, 'in this accursed place we cannot get any news'.

His school companions naturally resented his proficiency in French and his knowledge of Voltaire, as well as his wide and catholic taste in literature, ranging from Goethe and Sterne (absorbed from the American acquaintance in Sorrento) to Walter Scott, and Fenimore Cooper; and they took it out on him in their own way, forcing him to tell them stories during the evening on pain of further punishment[4]. The senior boy in his dormitory was fond of a good tale in bed and when Wilkie appeared as a newcomer, the other inmates had presumably been sucked dry. Wilkie rose to the bait on most occasions and, if not, was rewarded by a thrashing, or so he said.

'The oldest of the boys, appointed to preserve order', he later explained, 'was placed in authority over us as captain of the room. He was as fond of hearing stories, when he had retired for the night, as the Oriental despot to whose literary tastes we are indebted for *The Arabian Nights*, and I was the unhappy boy chosen to amuse him. It was useless to ask for mercy and beg leave to be allowed to go to sleep. "You will go to sleep, Collins, when you have told me a story. . . ." If I rebelled, the captain possessed a means of persuasion in the shape of an improved cat-o'-ninetails invented by himself. When I was obstinate I felt the influence of persuasion. When my better sense prevailed, I learnt to be amusing on a short notice'[5]. A painful beginning for our born story-teller. But he, at least, believed in the stimulus. 'It is a fact that it was this brute', he later explained, 'who first awakened in me, his poor little victim, a power of which but for him I might never have been aware. Certainly no-one in my "own home" credited me with it and when I left school I still continued story-telling for my own pleasure'[6].

He relished his school stories in after years, possibly more than he did at the time, and enjoyed even more explaining what happened to his tormentors. The school bully apparently died shortly afterwards in India;

while his companion who charged a penny for the spectacle of seeing him swallow a spider ended up as one of the leading lawyers of the day[7].

He was also fond of taking the 'bad boy' role himself. 'When I was at school', he told a friend in later life, 'perpetually getting punished, the master used to turn me to good moral account as a means of making his model scholars ashamed of their occasional lapses into misconduct. "If it had been Collins, I should not have felt shocked and surprised. Nobody expects anything of *him*. But *you!*" '[8] In short, he hardly settled down to Mr Cole's regime in the three years he was at Highbury and was still unclear as to what lay ahead of him when the time came to leave in 1841.

Willy had not only read more widely during his travels through Italy than his school friends; he had also been exposed to sights, events and feelings which had stirred the imagination and turned him away from the purely visual concerns of his father. Given the right stimulus at school, however brutal, he now found that he could conjure up plots and stories with little difficulty. It was something he quickly accepted and increasingly turned to as a pleasurable outlet.

His father may not have fully realised what was stirring within his elder son, but it was at least becoming clear that Charlie, not Willy, would be the real inheritor of William's artistic talents, thus fulfilling the predictions of Sir David Wilkie. At all events Charlie was soon entered at art school, prior to gaining the prestigious acceptance by the Royal Academy (in the year Holman Hunt was turned down). But what about Willy? His father's first inclination, he tells us, was for him to go to Oxford with a view to entering the Church.

The idea seems to have been pressed with remarkably little vigour: nor were Willy's own ideas particularly well received. 'I told my father that I thought I should like to write books, though how to write, or on what subjects, I don't believe at the time I had the smallest conception. However, I began to scribble in a desultory kind of way, and drifted, I hardly know how, into tale-writing. . . . This went on for some time, till an intimate friend of my father's remonstrated with him on the folly of allowing me to waste my time on a pursuit which could never lead to anything but the traditional poverty of the poor author and he mentioned an eligible opening in a tea-merchant's firm as a suitable position for me'[9].

William was going through a particularly bad patch. His health had already begun to deteriorate; his tetchiness was increasing in his letters home; and he plainly had difficulties in coping with the high spirits and independence beginning to be shown by Willy. The delayed effects of the rheumatism he had contracted in Italy were first shown in a severe inflammation of the eyes. One minor result was that a commission requested by the young Charles Dickens in the summer of 1839 was never completed. A more fundamental outcome was a decision to remove to a house with a drier foundation (gravel rather than clay) and by the autumn of 1840 they had moved from the outskirts of Regents Park (in Avenue Road) to the outskirts of Hyde Park (in Oxford Terrace).

Willy's future, however, was still the main focus of attention. Tea-merchanting resolved nothing. To William it was a possible means of livelihood; to Willy simply a place to revert to his old pursuit of putting pen to paper. Edward Antrobus, who had come to the rescue, was a well-to-do tea-merchant running his own business, with the royally approved description of 'Teaman to Her Majesty', from premises in the west end of the Strand. He was an expert at the top of his profession and William had painted his three children (for two hundred guineas).

Antrobus must have taken Willy on, fully aware of the likely outcome, if not from the clues given when William invited him to meet Willy over dinner, at least from Willy's subsequent behaviour either in the office ('whenever he found me tale-writing, I was always able to show that I had finished everything I had been given to do')[10] or when on leave, peren- nially seeking an extension of another week. If invoices, bills of lading and the state of the Chinese tea market passed Willy by, he was, according to one old friend, slowly trying his hand at 'tragedies, comedies, epic poems and the usual literary rubbish invariably accumulated about themselves by "young beginners"'[11].

The situation of Antrobus's office would encourage such enterprises. It was virtually in the heart of the publishing world. Next door were the publishers of the *Saturday Magazine*. Not far away were *Punch*, the *Illustrated London News*, the *Satirist*, the *Colonial Gazette*, Bell's *Life in Lon- don*, the *Observer* and Chapman & Hall's various monthlies. And only a couple of hundred yards towards Fleet Street were scores of small publishing offices. Willy had not far to go in offering his early journalistic efforts. By 1843 he had a signed article accepted by Douglas Jerrold's *Illuminated Magazine*[12] and a year later William was sending Willy's 'cut- tings' to his old friend Dr Norris, President of Corpus Christi College, Oxford, seeking his opinion, and discussing Willy's latest poem with Harriet.

Willy had got into his stride sufficiently to impress his father, though the twinges of doubt about his ability to earn a living continued, for William was soon sounding out Landseer again, presumably with a view to some opening at the Royal Academy. Behind these anxieties were the continual strains that had clearly built up between them as Willy's interests and intentions clashed with William's. His father's early attempts to entice him into his own artistic world had had only partial success, occasionally enthralling him with Landseer's tales over dinner, or introducing him to Edward Ward, a more rewarding younger companion.

William's anxieties were not helped by his failing health. Following the need to rest his eyes for a full six months in the late 1830s, his energy began to be sapped by increasing pain, especially around his heart. By the spring of 1842 his doctor had told him the truth: he had an 'organic disease of the heart' and he ought to ease up. So he did for a time; but it did not prevent him from taking Willy on a trip to the Shetlands to complete a series of sketches for Sir Walter Scott's romance *The Pirate*.

From all accounts they got on well together, Willy free from the drudgery of the tea-trade fully appreciating his father's dedication ('with one knee on the ground, steadying himself against the wind; his companion holding a tattered umbrella over him to keep the rain off his sketch-book')[13] and, in retrospect, storing up his own impressions of the scene of Clareland's shipwreck in Scott's romance, almost a preview of *Armadale*:

> 'The way thither, over vast treeless moors, intersected here and there by an arm of the sea, penetrated by nothing broader than a footpath, bounded by bleak hills, and overshadowed by wild stormy clouds, presented a monotonous grandeur, in its very barrenness'.[14]

Within a year William was seeking medical advice again and, at the same time, finally coming to terms with Willy's future. He wrote in his private diary, the first intimation that Willy might be tempted 'to furnish the world with a memoir of my life'. What had convinced William is difficult to say: Willy's persistence; his stream of printed articles; or perhaps even the completion (and the determination to complete) a full-length novel about Polynesia called *Iolani*. It must have caused something of a stir in Devonport Street (the more commodious house they had moved into), while it was being hawked around the publishers.

He went away to Paris with high hopes that the manuscript would help his parents to raise a hundred pounds on his account and even tried to borrow from them on the strength of it. But Chapman & Hall were evidently not impressed. 'My youthful imagination', Willy confessed later, 'ran riot among the noble savages, in scenes which caused the respectable British publisher to declare that it was impossible to put his name on the title-page of such a novel.'[15]

Eventually he induced his father to submit it to Longmans 'whose reader presently returned it with an intimation that the story was hopelessly bad, and that in his opinion the writer had not the slightest aptitude for romance-writing'. As Willy later recalled, 'I met the worthy man years after at a dinner party, when *The Woman in White* was running through *Household Words*, and I remember that neither of us could forbear from bursting out and laughing at the *rencontré*. What would have made them laugh even louder perhaps, as we shall see later, would have been the knowledge that it would take at least another 150 years before it was finally published.

After the failure of his first novel, according to Collins, 'everybody seemed to conspire to shut the gates of the realms of fancy in my face. Tea, however, seemed to lead to nothing and another friend of my father's suggested that I should go to the Bar which would make me eligible for the many Government appointments open to barristers, one of which my father's influence would easily procure for me. I assented at once to the proposition, and was accordingly entered as a student at Lincoln's Inn.'[16]

For a short spell Willy took his legal studies seriously. His father procured him a reader's ticket at the British Museum[17]. He was placed with a conveyancer who set him to studying Blackstone's Commentaries. 'I worked hard and conscientiously', he later explained, 'but at the end of two months I had conceived such a complete disgust for the law that I was obliged to tell my father that I could endure the drudgery no longer'. And it was not long before he was turning his Italian trip (and his British Museum ticket) to good account in the preparation of what was to become his first work of fiction, *Antonina*.

Such was Willy's later version. But in fact there is good reason to believe that he had already begun *Antonina* before he entered Lincoln's Inn. He himself puts the start on April 23rd 1846[18], a month after receiving his British Museum ticket and another month before he entered Lincoln's Inn. Whatever the truth, his father was already reconciled to Willy's writing, and simply anxious that his enthusiasm should not deprive him of a means of livelihood should his efforts prove unsaleable once more.

It seems to have been another period of strain within the Collins household. To William's advancing illness and Wilkie's doubtful future were added Harriet's apparent efforts at some independence. With the boys grown up she, too, was freer to move around as William had previously done, not on the smart scale of his patrons but among her relations and friends. Sometimes she took Charlie with her; sometimes she left both boys with William; occasionally the boys were on their own, with William here and Harriet there: not an unusual situation as a family grows up, and the children, and parents, taste their first bit of freedom, with the loosening of natural ties.

Willy's letters at this period showed a continued exuberance. The change from the moodiness described by his father when Willy had just left school, with William desperately arranging visits to the zoo and other distracting 'engagements' for Willy who complained of 'being dull', to the chirpiness of his later letters from his office in the Strand and from home to his absent parents, in his late teens and early twenties, was striking. It was a measure of how much he had grasped at the freedom slowly offered him.

In one letter he evoked an anxiety he can hardly have felt at the prospect of having to look after a couple of the family's female friends (plus his aunt) on his own with his parents away. 'What am I to do with this *seraglio* of women (six including the servants)? Good God, suppose they should want a change of chemises!!'[19] In another from the office, he laughingly describes a mix-up with the servants and the key to a house at one o'clock in the morning. ('Never had such fun in my life') and bursts into verse ('The virgin she leapt from her bed, As solemn as usual (confound her), With her nose looking devilish red, and Chemises by dozens around her . . .')[20]

His main exuberance, however, was reserved for his visits abroad – especially to Paris – from the age of twenty onwards. His first taste of the freedom (and anonymity) of the French capital opened up a world of distractions he could only contemplate in London. It was, in effect, his first real escape from the suffocating grip of his father.

'Paris!!!' he headed one letter to his mother and in another went on to enthuse at what he saw around him – Versailles, the Louvre, the Luxembourg Gardens – but added ambiguously 'We are dissipating fearfully – gardens; theatres and cafés being the conglomerate parts of the Parisian Paradise we are most inhabiting'. He was with Edward Ward, a young artist whose father was the family's bank manager at Coutts, and whose brother Charles was to become Willy's financial adviser. What else they got up to is hardly revealed in his letters to his mother. But the dissipation he admitted to and the freedom he enjoyed on these visits to Paris were to stand him in good stead when he and Dickens were to make the French capital the main target for their nocturnal escapades a few years later.

They took the rough with the smooth. Edward, he reported to his mother, had been plagued by bed-bugs, but 'not yet' Willy. He extolled a glorious subject for Charlie to paint' 'a dead soldier laid out naked at the morgue, like an unsaleable cold fish – all by himself upon the slab'. But the gatherer of future plots was active too, for he added 'he was a fine muscular old fellow who had popped into the water in the night and was exposed to be recognised by his friends'. The morgue was mentioned in all the guide books and the public display was one which Willy availed himself of on later visits and eventually made use of in *The Woman in White*.

He went to the theatre, good and bad. One play 'began with a chorus of manufacturers (sung out of tune) and indeed with thunder, lightning, fire from Heaven, smoking rains and a fat woman in tights and muslin petticoats who said she was Charity'. Another, *Le Médecin Malgré Lui*, left him 'weak with laughter'.

He adored returning to the same hotel, the Hotel des Tuileries in the rue de Rivoli. 'I have kept moving ever since my arrival; having shaken hands with every soul in this my beloved hostelry, taken a bath, ordered boots, eaten a dinner, changed a sovereign, smoked cigars, imbibed coffee, and procured one of the chambermaid's neckerchiefs, as an impromptu nightcap, within a couple of hours of setting foot 'in the capital of Europe!' And he hated leaving. 'I intend to stay in Paris as long as permitted – a very pleasant and necessary achievement considering that the Italian opera has begun and that *Pâtés de Foie Gras* are daily expected at the principal restaurants.'

He rarely forgot to give his mother news of the latest fashions or a description of her favourite bits of Paris. Recalling the family's visit nearly ten years earlier, he wrote of the crowds still cramming the Palais Royal.

'Paris is twice as full as it was last year. The Palais Royal is now encased in denser clouds of tobacco smoke than I saw it before. The children who assemble there are worth the journey from England, alone. An evening or two since, a creature (whether "masculine, feminine or neither", I know not) bowled his hoop against the top of my boot and made an apology (he seemed just able to walk and talk) so *elaborately civil* that I was perfectly astounded and took off my hat to him in the impulse of the moment! The men stick to their beards, their arguments, and their sugar and water, as usual; and the women eat as many bon-bons, wear as many "bustles" and make as many speeches, as ever. The gutters hold their rights infringed, the churches rejoice in their accustomed emptiness, the sugar plums still glitter in gorgeous indelicacy of design; each shopkeeper leaves his business to his wife and each *grisette* is redolent of sentiment and prodigal of smiles, as in the days of Sterne – in short (saving that it is more desecrated than usual by the presence of the beef-eating British) Paris flourishes its "flesh pots of Egypt" with the glory and perseverance of former days'[21].

His enthusiasm was, of course, blended with requests for extra allowances (both of money from his parents and leave from Mr Antrobus). But however they were received by Harriet, William found it all hard to live with. 'I do not like his flippant companion', he told Harriet on one of Willy's first continental trips. 'They seem to think of nothing but doing absurd things'. And it was not long before he was administering a few timely admonishments in one of Harriet's letters about eating 'plain food', reading Duncan's *Logic* and Butler's *Analogy* and about Willy's behaviour generally.

Willy was mildly repentant but he could hardly resist the last word – through his mother's safe intervention. 'I have always read your letters through', he told her. 'Considering that he is a lamb of Mr Dodsworth's flock, Mr Collins evinces a most unchurchlike disposition to scandalise other people. Heap coals of fire upon his head by giving him my love in return for his fabrications and behaviour'[22].

Harriet too occasionally felt William's brusqueness in his letters. At this period arriving at Stratton Park without his complete painting tackle, he rushes off a quick rebuke. 'I find of course that some important articles are not to be found. They are no doubt in your large basket. Look for them and send them immediately addressed to me here'.

Increasingly, of course, he had much to contend with, pushing himself into as normal a life as he could against an illness that was monthly taking a growing toll on his energies. As Willy himself later put it, 'The spring of 1844 brought with it a more distressing symptom of his malady than had yet appeared, in the shape of a constant wearing cough, which resisted all remedies; and constantly interrupting his repose at night, soon weakened his strength in a palpable and serious degree'. He struggled against it but to no avail. After dining out one evening in early July, his cough became so violent and unremitting later that night that his fitness for the excitement of normal society was at last put in doubt. 'I have dined out for the last time' he remarked next morning, and he never did thereafter.

He took his doctor's advice to seek country air when he could – the Isle of Wight, Devonshire, the South Coast, Buckinghamshire, all were visited in the interests of his health. Sketching and painting were also included when he could, through sheer determination. 'Sometimes the brush dropped from his hand from sheer weakness; sometimes it was laid down while he grasped for breath like one half-suffocated, or while a sudden attack of coughing disabled him from placing another touch upon the canvas; but these paroxysms subdued, his occupation was resolutely resumed'[23].

It could not last. The inevitable, though delayed several months longer than his doctors imagined, came on February 17th, 1847. He died 'quietly and painlessly', as Willy puts it, 'in the presence of his family'. He was only fifty-eight.

Willy had progressed as far as the third chapter of the second volume of *Antonina*, his romance of the Romans and the Goths, when his father died. He had been writing part of the chapter the night before his father's death[24], and did not take it up again until July of that year, and by that time he was already heavily engaged in collecting material for the promised *Memoir* of his father's life.

His father's death thus held up his first published fictional work, and he had the satisfaction of knowing that William had at least had the first third of the novel read out to him in his last months. William would have been even more satisfied had he realised that the *Memoir* of his life would establish Willy as a writer of some substance, though with few clues as to what was still in store.

CHAPTER SIX

Mother

WILLIAM COLLINS'S death left the family bereft. They had lived with his mild idiosyncracies and had grown used to his rigid code of living. But his love for them was never in doubt and the strains on them all as he coped with the last months of his terminal illness brought them closer together. In spite of their grief it was a family full of inner resilience.

William had left them comfortably off. Charles was establishing himself in his father's profession and both Harriet and Wilkie[1] had lives of their own still to develop. It was astonishing, given the poverty he himself inherited, how much William had managed to amass from his paintings and to leave to his widow and two sons. He eventually bequeathed over £11,000, thus ensuring an income of close on £700 a year for Harriet during the rest of her lifetime. It proved adequate for all their needs, was a godsend to both Harriet and Charles and, as things developed, a useful cushion for Wilkie until, a decade later, he was to strike the public's imagination with *The Woman in White*.

Devonport Street, with its large and impressive painter's gallery, (the best William had in his entire career), was too big for a mother and two sons and they moved for a couple of years into 38 Blandford Square and then into 17 Hanover Terrace, overlooking Regents Park. Both were to become, in their different ways, magnets to the young artistic and literary sets of the day, with Harriet at last coming into her own as one of the liveliest of hostesses. Harriet after all had entertained genuine stage ambitions of her own before her marriage, at a time when such ideas were frowned upon. So the boys' young friends and 'flippant companions' were welcomed.

It was as if a heavy load had been lifted from the family's shoulders. All three reacted differently. Harriet's independence and energy were suddenly given full rein. She encouraged Wilkie and Charles to pursue their talents and their friendships and kept open house for them. Charles was left to develop his painting talents without his father's guidance and, for a time, his friendship with John Millais gave him all he needed. Wilkie, who had had the double restraint of a desperately ill father and a growing rift between them, was at last able to pursue both his writing and his life in any way he wanted.

It may seem strange that young men of twenty and twenty-four should be willing to spend close on the next decade in a parent's house. With William perhaps so. Not, however, with Harriet, who immediately opened her doors to Wilkie's and Charles's friends, encouraged them to congregate in her presence, delighted in giving parties and in the lively gossip that went with them, and was more than interested in the serious discussions of art and literature that began to develop. Both brothers had interesting friends, and both were delighted to bring them home on an informal basis.

Wilkie was soon plunged into the business of collecting details of his father's life from friends and acquaintances. William had apparently not had the time or energy to make the notes he had promised three years earlier, but within a matter of months Wilkie had filled in much of the background and was making progress with William's earlier diaries and papers. It was a labour of love, in spite of holding up his other efforts to entrance the public with the Romans and the Goths. The *Memoirs* were finally completed just over eighteen months after William's death and immediately posed a problem for the family.

The publishers were not keen to underwrite the whole issue and Harriet was faced with the problem of putting up a few hundred pounds to launch the book. She never hesitated and sales eventually crept up towards the seven hundred and fifty mark and beyond, turning a potential flop into a modest commercial success. It received good notices from friends in the artistic world and several critics have subsequently detected shades of *Armadale* or *The Woman in White* peeping out of the descriptive passages. Perhaps. The fact is that Wilkie had shown he could sustain a full length book successfully and had been drawn to the attention of the literary world.

The *Memoirs* revealed more about Wilkie's relations with his father than they did about Wilkie himself. He knew, of course, that he had a problem on his hands at the outset. As he put it, a biographer of a father is inevitably 'perplexed by being called on to delineate a character which it has hitherto been his only ambition to respect'[2]. There was another difficulty: how was he to cope with the facets of his father's character which he found difficult to respect, certainly difficult to admire? The way out was plainly to remain unobtrusive. Thus in the *Memoirs* Wilkie rarely intrudes, but in his choice of material and his assembly of it he unwittingly shows only one side of his relationship.

Mr Verlyn Klinkenberg[3] has carefully compared the letters printed in the *Memoirs* with the originals in the Pierpont Morgan Library in New York. His conclusion is that parts of the biography are 'as fictional as his father's paintings of childhood scenes'. This is probably a trifle harsh but Wilkie certainly omits any reference to the family's relationships, and above all, in editing William's letters so severely, 'he seems to have recognised his father's strengths and shortcomings quite as readily as the Royal Academician's peers. Like them, he was caught between esteem for the painter and frustration with the man'.

Once the *Memoirs* were finished, Wilkie quickly took up *Antonina* where he had left off. He finished it a year after the *Memoirs* and, even before completion, promptly sent the first volume round to Colborn, the publisher, who just as promptly sent it back with a chilling 'declined with thanks'. But he soon struck lucky. 'Next I tried Bentley who, to my surprise and delight accepted the first volume, all I had completed, eagerly; and with a liberality unheard of in those days to an unknown beginner actually gave me £200 on the completion of the book.'

It ultimately received reviews rather better than it probably deserved. Later critics have been more severe. Dorothy Sayers[4] thought Wilkie's Goths and Romans hailed from Wardour Street and that his fifth century Christians were nineteenth century protestants. But the novel launched Wilkie Collins on the writing career he had longed for; and he was particularly enthralled at a crowded Lord Mayor's reception to be mistaken for a member of the Pre-Raphaelite Brotherhood and to be asked whether the author of *Antonina* was present. Through his new publisher Bentley, his book introduced him to a growing range of literary men of the day. Edward Piggott, who was to become a firm friend for years and was to found *The Leader* in 1850, was one of them. And soon both they and Charles's friends, Millais, Holman Hunt, the Rossettis, Frith and others were thronging Blandford Square.

Through Charles (as well as Harriet's interest and encouragement), Blandford Square and, later, Hanover Terrace, became one of the hubs of the Pre-Raphaelite movement. Charles had met John Millais and Holman Hunt at the Royal Academy where they were actively discussing and developing their new outlook and, while never being admitted to the inner circle, he shared their views and the public's critical reaction to them, particularly after the exhibition of his painting *Berengaria*[5]. They and the Rossettis saw a great deal of each other, in London and in visits to mutual friends in Oxford, Worcester Park Farm (between Kingston and Ewell) and Scotland. And it was at Worcester Park Farm in the summer and autumn of 1851 that, in the company of Charles, Millais found his inspiration for *Ophelia* and *The Huguenot* and Hunt discovered the scene for *The Light of the World.*

Charles in his early twenties retained the twin characteristics his father had pronounced at birth: flowing red hair and blue eyes. As Holman Hunt described him on their first acquaintance at the British Museum: 'He was then a remarkable looking boy with statuesquely formed features, of aquiline type and strong blue eyes. The characteristic that marked him out to casual observers was his brilliant bushy red hair, which was not of golden splendour, but had an attractive beauty in it. He had also a comely figure. While still a youth he imported to me his discomfort of the striking character of his locks and was anxious to find out any means of lessening their vividness'.

Charles, in fact, lived most of his life moving from one anxiety to another, most of his own making. His friends teased him in friendly fashion but both they and Wilkie were also concerned at the excesses of fasting and other unhealthy disciplines that his religious convictions drove him to. Quite often they were fleeting idiosyncracies like his refusal to eat blackberry pudding. In Hunt's view his nature 'yielded itself to the survey of the current fashion', and it was only later that he found out how this had led him into 'unanticipated perplexities'.

It may have explained why, to Charles's bitter regret, his friends never accepted him as one of the Brotherhood. He who had sat at the knee of David Wilkie, John Constable, John Linnell, even Turner, had perhaps had it too easy, too soon. He realised it himself. 'You saw the peril of becoming one of those who faint by the way' he told Hunt, 'and you were prepared to encounter obstacles; you put out all your strength to arrive at the desired goal. In doing this you were forced to tread new ground, and you acquired the habit of doing so. The difference with me was that I was already enjoying the brightness and glory of the haven where the crowned ones were resting, talking of the race they had run as only part of their youth. I was dandled on their knees. I took to drawing from mere habit and they all applauded my efforts. I looked upon the diadem as a part of manhood that must come, and now I begin to doubt and fear the issue'[6].

Charles could easily have been contrasting his own career and beliefs, moulded so closely on those of his father, with those of Wilkie who had deliberately set out in new directions, in opposition to his father, and had found that a far sharper cutting edge was necessary to make the progress he wished.

Millais and Hunt were naturally frequent visitors at Hanover Terrace, staying overnight or, in the case of Millais, a week at a time. Both clearly found Harriet an attractive woman as well as an encouraging listener. She told Holman Hunt of the occasion when as a young girl Samuel Taylor Coleridge had singled her out at an evening party and had talked with her for twenty minutes 'in the highest strains of poetical philosophy', of which she understood not a word. She wondered why he should have chosen to talk to her. When Hunt saw her portrait by her sister, Margaret Carpenter, showing her in all her girl-like beauty, 'the portrait explained the riddle'. Millais too mockingly courted Harriet on every opportunity. 'Give my love to Harriet', he would tell Charles, 'and tell her that I shall soon want her to fix the day for the wedding'. She took it all in good part.

All of them had the happiest memories of the dinners and parties Harriet gave for the young friends of her two sons. 'Nothing could well exceed the jollity of these little dinners', Holman Hunt later recalled. 'Edward Ward and his pleasant wife would sometimes be of the party. In any case Mrs Collins did not often make our smoking after the meal a reason for her absence from our company. We were all hard-worked people enjoying one another's society and we talked as only such can'[7].

John Millais had similar recollections of a dance at Hanover Terrace. 'It was a delightful evening. Charlie never got beyond a solemn quadrille, though he is an excellent waltzer and polka dancer. Poor Mrs C was totally dumb from a violent influenza she unfortunately caught that very afternoon. She received all her guests in a whisper and a round face of welcome. There were many lions – amongst others the famous Dickens, who came for about half an hour and officiated as principal carver at supper'.

Millais was in fact the most frequent visitor, being for a time almost part of the family. 'I still half reside with Mrs C' he once confided. On another occasion: 'I scribble this at Collins's house being totally incapable of remaining at my own residence after the night's rest and morning's "heavy blow" of breakfast'. And again, referring to dinner: 'This revives just strength enough to walk to Hanover Terrace in a night so cold that horses should wear greatcoats. Upon arriving there I embrace Collins and vice versa; Mrs Collins makes the tea, and we drink it; we then adjourn upstairs to his room and converse till about twelve when we say goodnight'[8].

They were a hard-working, loyal group of friends, accepting Harriet as one of themselves. She for her part defended them whenever she could. On one occasion, when Holman Hunt's *The Light of the World* was causing its initial stir at the Royal Academy, she was accosted by an old friend. 'Ah,

Mrs Collins, you are the very person to tell us whether it is true that Holman Hunt has found some fool to give him four hundred guineas for that absurd picture which he calls *The Light of the World*?' Harriet was quickly on the attack. 'It is quite true. And you will perhaps permit me to introduce you to the wife of "the fool" who will confirm the statement.'

All these friends were inextricably linked with each other, through art or literary endeavours. Some were Charles's friends, some Wilkie's, others Harriet's. The Wards, for example, were a combination of all three.

Charles Ward was their bank manager at Coutts and his brother Edward, who had become a close companion of Wilkie's in London and Paris, and Edward's girlfriend Henrietta Ward (who was no relation) were artistic friends of them all. So it was natural that Wilkie, Charles and Edward Piggott should have been part of the plot to further the romance of Edward and Henrietta when she was well below age, Wilkie himself making most of the wedding arrangements.

Wilkie 'impressed great caution and secrecy,' Henrietta later recalled, 'as he planned the whole affair with zest and enjoyment . . . my sister-in-law called for me and we walked to the Church of All Souls, Langham Place. It was May 4th, 1848 and I was not yet sixteen years of age. The first person we saw was Edward gaily attired in bridal array . . . Wilkie arrived soon after, well in his element. The spice of romance and mischief appealed to him; he gave me away to the best of men, with a hearty good will'[9].

It was not until three months later that they ran away on honeymoon, Wilkie again orchestrating affairs, seeing them into a cab, booking the rooms and relishing the whole secret affair. They remained firm friends, Wilkie gracing the christening of their first child, Alice, by becoming her godfather and a little tipsy in the process ('the baby seems to be moving in a very odd way, and is making funny faces. Why, 'pon my soul, the baby's drunk! The baby's drunk!!!)[10] Leslie, their second child, not only became a favourite of Wilkie's, but eventually emerged as 'Spy', the well known cartoonist of *Vanity Fair*.

Other romances hardly had such happy outcomes. Charles had caught the eye of Maria Rossetti, the sister of Christina Rossetti, after she had had a short romantic attachment with John Ruskin whom, she said, had for a time 'engaged her warm heart'. She was an attractive girl but, like Charles, had become imbued with the high ritual of the Roman and Anglican churches[11]. Whether it was her looks or her beliefs that appealed to Charles, it is difficult to say. Whatever it was, she eventually chose the Church and later entered the Anglican Sisterhood of All Saints Home. Both of them were to die young from internal tumours, within a few years of each other, and to be buried not far from each other in Brompton Cemetery.

Blandford Square had thus become the focal point of a lively and talented group of friends, some writing, some painting, some dabbling in a variety of diversions. It was almost inevitable that amateur theatricals should be one of them.

Just after Edward and Henrietta Ward had moved into Harewood Square, round the corner from Blandford Square, he and Wilkie developed a mutual enthusiasm for putting on plays, which was rarely to wane. Wilkie had been attracted to the stage and to the play as an alternative form to the novel on his visits to Paris; and he had long wondered why the London stage and London playwrights were in such dire straits. But it was enthusiasm, rather than any reforming zeal, that brought theatricals to the back drawing room of Blandford Square.

Apart from Edward Ward, who initially designed all the costumes, the other enthusiastic recruits included William Frith and John Millais. They put on Goldsmith's *Good-natured Man* and Sheridan's *The Rivals*, to friendly and encouraging audiences, Wilkie acting as stage manager, with Charles, Millais and Frith taking the main parts. They had the usual theatrical tantrums with, on one occasion, both leading lady and leading man determined not to act with each other, one regarding her partner as 'hideous', she being accused of being an 'ogress'. Wilkie accepted both resignations with good humour and still had a success on his hands.

Whether these theatrical successes were the reason, or simply Wilkie's growing name as a novelist, his interest in the stage brought him into direct contact for the first time with Charles Dickens. The go-between was Wilkie's artist friend, Augustus Egg, who had been drawn into the Dickens circle three years earlier as part of his touring theatrical group. Early in 1851 Dickens, already basking in the fame of *David Copperfield*, was seeking an extra actor for his own theatrical venture, Sir Edward Bulwer Lytton's *Not So Bad As We Seem*. He wondered whether Egg's friend, Wilkie Collins, whose father he had known, would like the part of Smart, 'a small part, but what there is of it, decidedly good'. Wilkie was delighted to be asked and was soon absorbed into the part.

The play[12], specially commissioned from Sir Edward, was intended as part of a fund-raising effort for special housing for artists and writers under the patronage of the newly established Guild of Literature and Art. Sir Edward was President and Charles Dickens, Vice President.

Dickens put all his energies into the construction of a special stage for the play, commissioned the actors, arranged the insurance and pressurised the Duke of Devonshire to provide Devonshire House for the occasion, 'plainly telling him what we wanted' (ie the use of his house for a first night with the Queen in attendance). Within a couple of hours he had the Duke's reply that his services, his house and his subscriptions would be available.

No one stinted. Several R.A.s (including Edwin Landseer) painted the scenery. Augustus Egg prepared the detailed drawings for all the costumes. And the actors, Wilkie included, were soon hard at it, rehearsing 'three days a week, all day long'.

The first night, on 16th May, 1851, was a glittering occasion in the presence of Queen Victoria and Prince Albert to which Wilkie invited his mother, brother and Edward and Henrietta Ward. Dickens's overwhelming presence on stage assured the play an immediate success and over a thousand pounds was raised for the charity.

Wilkie had become absorbed not only in a successful play, but in a new and exciting milieu. These theatrical ventures were to continue throughout Dickens's friendship. It was the need for each other's company at home and abroad and particularly Dickens's need for the lively companionship that Wilkie could provide that led to the closeness of their developing relationship and to some of the later jealousies among Dickens's older friends.

Wilkie was not the most professional Thespian to tread the boards, but he worked at it and, with his enthusiasm and Dickens's unbounded energy, they got on famously. It was hardly a bad introduction to the theatrical world – even the amateur – for a twenty-seven year old and Wilkie was clearly determined to make the most of it. Few, if any, of his subsequent theatrical enterprises ended so quickly or so grandly with a Royal Command performance to which Wilkie could invite his family and friends to supper in the dining room of Devonshire House. But there were other memorable occasions ahead.

Further performances of the Lytton play followed in the provinces and soon Wilkie was writing enthusiastic letters to his friends from Bristol, Manchester, Birmingham, Newcastle, Shrewsbury and Liverpool. 'We have had a wonderful theatrical campaign' he told Edward Piggott. 'Even a Bristol audience is beaten in enthusiasm by the audiences of Manchester and Liverpool. They even laughed at "Dimidum me!" We filled the Philharmonic Hall at Liverpool two nights following – Jenny Lind in the height of her vogue in the provinces was afraid to try what we have accomplished. King Public is a good thing for Literature and Art'.

Once started, these theatrical ventures with Dickens seemed to take on a momentum of their own. Wilkie was given small parts in the other two plays in the touring repertoire. Then less than two years later came a bigger role still. Towards Christmas 1854, Tavistock House was beginning to reverberate to the preparations for a children's pantomime. Mamie Dickens[13] has stressed how fond her father was as a child of singing, reciting and acting. 'These tastes clung to him all his life, and he was constantly getting up private theatricals; and when his children were old enough to join in them, he took quite as much pains in getting up fairy pieces for them as he did with grown-up pieces.' In this particular year the fairy tale of *Fortunio* was to be played. 'All the children, even the Plorn[14], who was so small that he could hardly stand in the little top boots which were made for him, took part in the pretty play. The children were wonderfully well taught and the whole performance was a great success'. And once again a part was found for Dickens's new friend, Wilkie. He had only a dozen words to say but was given a nice prominence in the playbill as Wilkini Collini.

Wilkie had wider ambitions too. He had been considering for some time whether he might not turn his hand to a play, rather than a novel. He was perhaps naturally fearful of the outcome and confided solely in Charles Ward (Edward's younger brother who worked at Coutts Bank) before its completion. Its reception was eventually far better than he could have hoped for and before long Dickens himself was taking the play – entitled *The Lighthouse* – under his wing. 'I have a little lark in contemplation, if you will help it to fly,' he wrote to Clarkson Stanfield, the artist. 'Collins has done a melodrama (a regular old-style melodrama) in which there is a good notion. I am going to act in it, as an experiment, in the Children's Theatre here – I, Mark, Collins, Egg and my daughter Mary, the whole *dram. pers.*; our families and yours the whole audience; for I want to make the stage large and shouldn't have room for above five-and-twenty spectators'[15].

It seems to have had a reasonable reception. Dickens told Angela Burdett-Coutts in June that the audience had not been so demonstrative the night before as on the previous Saturday and the drama critics thought it 'flat'. But he added 'I heard they were crying vigorously – Mr Longman, the bookseller, was seen to cry dreadfully – and I don't know that anything could be said to be beyond that!'

The upshot was that Wilkie had broken through into a difficult new genre and in the best of company. Carlyle, who was one of the enthusiastic first-night audience, gave high praise both to the play and to Dickens's performance. *The Lighthouse* became the talk of the town and Dickens remarked that, at a dinner party at Lord John Russell's, it was 'the chief topic of conversation'[16]. But it was not until two years later that Dickens managed to get a commercial theatre, the Olympic, to put it on professionally and Wilkie had his first thrill, as author, of being called for by the audience from 'his private box'. It was in fact only a moderate success but he had touched the first rung of a ladder that was to take him to many more London theatres and first nights.

It was Wilkie's passion for writing, however, that Charles Dickens had touched at a crucial time. He had begun to contribute more widely to the periodicals and he was soon not only offering short stories and essays to *Bentley's Miscellany* but acting in a much more journalistic, if not editorial, capacity in *The Leader* which his friend Edward Piggott was then running.

His literary output, at this time, like that of so many young writers, was necessarily catholic and varied. He took opportunities when they came and created a few of his own. In the early 1850s they ranged from full length novels to Christmas sketches, from plays to drama criticisms and from a travel book to paragraphs on art – all in the interest of experience and the necessity to make a living. He was also making friends in this new world – through Dickens, through his own writings and interests and through Charles.

He was not the first writer to be tempted to combine a well-earned holiday with a spot of lively travel writing. And it was not long after the successful launching of *Antonina* that he persuaded an artist friend, Henry Brandling, to go off to the wilds of Cornwall – the only rival in his view to the most eastern states of Russia as an untrodden territory. Or, in other words, the only part of the British isle still unblessed by the railway. Hence his title, *Rambles Beyond Railways*[17].

They arrived in Cornwall with their packs on their backs and notebooks and sketch pads in hand. The result was a mixture of lively descriptive writing, a few bizarre touches (how the people of Looe got rid of rats on Looe island by eating them and why there were no dogs to be seen in the Lizard district), some intrepid plunges into the mines, even beneath the sea, and a friendly description of their reception by the locals who clearly found it difficult to accept that two young men should actually be walking from town to town for pleasure. It was a pleasantly written book which had a modest success running into a second edition and which saw its last edition as late as 1948[18].

On his return to London Wilkie was quickly absorbed in the work of *The Leader*, further amateur theatricals, as well as the commitments for contributions to *Bentley's Miscellany*. Most of these involvements were to grow further and to coincide a year later – in 1852 – which turned out to be a remarkably active year. Apart from the provincial tours of Dickens's theatrical group, he was already turning out what could no longer be termed entirely short stories – *Mr Wray's Cash Box* was published in book form for the Christmas of 1851 (or at least was so intended), and *A Terribly Strange Bed* became his first contribution to *Household Words* in the spring of 1852. And throughout this period he continued to make progress with *Basil*, a new novel, and to lend a hand to Edward Piggott, at *The Leader*, where he had clearly risen to drama critic, art critic, book reviewer and general factotum on the literary side of the paper. He plainly relished his press ticket for the Adelphi, the piles of new books to review and the possibility of going to the opera and attending art reviews, whether at the Suffolk Street Gallery or the Royal Academy[19].

His enthusiasm and devotion extended to the early hours. 'I have just returned from a very jovial dinner party at Lord Boothby's' he wrote to Edward Piggott at two o'clock one morning, 'and I am in the worst possible condition for making alterations of any consequence in a proof sheet. I have put in the poetry from Tennyson, as you wished – though I think such an expression as "wilful thorns" hardly suits the character of our sweet-tempered and lovely Alice! N.B. This is written in a very maudlin Bacchanalian state – Oh! if Alice were here at this moment'.

He even extended his help to advice on how religion should be treated (or rather *not* treated) in the magazine. 'What business has religion in a paper at all?' he asked Piggott in a lengthy letter, distancing himself from two recent articles. 'I go with you in politics, I go with you (saving in one or two exceptional cases) in social matters, I go with you in your judgment of literature, but in regard to mixing up the name of Jesus Christ with the publications of the day, I am against it. I make no claim to orthodoxy. I am neither a protestant, a catholic nor a dissenter. I do not desire to discuss this or that particular creed but I believe Jesus Christ to be the Son of God'. Strong sentiments from someone who was not on the editorial staff – but perhaps he knew his man. At all events, he was still writing for *The Leader* four years later and continued to sail with its editor for many years after that.

It was a symptom of Wilkie's strong views[20] plainly expressed on an issue he felt passionately about, at a time when he was mentally active and widely stimulated. He was clearly turning his mind to a variety of topics beyond his own imaginative writings. Soon he was advising Piggott on how to re-organise *The Leader*, stressing the political and literary strengths of the paper; then he was criticising the contemporary woolliness of socialism and what it implied; finally, he was promising an inside story about Pre-Raphaelitism based on his intimate friendship with John Millais and the possibility of borrowing his personal diary. (They had both been 'cut up', he confessed, in the previous week's issue of *The Atheneum*.)

He was also on good terms with Richard Bentley and offering articles both by himself and by his literary friends (one in France) for the *Miscellany*. Little wonder that work on *Basil* dragged on and that on completion in September he called it this 'hitherto interminable book'. He was beginning to learn, like all young writers, that it is easy to accept commitments to the papers of the day; much harder to fulfill them and to undertake the more serious writing of books at the same time.

In retrospect, his first novel, *Antonina*, stands out as an isolated phenomenon. In it he had drawn on his own travels to Italy and his subsequent research and imagination. His next major novel was to break away in plot, in timing and in its handling of characters. It was also to reveal far more of himself for the first time – how much is still in dispute.

Basil is the story of a youth from an upper class family who falls in love with the daughter of a rich man in the clothing trade (they had met on the top of an omnibus). They marry, but only on the understanding that the marriage is not consummated for a year and that Basil will try to get his own father's consent. A foolish decision perhaps, but worse was to follow. The girl is seduced by the head-clerk of her father's firm, and, in a remarkable scene, Basil deliberately listens to the couple through the thin wall of a cheap hotel bedroom. Basil attacks and maims the head-clerk; Basil's father disowns him; the girl dies of typhus; and Basil retreats to Cornwall where he evades a final attack from the head-clerk.

It is all rather melodramatic, although the early part of the novel is allowed to develop with insight and compassion. What set the tongues wagging, however, and has kept them wagging ever since is that Collins wrote a preface to the novel in which he stressed that the main event had been founded 'on a fact in real life which had come within my own knowledge' and the rest of the narrative had been guided by his own experiences and those of others.

This double emphasis on 'knowledge' and 'experience' has intrigued everyone since: had Collins actually married in this fashion at an early age or perhaps had a similar, though less traumatic, experience? Some feel that he simply borrowed some of the incidents from the life of a well-known Peer, the fourth Earl of Chesterfield; others that he was putting together material from the lives of his brother and friends; others again that it represented an emotional experience, deep enough to be transformed into fiction and even to explain why he never married[21].

For the first time the writing reveals strong hints of autobiography (the hero undergoing legal training at the bar, writing a historical romance, travelling on omnibuses, touring the Continent, grappling with a proud, rigid father) as well as evidence of growing sexual awareness. From his first admitted infatuation at the age of eleven or twelve in Bayswater, through his startling boast to Dickens that his first 'affair' had occurred during his family visit to Rome at the age of thirteen, to his first visits to Paris with Edward Ward, Collins had rarely hidden his predilections. He was decidedly heterosexual. A pretty face and figure were current attractions. 'I think the back view of a finely formed woman the loveliest view', he was later to confess to his American photographer friend, Sarony, 'and her hips the more precious parts of that view. The line of beauty in those parts enchants me'. And, commenting on Sarony's latest nude work, he added: 'From the small of her back to the end of her thighs, she has escaped the detestable restorers – and my life has been spent in trying to find a living woman who is like her – and never succeeding'[22]. He was then sixty-three. His quest, according to his boasts to Charles Dickens and Augustus Egg, must have started all of fifty years earlier.

Basil introduced these yearnings to the public for the first time. The sensuous theme which offended some of his critics would certainly have shocked his father. It was, in essence, a novel that could not have been written, or at least published, while his father was alive. It was also a novel that contained the seeds of his own developing habits. As with his school stories, one has to sift fact from fiction. Was it all true or were solid facts being slightly embellished in the telling? *Basil* strongly suggests that both interest and experience, of some kind, were basic ingredients.

CHAPTER SEVEN

Dickens

AMATEUR THEATRICALS had brought Dickens and Collins together for the first time in 1851; writing kept them in close touch. Within twelve months Wilkie had written his first contribution for *Household Words* (as it happens it was one of his best short stories, *A Terribly Strange Bed*, which is still occasionally reprinted in anthologies); within another twelve months they had gone abroad together; and within four years Wilkie was on the permanent staff of *Household Words* and cooperating directly with Dickens on each year's special Christmas number.

The two were soon to be exploring areas of London and Paris with such diligence as to suggest a common need for diversions of varying kinds. They were an unlikely couple to become such firm friends and collaborators. Dickens, twelve years' Collins's senior, was at the height of his fame, Collins still making his way; Dickens the affluent lion of literary society, Collins still rather dependent on his mother's allowance. Dickens could walk twenty miles a day; Collins eschewed violent exercise and preferred to be under sail. Dickens was punctual, tidy and generous; Collins tardy, Bohemian and a trifle penny-pinching. Yet within a few years, Dickens's firmest friends, especially John Forster, had to recognise that he had in some way found a new and lively companion.

Dickens explained part of the conundrum years later in simple literary terms saying that he felt he had discovered a new exciting novelist. He candidly told Collins, 'As you know, I was certain from the *Basil* days that you were the writer who would come ahead of all the field – being the only one who combined invention and power, both humorous and pathetic, with that invincible determination to work, and that profound conviction that nothing of worth is to be done without work, of which triflers and foreigners have no concept'[1].

It may have been the successful novelist talking, but it also has a touch of the alert editor about it too, looking for new talent, keen to work, willing to be flexible and full of ideas, large and small. Wilkie fitted in admirably to Dickens's needs on *Household Words*. He was a swift worker. He took a point quickly and was willing to turn his hand in any particular direction. Soon the subtle directives with which Dickens ran *Household Words* were flowing to Wilkie, sometimes through Wills, the sub-editor, sometimes direct.

Dickens was a journalist turned novelist, and he rarely overlooked his earlier training. He had worked in harness with William Henry Wills, very briefly, on the *Daily News* and both had magazine experience behind them. There was never any doubt who was in the editor's chair. As Wills, perhaps over politely, put it almost at the outset of their collaboration on *Household Words*, 'When I make an objection to any article I do it suggestively'. Wilkie Collins too felt the impact of the editor's final decisions from time to time, either by outright rejection (of *Mad Monckton* for example) or by subtle suggestions of changes.

Dickens was conscious of the susceptibilities of his readers and protected them assiduously, whether on sex, marriage, religion or class. In one early case he felt Wilkie was in danger of offending the public's attitude to hereditary insanity and on another occasion it was class. 'I particularly wish you to look well to Wilkie's article about the Wigan schoolmaster', he wrote to Wills, 'and not to leave anything in it that may be sweeping and unnecessarily offensive to the middle class. He has always a tendency to overdo that – and such a subject gives him a fresh temptation'[2].

The collaboration, however, prospered. 'He is very suggestive,' he explained to Wills when considering Wilkie's possible new role in *Household Words*, a few years later, 'and exceedingly quick to take my notions. Being industrious and reliable besides'. So he proposed even closer collaboration. But Wilkie was not so easily tempted, having, as he thought, a growing reputation as a writer which needed encouraging. The upshot was that he accepted Dickens's monetary offer, while insisting on rather better terms, especially publicity, for his serialised pieces.

The eventual agreement to join the staff of *Household Words* meant another five pounds a week to Wilkie. It also meant, as Dickens put it succinctly to Wills, 'dining three instead of two'. In short, Wilkie was accepted as one of the inner three on the editorial staff. It hardly introduced Wilkie to Dickens's table or indeed to his social life. That had already developed rapidly over the intervening years, extending from dinners in the City at the *Cock Tavern* or the *Ship and Turtle*, followed by nocturnal prowls round Whitechapel, to visits to the theatre, strolls on Hampstead

Heath and the traditional whitebait suppers at Greenwich. Sometimes together ('I think we may forage pleasantly for a dinner in the City, and then go and look at Christmas Eve in Whitechapel, which is always a curious thing')[3]; sometimes with others, the two writers grew closer and more intimate.

Edmund Yates, who later became a regular contributor to *Household Words*, and founded and edited *The World*, has described one of these joint trips to see how the other half lived, in graphic detail:

'We went on what would nowadays be called a "slumming" expedition, quite original in those days, but long since done to death. A friend of Dickens's, a certain M. Delarue, a banker in Genoa, who was on a visit to Tavistock House, had a great desire to see some of the low life of London: and Dickens accordingly arranged with the police for a party of us, of which I was one, to dine early together, and then "go the rounds" of the thieves' quarters in Whitechapel, the sailors' and German sugar-bakers' taverns in Ratcliff Highway, the dens of the Mint etc. It was a curious experience. . . .'[4]

The more Wilkie's collaboration grew and prospered, the more Dickens's existing friends noticed the growing intimacy with the newcomer. John Forster, as one of Dickens's closest companions and literary colleagues, probably felt the change most. They had first met in the mid-1830s, when Dickens was half way through *Pickwick Papers* and was about to start his editorship of *Bentley's Miscellany*. They had a number of mutual friends and common interests. 'Both were lively men, passionate about the theatre, keen on drinks and company and excursions, on being intensely gay, relaxing strenuously, responding vehemently'[5].

While Dickens's animal spirits and vast energy persisted, Forster's, however, clearly moved into a different mould and increasingly, we are told, 'he spent his late thirties and early forties lying bed-ridden and alone in his stylish chambers in Lincoln's Inn Fields'. They remained firm friends, Dickens relying on his advice on most of his major difficulties, both business and emotional. But Forster, especially following his marriage, was edging closer and closer to sober and respectable habits. And as he moved away from weekly and monthly writing towards more scholarly ambitions, first Wills and later Collins took his place as Dickens's confidant on day-to-day magazine issues.

Yet it was not so much what went on at the office, as what they did outside it that brought Wilkie closer to Dickens, at home and abroad.

Wilkie provided what Dickens was beginning to lack: fun and excitement.

Dickens and Collins were gradually getting to know each other in all manner of circumstances. In the early part of 1853, both were suffering from the onset of illness, Dickens from a recurrence of an old kidney complaint, Collins probably from the first sign of his rheumatic and gout torments to come. It led to an invitation, the first of many, for Collins to join Dickens at his newly discovered rented property in Boulogne, and to the first of their many joint trips to France.

The Château des Molineaux was to be Dickens's base in Boulogne for several summers to come. There was more than one house in the grounds and several amenities ('excellent light wines on the premises, French cookery, millions of roses, two cows (for milk punch), vegetables cut for the pot, and handed in at the kitchen window; five summer houses, fifteen fountains (with no water in 'em) and thirty seven clocks (keeping, as I conceive, Australian time')[6]. So he rarely lacked visitors; nor stinted with his invitations.

Wilkie was there throughout August and the early part of September as Dickens was putting the final touches to *Bleak House*. They were also plotting a much bigger excursion, along with Augustus Egg, to Switzerland and Italy. Their work and planning was occasionally interrupted by a local diversion, which they always entered into with enthusiasm. A *fête des enfants* found particular favour. It began at 'half past three and ended at twelve at night,' Wilkie told his brother, 'and the admission was *five pence*. For this entrance fee we had provided an orchestra of forty performers – thousands of variegated lamps to be lit as it grew dark – statues, amusements of every kind, racing in sacks, greased poles, donkey races, balloons, fireworks and a grand lottery. The children danced on the grass with the grown people sitting round them'. Something, Wilkie felt, that they might do at home if only their 'stupid dignity' would let them.

Soon Dickens and Collins were going back to London to tidy up loose ends at the office and at home and to pick up Augustus Egg. They were to suffer, en route, one of the worst crossings of the season, with Dickens as sick as anyone on a crowded boat, but with Wilkie, in no particular trouble, 'raised aloft on a high pile of luggage', surveying the after deck where the ladies, who were lying wet through in all directions, 'looked like an immense picnic party with everybody intent upon a pigeon pie of their own – from the immense number of white basins'. Dickens was still feeling the after effects days later, and probably brooding on the next crossing. Wilkie's sea legs were already attuned to most things afloat.

The three companions were on their way back to Boulogne by early

October and then on to Paris, Strasbourg, over the Alps to Milan and Genoa, down to Rome and Naples and finally to Venice. Dickens was essentially the leader, the organiser and the holder of the real purse strings (though Wilkie was eventually given the privy purse for tips and smaller items such as 'picnic eatables and drinkables between breakfast and dinner'). Both Augustus Egg and Wilkie were younger, less travelled and certainly less used to the luxuries Dickens introduced them to en route, from the use of a personal courier to some of the hotels they stayed at.

The trip hardly went undocumented. Both Wilkie and Dickens wrote continually to friends as they moved along, with Wilkie also mentally preparing a travel series for *Bentley's Miscellany*, and Augustus Egg religiously writing their every movement in a small working diary. In many ways this particular diary, which seems to have vanished completely, dominated so much of their life that at Egg's death a decade later, Dickens was still talking of it. 'In my memory of the dear gentle little fellow, he will be (as since those days he always has been) eternally posting up that book at the large table in the middle of our Venice sitting room, incidentally asking the name of an hotel three weeks back!'[7]

For such a long trip, the assorted trio got on remarkably well together. Both Egg and Wilkie were lively companions, with enough idiosyncrasies to keep Dickens amused rather than annoyed. He poured most of them out to his wife Catherine. He quickly had Wilkie down as the better traveller. 'He takes things easily and is not put out by small matters'. He 'eats and drinks everything, gets on very well everywhere and is always in good spirits.' On the other hand, he 'sometimes wants to give people too little for their troubles'.

Egg was always demanding trifles in the wrong places. Both tended to meanness. 'It is the drollest thing in the world to see Egg and Collins burst out into economy – always on some wretched little point, and always on a point they had previously settled the other way.' The trouble was that Dickens, who could well afford everything they were experiencing, did not always appreciate the anxieties of his impecunious companions. They nonetheless remained 'the best of friends'.

Dickens joined in one of the trip's idiosyncrasies himself. Relaxed foreign travel quickly brings out strange personal initiatives. The growing of moustaches had become something of a fad at that time and, under Dickens's enthusiasm, quickly took on a competitive edge among the trio. We only have one account of the contest, however, from Dickens, who clearly won hands down. Giving Georgina his sister-in-law the latest report from Milan on Egg's and Collins's moustaches, he told her: 'They are more distressing, more comic, more sparse and meagre, more straggling, wandering, wiry, stubbly, formless, more given to wandering into strange places and sprouting up noses and dribbling under chins than anything in that nature ever produced, as I believe, since the Flood. Collins has taken to wiping his (which is like the plornishghenters eye-brows) at dinner; and Egg's are not near his nose, but begin at the corners of the mouth, like those of the Witches in *Macbeth*'[8].

He clearly could stand the situation no longer and in an attempt to force the pace, shaved off the whole of the fringe under his chin. 'The moustache remains, and now looks enormous; but the beard I have sacrificed as a dread warning to competitors.' What the competitors thought is not recorded.

Whereas Dickens stuck to people and events in his letters home, Wilkie concentrated on the scenery, the pictures and occasionally the bizarre. They found Paris overflowing with English visitors and were astonished at the way the new boulevards were being thrust through the centre of the French capital. 'Old houses are being demolished, and new houses springing up, over nearly a mile of space in the heart of Paris. The main street will be the broadest, longest and grandest in the world when it is finished'[9].

They were quickly through Strasbourg and into the Alps where Wilkie let his pen flow freely in his letters home. 'The mighty peaks rose dark and dim, with the sun behind them, rough masses of thick white cloud, rolling far below their summits, and far above the morning mists smoking up from the valleys beneath'. Then they were through Geneva, skirting Mont Blanc, going down the valley of Chamonix and finally ascending the Mer de Glace on mules, the beasts 'preferring the extreme edge of every precipice all the way up'.

It was an exhilarating journey spoilt, for Wilkie alone it seems, by some of the Swiss valleys. Once again his eye for the bizarre was constantly alerted. 'The beautiful valleys,' he noticed, 'are nests of pestilence and the people who inhabit them are hideous with disease and deformity. . . . Many of the people are born idiots as a matter of certainty, if they are born in the valleys. The first of these miserable creatures that I saw,' he told his mother, 'was about the height of Ward's eldest child, had the face of a monkey, and could utter no articulate sound. I asked the postillion how old he was, and was told that he was twenty years of age. There are hundreds and hundreds of creatures like this in all the Swiss valleys we passed through. . . . Still more frequent is the hideous deformity called the goitre – a bag of flesh growing from the throat, generally . . . the size of a carpet bag, and affecting the women particularly. Some of them walk with the goitre actually over their shoulders . . .'

By the time they reached Lake Maggiore and had been ferried across and serenaded by an old blind fiddler, reminding Wilkie of old times in Italy, his emotions were beginning to get the better of him. 'I never felt nearer astonishing everybody by bursting out crying than I did while we were ferrying over the river and listening to the blind fiddler's Italian songs.'

It is remarkable how well they all coped with the journey and with the troubles they were bound to meet with en route. The beginning between Paris and Strasbourg offered no difficulty, for they travelled, according to Dickens, on 'the very best railroad I have ever seen'. But it was not long before they were teetering on the edges of precipices on mules. As they crossed the Alps they changed from one mode of travel to another using 'the most extraordinary vehicles – like swings, like boats, like Noah's arks, like barges and enormous bedsteads'. And prior to entering Milan they ended up in a carriage with their luggage on top, but each piece with a string attached, to which they held on throughout the night – to frustrate thieves along the route – 'exactly as if we were in three shower-baths and were afraid to pull the string'[10].

On the Swiss side of the Simplon their sleep was shattered by the arrival of fifty cats which tumbled into the corridor outside their bedrooms all at once in the middle of the night, whether through the roof was not clear, 'and made such a horrible noise that we started out of our beds with panic'. Obviously a crisis for the courier to deal with. He opened his door and 'laid about him until they dispersed'. Then all was calm again as they reached the oasis of Genoa and a remarkable number of Dickens's old acquaintances.

They were entertained by the de la Rues, a Swiss banker and his wife, with whom Dickens and his wife Catherine had stayed nine years earlier, and whom Dickens had escorted through London. Although they were there only a couple of days, it was enough to jog Dickens's memory, even prick his conscience, about his earlier behaviour. He had had a remarkable relationship with Madame de la Rue using his mesmeric powers to cure her, even if temporarily, of her nervous headaches, convulsions and other neurasthenic symptoms. The dependence grew and the doctor/patient relationship deepened to a point which was unlikely to recommend itself to Catherine.

How she showed her resentment is far from clear but, after Madame de la Rue had politely declined any further treatment on this second trip, the reverberations began to echo down the years and finally came out in a particularly bitter letter he wrote to Catherine several weeks later from Turin[11]. He suddenly poured out his resentments at her behaviour nine years earlier and even persuaded Catherine to send the de la Rues an apology. Catherine acquiesced. It was just a first taste of the bitterness that was to overwhelm them both only five years later.

The three companions needed the break in Genoa, for the sea voyage by P&O down to Naples was hardly what they had bargained for. The ship was badly over-booked even in first class. By the time the ship sailed, according to Dickens, there were 'ladies on the tables, gentlemen under the tables, and ladies and gentlemen lying indiscriminately on the open deck, arrayed like spoons on a sideboard. . . . We were all gradually dozing off when a perfectly tropical rain fell, and in a moment drowned the whole ship.' The next night was infinitely better for Dickens who, with charm and tact, got himself into a state room but did only marginally better for Wilkie and Egg. 'The store room down by the hold was opened for Egg and Collins,' Dickens later reported, 'and they slept with the moist sugar, the cheese in cut, the spices, the cruets, the apples, the pears – in a perfect chandler's shop; in company with . . . a cat, and the steward, who dozed in an armchair and all night long fell head-foremost, once in every five minutes, on Egg, who slept on the counter or dresser'.

There were many compensations and diversions to make up for these discomforts: a huge evening party among Dickens's old friends in Lausanne; a visit to La Scala in Milan (where the tenor was laughed at and the prima donna was hissed at); a picnic among the ruins at Pompeii; the inevitable climb up Vesuvius on horseback and a moonlight descent with Capri and Sorrento stretched out before them; a better prima donna at the San Carlo in Naples; vespers at St Peter's and a chance meeting with the Pope (who according to Wilkie, 'looked straight at me as he passed and bowed as he saw me with my hat in my hand').

Wilkie's first wave of Italian nostalgia plainly hit him crossing the river with the blind fiddler. It was renewed with greater intensity once they reached Rome, sixteen years after the family's first visit. 'Nothing has astonished me more', he wrote to his brother, 'than my own vivid remembrance of every street and building in this wonderful and mournful place. . . . This place seems, and really is, unaltered. I recognised this morning all the favourite haunts at the Pincian hills that we used to run about, as little boys – I saw the same bishops, in purple stockings, followed by servants in gaudy livery, the same importunately impudent beggars, the same men with pointed hats and women with red petticoats and tights and swaddled babies that I remembered so well in England since 1837 and 1838. . . . I can hardly help fancying that I must have gone to sleep at fourteen years old and woke up again at the comparatively mature age of twenty nine'.

The trouble was that, as nostalgia nudged Wilkie, it all began to be shared with his travelling companions and Dickens at least began to find it all a trifle overdone. 'He tells us about the enormous quantities of Monte Pulciano and what not, that he used to drink when he was last here', he complained to his wife, 'and what distinguished people said to him in the way of taking his opinion, and what advice he gave them and so forth – being then exactly thirteen years old'.

It was, however, a trifling irritant. The major difference between them was basically in their attitude to art galleries and museums. 'The Fine Arts,' Dickens confessed, 'afford a subject which I never approach; always appearing to fall into a profound reverie when it is discussed. Neither do I even go into any gallery with them'. Egg and Wilkie meanwhile had some profound discourses on Art, Colour, Tone and so forth. 'But I keep out of the way when pictures are in question and go my own path.' It was a natural reaction, but he missed some of Wilkie's basic enthusiasms as a result, as well as his judgements, as he and Egg visited Milan Cathedral ('a compromise between the Gothic and the classical styles . . . and noble in its gloom and mystery'), Leonardo's *Last Supper* ('the utter ruin of something which was *once* a picture'), Raphael's *Spolsalizio*, ('a picture that really deserves its reputation'), Tintoretto's *Crucifixion* ('without a parallel in the world'), and discussed the Venetian painters ('the most *original* race of painters that the world has yet seen').

Venice, however, as so often, seemed to exert its special charm and they were determined to make the most of it, staying at Dickens's favourite hotel, the Danieli, at the mouth of the Grand Canal near the Bridge of Sighs and close to St Mark's. They took up a large sitting-room[12], with two front windows, and three bedrooms close to the small canal by the Bridge of Sighs. 'We lead the luxurious dandy-dilletante sort of life here', Wilkie told his mother. 'Our gondola (with two rowers in modern footmen's liveries!) waits on us wherever we go. We live among operas, ballets and cafés more than half the night.' The gondola had one particular perk attached to it – the gondolieri were expected to light the customer all the way to his box at the opera with an enormous lantern.

'Imagine the procession,' Dickens urged his wife, 'led by Collins with incipient moustache, spectacles, slender legs, and extremely dirty dress gloves – Egg second, in a white hat, and a straggly mean little beard – Inimitable bringing up the rear, in full dress and big sleeved great coat, rather considerably ashamed'. But they enjoyed the opera and much more besides.

They all eventually returned briefly through Paris, Dickens picking up his son Charley, who was on his way back from Leipzig. They had managed to maintain their friendships, in spite of their natural differences. Wilkie and Dickens in particular had grown still closer as was to be proved by their next Continental excursions. How far they had indulged in the kind of relaxed enterprises that were clearly to follow, in London and Paris, remains unclear, though Augustus Egg, significantly, was not to accompany them again in the same way.

They returned to London, refreshed but hardly lacking potential work. Dickens was soon faced with the possibility of a further decline in the circulation of *Household Words* and, within four months, was doing his best to revive flagging interest with the serialisation of *Hard Times*. Wilkie too was soon picking up the threads of his unfinished novel, *Hide and Seek*, delayed partly through illness and partly by his Continental trip.

He was also giving much thought to the series of travel articles promised to *Bentley's Miscellany*. He had clearly worked on them during his travels and spent some time over Christmas and New Year sorting out his ideas. By early January he was writing to Richard Bentley again enclosing drafts of some of the articles, along with detailed suggestions about their use in the magazine. They would, he explained to Bentley, eventually cover his travels in Italy, describe various papist ceremonies, and include art criticism and a true love story.

Their reception, however, came as something of a shock. The *Miscellany*, unknown to him during his absence, had been running just such a series on art developments in Italy and could not, therefore, entertain Wilkie's proposed series. So all his ideas of paying for part of the Italian trip, through a series in the *Miscellany*, collapsed.

What became of his prepared series remains a mystery. When correspondence between Wilkie and the editor of the *Art Journal*, S. C. Hall, an old friend of William Collins, recently came to light in London, along with a letter discovered by a London art-dealer, Jeremy Maas, it was strongly suggested that Wilkie was the author of a series of articles in the *Art Journal* starting in June, 1854[13]. The letter was brief. It simply stated: 'May the bearer have a copy of the *Art Journal* of this month to be sent to the writer of the article on the *Studios of Rome*?' and was signed W. Wilkie Collins.

The first impression was that Collins was the author and that the puzzle of the missing articles had been resolved. But the solution has proved rather more elusive. The subsequent discovery of a second, and earlier, letter to S. C. Hall seems to suggest that at least the first article (of seven) was written by a friend of Wilkie's in Rome. Who then was it?

A detailed analysis of all the articles, while providing a few doubts of Wilkie's full authorship, initially seemed to produce circumstancial evidence supporting it. He had prepared just such a series. He had visited the studios concerned. He had sufficient knowledge of art to attempt such analysis. He could in fact have prepared and planned the articles and encouraged a local friend in Rome to complete the visits and send him notes from which he wrote up the final versions in London.

There is also the evidence of the 'true love story'. In the middle of his artistic visits, the author of the articles and his companion stumble on a human tragedy. The story goes on: 'A sad change was now to meet us as we picked our steps along an utterly broken-up, dirty lane, and then grasped our way up a dark winding staircase to the next studio on our list.' They were greeted by a pretty woman (evidently the painter's wife) who received them and then instantly withdrew. The artist himself ('one of the best animal painters alive, after Landseer') was 'pining, old and broken-hearted'. Why? In a corner of the studio stood a lovely female face, just sketched in. 'I shall never finish that portrait, begun twenty years ago now,' the artist sighs. It had been started when he was young and when his present wife had been the beautiful model, whom he had regarded 'with the lover's as well as the artist's eye'.

He had just begun to be accepted in the noble society of Rome; he married his model; and then made the fatal mistake of introducing her to his new society friends. They quickly recognised her.

'A buzz went round the room of wonder and admiration, but with these mingled gradually a whisper that the beauty had been a model. Both husband and wife were desired to withdraw and from that day the painter's fate was sealed; no-one employed him, no-one received him; solitary and poor he worked on, and children were born, and debts contracted, and misery gathered like a dark cloud around his household, until he became the poor, pinched, faded man whom I now saw. It was his beautiful wife who had opened the door and had then quickly left us. Time had laid his heavy finger on her too. We had no opportunity of seeing more of her, for she never showed herself again at our departure. What a world of wretchedness there is in all this, even as I write it, and yet every word is strictly, positively true.'

Is this then the 'true love story' Collins had promised Bentley? One rather hoped so, if only to resolve the mystery of the articles he wrote in Rome. The key to the *Art Journal* articles, however, has been shown to be the letter referring to a friend of Wilkie's in Rome. There was such a friend who was also a regular contributor to the *Art Journal*: Frances Dickinson, who wrote under the pseudonym 'Florentia' and later reproduced excerpts from the articles under her own name.

Whatever the truth about the missing articles, it is unlikely that Wilkie would have spent so much time in preparing them and not placed them somewhere. Over the same period Wilkie was also discussing articles and illustrations for Punch, sometimes by correspondence, sometimes over lunch at the Garrick Club, with Mark Lemon. It all went to explain how he managed to keep money flowing in (to top up his allowance from his mother) in his efforts to keep pace with the demands of his new found companion, Charles Dickens.

CHAPTER EIGHT

Diversions

BY THE SUMMER of 1854, with the Crimean War only a matter of three months old, Wilkie and Dickens were emerging from their latest writing efforts and Dickens was once again established in Boulogne, where Wilkie was to spend several weeks in the later summer and autumn. But even before Wilkie's departure from London, Dickens was popping back across the Channel for a night or two out together. He had just finished a long session with *Hard Times* and needed a bit of relaxation. Who better to spend it with than Wilkie, in London, prior to their returning to Boulogne?

'The interval,' he wrote to Wilkie from Boulogne, 'I propose to pass in a career of amiable dissipation and unbounded license in the metropolis. If you will come and breakfast with me about midnight – anywhere – any day, and go to bed no more until we fly to these pastoral retreats, I shall be delighted to have such a vicious associate'. That he could have written such a letter to few, if any, of his other friends is a commentary not only on their growing intimacy, but on Dickens's changing domestic situation. Dickens's appetite for living life to the full had begun to be satisfied by a pleasure-loving companion who knew where to seek it out.

After their escapade in London, Wilkie accompanied Dickens back to Boulogne where other literary friends were invited throughout the summer. Napoleon III also visited Boulogne in the early autumn, encouraging military manoeuvres all round the villa and stirring a certain patriotism among the visitors, to the extent of flying the Union Jack alongside the Tricolour, and illuminating the house 'the English way' and 'astonishing all Boulogne by the spectacle'.

The French apparently used oil lamps to light up their houses outside in honour of the Emperor. Dickens and his friends were determined to go one better and to avoid the interference of the wind. 'We shut all the front windows in the English way,' Wilkie told his brother Charley, 'and put candles in them. This house is all windows. We had 114 candles burning, in 114 clay candlesticks, stuck on 114 nails, driven into the window sashes. When we were ready to light up, every soul in the house (except the children) were stationed at a window – Dickens rang a bell – and at that signal we lit up the whole 114 candles in less than a minute. The effect from a distance was as if the whole house was one steady blaze of light. It was seen for miles and miles round. The landlord went into hysterical French ecstasies – the populace left their illuminations in the town, and crowded to the ramparts opposite our hill, to stand in amazement. We let off fireworks besides, and to crown all we had not the slightest alarm or accident'[1].

Wilkie was in his element. He was later to say that these were some of the happiest years of his life. He was making a name for himself; he was associating with the most successful novelist of his day; he had an understanding, and encouraging, mother; and he was beginning to enjoy himself, doing the things he loved best in stimulating company. His friendship with Edward Piggott had brought him the opportunity of writing for a political weekly and of sailing in his father's yacht, and his friendship with Dickens developed along similar lines, at work and play, usually in London, occasionally in Folkestone, sometimes in Boulogne, increasingly in Paris.

It was while staying with Dickens in Folkestone, among such guests as Thackeray and Kinglake, that Wilkie began to discuss his next book, *After Dark*, and his mother's manuscript which was to form the basis of it. It is odd that her diaries have been generally overlooked, even by Wilkie himself in the case of his biography of his father (his description of their visit to Italy was entirely based on his father's writings). It is even odder that he never publicly acknowledged her initial involvement in the series of separate stories which eventually made up *After Dark*.

His mother had clearly given him a diary of reminiscences based on her life as an artist's wife, and he had taken it with him to Folkestone. After working on it and discussing it with Dickens, he wrote to her at Hanover Terrace reporting progress. 'After I had done fifty pages,' he told her, 'leaving out many things and transferring others, but keeping as close as I could to the simplicity of your narrative, I began to have my doubts whether it would not be necessary (with the public) to make a story to hang your characters and incidents on'[2].

He had told Dickens the history of the manuscript and had read his own amended version to him. He obviously agreed with Wilkie's judgment but felt, as Wilkie did, that 'without more story, it would not do with the public'. As Wilkie told his mother, 'strangers could not know that the thing was real – and novel readers seeing my name on the title-page would expect a story'. The upshot was that five stories, published in *Household Words*, coupled with a sixth, specially written (*The Lady of Glenwith Grange*), were linked together by the introduction of a diary by an artist's wife. So Harriet's efforts eventually saw the light of day. But clearly not in their original form, and not directly acknowledged by Wilkie in the Preface. Perhaps the truth is that little of her original manuscript was left, following his extensive revisions and the addition of his own stories[3].

During his stay in Folkestone, Wilkie began to plan his next sailing expedition with Edward Piggott. As usual he wanted to know the cost: 'If the yachting is to come off,' he wrote to Edward, 'can you find out before we leave London, about the size of the vessel, the number of amateur sailors to go, the time of starting and, last but not least, what is likely to be the expense per man of the trip? This last item, so far as I am concerned, is an important one'[4]. On the other hand he had no intention of stinting on food. 'Let us by all means take some stores at least with us from Fortnum and Mason's. We can be certain of *their* preserved provisions – and that certainly is worth paying a few shillings extra for.'

Wilkie was clearly in charge of food and drink from the outset. As he said later, 'when grog is to be made or sauces are to be prepared,'[5] he was monarch of all he surveyed. But it did not prevent him from having a few anxieties on more purely nautical matters. He began to worry about the Equinox. 'I find by my Almanack that it begins on the 23rd September. Surely,' he asked Edward, 'we shall not have time for the Scilly Islands, starting only on the 18th or 19th? And as for returning in an Equinoctial gale in a boat of 8 tons with one able seaman on board, is that not rather "tempting Providence" by making a toil of a pleasure? Had we not better make a brief burst upon the Welsh coast and get back before the Boreas can overtake us?'

In the event they took a crew of three from Bristol and did make it to the Scillies, in spite of a spot of bad weather. It was a form of relaxation which Wilkie continued to indulge in virtually to the end of his life, almost entirely with Edward Piggott, an enthusiasm which he eventually passed on to his young solicitor, Henry Bartley.

Whether Edward Piggott shared in the other relaxations which Wilkie pursued so vigorously with Dickens is not entirely clear, but their closeness to each other and to the young friends attracted to Hanover Terrace at this period comes out in much of their correspondence. On one occasion he is the convivial companion. 'What a night! What speeches! What songs! I carried away much claret and am a rather seedy barrister this morning,' confessed Wilkie. On another occasion, he is concerned with one of their friend's preparations for his marriage, and is clear about the right formula. 'As to George, nothing ought to pass his lips on Wednesday but oysters and the strongest port wine.' And he soon wants to know the results. 'Any news (erotic or otherwise) of dear old George will be welcome.' And in preparation for John Millais' wedding, they have a similar interest. 'We dine at six, and shall drink limitless potations. May he consummate successfully! And have the best cause in the world to lie late on Wednesday morning'.

It is hardly surprising that Collins and Dickens would have begun to develop their comradely jaunts in Paris, as well as in London. Wilkie had clearly grown to love the freedom of the French capital, and had plainly pursued all manner of distractions there, even when his father was alive. To Dickens Paris had simply become an extension of his family visits to Boulogne. Both had literary and theatrical business to undertake and both did some of their writing there. But the ease with which they could go to the theatre when they wanted, eat when they wanted and generally do as they pleased, coupled with the cafés and dance halls they liked to frequent, inevitably made a visit to Paris one of their favourite relaxations for close on a decade. This was where, if anywhere, that their differing needs merged together.

Paris had a variety of theatres, catering to a variety of tastes, from the classics put on at the Théâtre Français to the melodramas and tragicomic pieces that, according to Galignani's contemporary guide, formed 'the standard of dramatic excellence to the lower orders' at the Théâtre de la Porte St Martin. The restaurants (for dinner) were far more relaxed about the entertainment of women than they were in London. Ladies were welcome, accompanied or alone, without attracting undue attention.

Only in the *estaminets*, where smoking was allowed, were ladies not encouraged. And after the theatre and dinner, there were the public gardens and dance halls ('all frequented by Lorettes who are admitted gratis') and the public masked balls at the Opera House or the Opéra Comique, where the chief attration was the congregation of actresses from most of the theatres, with whom to while away the night[6]. There was also a happy mixture of entertainments, the dance halls sometimes including wrestling, circus acts and acrobats. Drinking was common to them all. While gambling had been officially banned since 1837, the diligent could still discover whatever they needed in the boarding houses and smaller hostels. Wilkie had long been at home in such a milieu.

The first extended visit to Paris planned jointly by Dickens and Collins seems to have been in the early months of 1855. Dickens was in no doubt what they wanted to do and how it should be arranged. 'Now, *mon cher*,' he wrote privately to his old friend Regnier, the well-known actor at the Théâtre Français, 'do you think you can, without inconvenience, engage me for a week, an apartment – cheerful, light and wholesome – containing a comfortable *salon et deux chambres à coucher*. I do not care whether it is an hotel or not, but the reason why I do not write for an apartment to the Hotel Brighton is that there they expect one to dine at home (I mean in the apartment) generally; whereas, as we are coming to Paris expressly to be always looking about us, we want to dine wherever we like every day. Consequently, what we want to find is a good apartment, where we can have our breakfast but where we shall never dine. . . . I want it to be pleasant and gay, and to throw myself *en garçon* on the festive *diableries de Paris'*.

No doubt Regnier understood the message, for by mid-February they were warmly established in an elegant apartment at the Hotel Meurice, facing the Tuileries Gardens. Unfortunately, Wilkie had been struck down by one of his bouts of illness again and Dickens was forced to make the best of it, largely on his own. 'We breakfast at ten,' he wrote home, 'read and write till two, and then I go out walking all over Paris, while the invalid sits by the fire or is deposited in a café. We dine at five, in a different restaurant every day and at seven or so go to the theatre – sometimes to two theatres. Sometimes to three. We get home about twelve, light the fire, and drink lemonade, to which *I* add rum. We go to bed between one and two'.

On this occasion they visited the Opéra Comique and the Théâtre Français and were driven out of the Théâtre de la Porte St Martin by the awful stench. 'The whole theatre must be standing over some vast cesspool.' They frequented Franconi's restaurant and with Regnier's encouragement had every intention of attending the masked ball at the Opera House.[7] It had a reputation for beautiful women and lively entertainment. 'The strict etiquette which presides in the aristocratic *Salons* of the Faubourg St Germain,' a contemporary pointed out in explaining the true basis of the Opera House's attractions, 'is occasionally lost sight of in the exhilaration of the moment and that "chilling reserve" is by no means the predominant characteristic of the fair who resort to this pleasantest of pandemoniums'. Whether Wilkie managed to make it from his convalescent fireside on this occasion is not recorded. There would, in any case, be many other opportunities.

Collins and Dickens were sometimes in Paris alone, sometimes with Dickens's family. The arrangements, and above all the diversions, changed accordingly. Dickens was back in Paris later that year, 1855, with his family, and after looking at apartments in the rue St Florentin and the Faubourg St Honoré, finally settled on one in the Champs Elysées, with the windows overlooking the thoroughfare, close to the Jardin d'Hiver and not far from Franconi's, one of his favourite restaurants. He took the rooms which were on two floors for six months until the following spring.

Wilkie was there with them for several weeks, in a charming bachelor apartment a few doors away, in one building 'like a cottage in a ballet' with smart green gates 'outside of which the stir and bustle of the Champs Elysées goes on from morning to night'. But before Wilkie's visit, Dickens was back in London briefly, attending to *Household Words* and, once again, in need of entertainment. 'If you are free on Wednesday,' he wrote from the Champs Elysées, 'and will meet me at the *Household Words* office at half past five, I shall be happy to start on any Haroun Alraschid expedition'. Presumably Wilkie planned their night out accordingly. Dickens was also back in London again for a similar purpose ('to survey mankind from China to Peru') a month later.

Thereafter Dickens and his family settled down in Paris for several months, Wilkie staying with them for a few weeks. The time was amiably spent in theatre-going ('an infernal dose of ditch water' at the Odéon, strange melodramas at the Porte St Martin and a rather disappointing attempt at *Paradise Lost* at the Ambigu which prompted 'the wildest rumours as to the un-dressing of our first parents'), Dickens dining out with his family at favourite restaurants (Franconi's, Les Trois Frères and Giradin's) and, when alone, simply walking round Paris for the sake of it. 'Yesterday,' Dickens wrote to a friend, 'I turned to the right when I got outside the Barrière de l'Etoile, walked round the wall till I came to the river and then entered Paris beyond the site of the Bastille. Today I mean to turn to the left when I get outside the Barrière and see what comes of that. . . .'

Wilkie had personal experience of Dickens's determination to walk the streets of Paris at the slightest provocation. He later spoke of 'Dickens's impatience of the long melodramas' which he use to take him to see when they were both in Paris. He recalled many years later: 'The second act generally exhausted his powers of endurance. I implored him to respect the *Development of Art*. He generally answered, "You shall tell me the story of the piece, when you get back to the hotel. I'm off for a walk in the streets" '[8].

Dickens was also busy discussing translations of his books, and planning new ideas for *Household Words*, including arranging a demonstration of the guillotine and the opening up of the catacombs. But other distractions called him too, plunging him 'into some of the strange places I glide into of nights in these latitudes'. One of them was a dance hall where he and Wilkie had watched some wrestling on an earlier occasion. On this particular night there was a ball on and Dickens paid his three francs at the door. He found the entertainment much the same as at the National Argyll Rooms in London. 'Some pretty faces, but all of two classes – wicked and coldly calculating, or haggard and wretched in their warm beauty. Among the latter was a woman of thirty or so, in an Indian shawl, who never stirred from a seat in a corner all the time I was there. Handsome, regardless, brooding, and yet with some nobler qualities in her forehead. I mean to walk about tonight,' he wrote to Wilkie, 'and look for her. I didn't speak to her there, but I have a fancy that I should like to know more about her. Never shall, I suppose'.

This easy relationship, both with each other and with whatever they found about them, continued for several years, and is reflected in much of their correspondence. A year later in London Dickens is clearly in need of another diversion. 'Will you come and dine at the office on Thursday at ½ past 5', he writes to Wilkie. 'We will then discuss the Brighton or other trip possibilities. I am tugging at my Oar too – should like a change – find the Galley a little heavy – must stick to it – am generally in a collision state'. Just over two weeks later Dickens is immediately responding, somewhat ecstatically, to a clear plan suggested by Wilkie. On its receipt, 'I immediately arose like the desponding Princes in the Arabian Nights, when the old woman – Procuress evidently, and probably of French extraction – comes to whisper about the Princesses they love, and washed my face and went out; and my face has been shining ever since. Ellis (the proprietor of the Bedford Hotel, Brighton) responds to my letter that rooms shall be ready. There is a train at 12 which appears to me to be the train for distinguished visitors. If you will call for me in a cab at about 20 minutes past 11, my hand will be on the latch of the door'.

A couple of months later, on the completion of his latest novel, *Little Dorrit*, he writes to Wilkie, 'I have finished! On Sunday last I wrote the two little words of three letters each. Any mad proposal you please will find a wildly insane response in – yours ever'. Two weeks later he is even more insistent. 'On Wednesday, Sir – on Wednesday – if the mind can devise anything sufficiently in the style of sybarite Rome in the days of its culminating voluptuousness, I am your man . . . If you can think of any tremendous way of passing the night, in the meantime, do. I don't care what it is. I give (for that night only) restraint to the Winds'[9].

[83]

Wilkie had thus became something of a safety valve for Dickens. While family life continued, though visibly deteriorating, Dickens took what opportunities Wilkie was able to offer in London, Paris or elsewhere. For Wilkie, Paris was his favourite watering place. He was free; he could indulge his needs in any way he wished; he could do some writing; and all without offending his mother. *The Rogue's Life* was written there during one of his visits with Dickens and remained, for that reason, one of his favourite stories, even if not his best[10].

They did not, however, confine their joint expeditions to London, Paris or Boulogne. One particular excursion, which was recorded in some detail both in *Household Words* and in their individual correspondence, took them to Cumbria, or rather what were parts of Cumberland and Lancashire in those days[11]. It was one of their last jaunts together and, for Wilkie at least, proved far too strenuous. For Dickens it was a last desperate effort to escape from the pressures at home.

He had recently returned from the touring successes of Wilkie's *The Frozen Deep*, during which his feelings for Ellen Ternan had developed apace and after which his relations with his wife Catherine had dramatically deteriorated. He was in need of a distraction and, once again, he felt that Wilkie might share it with him, though in the circumstances not the kind they had so often pursued together.

Not long after his return from the theatrical tour he wrote to Wilkie: 'Partly in the grim despair and restlessness of this subsidence from excitement, and partly for the sake of *Household Words*, I want to cast about whether you or I can go anywhere – take any tour – see anything – whereon we could write something together . . . Will you rattle your head and see if there is any pebble in it which we could wander away and play marbles with?'

Collins thought of the Norfolk coast and of the sea. Dickens, glancing through *The Beauties of England and Wales*[12], was taken with the Cumberland hills and the 'nearby coastline'. On closer inspection they discovered they could get to Carlisle by train in a day and that Carrock Fell, not far away, had all the attraction they needed. It was not far from Skiddaw, not too great a challenge ('520 yards above the surrounding meadows') and with a mystery of its own ('the top covered with masses of granite, some not less than 300 tons in weight, named locally "the Sunken Kirks"').

That quickly became their destination and they arrived in Carlisle late one evening and were greeted by the landlord of *The Queen's Head* at Hesketh Newmarket, at the foot of Carrock Fell, next morning. It was a prosperous mining town in those days, supporting five pubs and a whisky distillery. (Lead and copper had been found in the hills thereabouts.)[13] But the prosperity was difficult to appreciate in the incessant rain that greeted the intrepid visitors. And their enthusiasm to go up the nearest mountain in that weather fell on deaf ears – all except those of their obliging landlord, Joseph Porter.

Why they insisted on leaving the cosy sitting-room he showed them into with its comfortable furnishings, agreeable books (Fielding, Smollett, Steele and Addison), oatcake, whisky and water, only Dickens can explain. Wilkie can hardly have been the enthusiast. But a few hours later all three were slowly making their way, utterly wet through, up the mist-shrouded hillside.

'The mist was darkening, the rain was thickening, the trees were dotted about like spots of faint shadow'. Still they persisted until, having reached a cairn of stones (which the landlord at least must have known was not the summit), they decided to descend. At which point the landlord admitted he did not know the way down and Dickens broke his compass. 'It is the practice,' Dickens wrote later, 'of the English portion of the human race to receive all great disasters in dead silence'. In this case one disaster led to another, for they eventually decided to follow the course of a stream downhill. 'Watercourse followed accordingly' reported Dickens. 'Leaps, splashes and tumbles for two hours. C. lost. C.D. whoops. Cries for assistance from behind. C.D. returns. C. with horribly sprained ankle, lying in a rivulet'[14]. How they managed to get Wilkie down again and into a dog cart and then back to *The Queen's Head* was easier to write about later than to endure at the time. They bundled up his rapidly swelling foot in a flannel waistcoat and, sensing that Hesketh Newmarket was hardly the best overnight stop for an invalid, set off through the rain in an exposed conveyance to Wigton.

Once again they had a remarkable choice of accommodation, Wigton boasting of at least twenty-five pubs. They chose the King's Arms and as soon as Wilkie was comfortably stretched out on a couch in their sitting-room, overlooking the pump in the market place, Dickens reported mournfully what he could see from the window. It was a rather damp, empty scene. 'I see', he told Wilkie, 'what I hope and believe to be one of the most dismal places ever seen by eyes. I see the houses with their roofs of dull black, their stained fronts, and their dark-rimmed windows looking as if they were all in mourning'. He later reported that Wigton had 'no population, no business, no streets to speak of; but five linen-drapers within range of our windows, one next door and five more round the corner'[15]. He was probably right. Wigton at that time was the centre of the gingham and check trade and drapers' shops still abound near the King's Arms. There is still one next door[16].

They hardly lingered in Wigton, Dickens allowing himself a short stroll down the main street picking up material for their later contributions to *Household Words*, before they carried Wilkie down to the carriage which took them on to the coast at Allonby – and to a familiar landlady, Mrs Partridge, whom Dickens had previously met at Greta Bridge in Yorkshire when he was preparing for *Nicholas Nickleby*. Her husband was now the landlord of The Ship, 'a capital little homely inn', overlooking the sea and the Scottish mountains across the bay. To Dickens, Allonby was 'a small untidy outlandish place . . . very much what Broadstairs would have been if it had been born Irish, and had not inherited a cliff'.

While Wilkie remained necessarily idle, Dickens strode the seafront to Maryport and back (close on twelve miles the round trip) to pick up their mail, and began to plan their joint contributions to *Household Words*. But they soon tired of the sea and Dickens was soon tiring of, as he put it, another version of the sea in their room ('Collins is perpetually holding his ankle over a pail of salt water and laving it with a milk jug')[17]. But he put up with the discomfort, 'carrying C. melodramatically everywhere; into and out of carriages; up and down stairs; to bed; every step'.

Somehow he got him back to Carlisle and thence to rather greater comfort at the *King's Arms*, Lancaster, where Dickens secured a state bedroom with two enormous red four-poster beds for himself, a bedroom for Wilkie and a large sitting room. And the first evening the landlord presided over dinner consisting of two small salmon trout, sirloin steak, a brace of partridges, seven dishes of sweets, five dishes of dessert and, in the centre, an enormous bride-cake. 'We always have it here, sir,' said the landlord, 'custom of the house'. Wilkie turned pale, estimating the dinner would be at least half a guinea each. He later consoled himself with the thought that he had eaten the bride-cake 'without the trouble of being married, or of knowing anybody in that ridiculous dilemma'. A recurring Collins sentiment.

Lancaster, however, like Carlisle, was only a stepping stone to the Doncaster races where Dickens had planned they should end their expedition with something of a flourish. He had already alerted Wills, back in London, that they would have to pay all of twelve guineas for a couple of bedrooms and a sitting room during race week. But like many a correspondent before and since, he convinced himself that their 'grotesque idea of describing the town under those circumstances' would justify the expense. They got the rooms he wanted at *The Angel* and could look down on the main street as it filled up with 'horse jockeys, bettors, drunkards and other blackguards'; and, by this time, Wilkie's ankle had improved sufficiently for him to get into hotels and up the stairs with two thick sticks, 'like an admiral in a farce'. He went out for the first time to the theatre in a cab and was then ready for their first visit to the races in the carriage and pair Dickens had engaged.

They hardly approved of what they saw at the races. Wilkie later expressed his profound antipathy to horses. 'Taking the horse as an animal in the abstract, I cordially despise him from every point of view'[18]. And Dickens thought little of those who were attracted to the horses, dubbing them cruel, covetous, calculating, insensible and wicked. But it did not prevent them from entering into the spirit of the race meeting nor from picking the odd winner. Dickens in particular was clearly on a winning streak. On the day of the St Leger he bought the race card, quickly chose the names of three horses for the main three races and, as he exulted later, 'if you can believe it without your hair standing on end, those three races were won, one after another, by those three horses!'[19]

Their excursion to the north was not in their normal mould but it had served its purpose – offering Dickens the distraction and companionship he needed and *Household Words* a blend of travel articles and short stories from their joint pens over a period of five consecutive weeks. It had also kept Dickens's domestic troubles at bay a little longer.

As for their earlier escapades in London and Paris, they were, in many ways, an ill-assorted pair, plunging into their nightly adventures with different purposes, different needs: Dickens, unhappily married, increasingly conscious of his wife's deficiencies, driving himself into a frenzy of work as a way out, and as quickly needing immediate distractions; Collins, with a relaxed attitude to sexual morality, persuaded of the futility of marriage, avoiding it at all costs, often bent on the good life with an openness that fitted oddly with Victorian morals.

Yet for several years their needs coincided, just as did their literary interests and aspirations. Who else could Dickens have written to in such terms as these and who else but Collins could have prompted them: 'O misconstructive one', Dickens wrote from the Swan Hotel, Worcester, 'the mysterious addresses merely refer to places where Arthur Smith did not know aforehand the names of the best hotels. As to that furtive and Don Giovanni purpose at which you hint, that may be all very well for *your* violent vigour, or that of the companions with whom you may have travelled continentally, or the Caliph Hamoun Alraschid with whom you have unbent metropolitanly; but anchorites who read themselves red hot every night are chaste as Diana (if I suppose *she* was by the by, but I find I don't quite believe it when I write her name)'.

Not perhaps surprisingly it was in this period that both met women who were to fashion the rest of their lives, and in ways that reflected their differing temperaments. Collins met Caroline Graves in the mid-1850s; and Dickens was introduced to Ellen Ternan in the green room of a theatre in 1857. The repercussions in each case were again true to type, Dickens finally plunging into an almost self-destructive frenzy, involving the public renunciation of his wife, Collins absorbing Caroline quietly into his life in a style that suited him, merely shocking a few friends by the intricacies of his household.

CHAPTER NINE

Caroline

AT WHAT PRECISE date Wilkie Collins finally left home is difficult to establish. He might have had difficulty in pin-pointing it himself. His mother's influence was deep and the lively atmosphere she created in Hanover Terrace was enticing. Yet some time in the mid-1850s he slowly prised himself free to live a life of his own.

Though his real freedom began in 1848, he was careful not to show it too soon in a way that would offend his mother. Even when he could afford some independence, he seemed reluctant to make the final break, answering formal social invitations particularly to friends of his mother, from Hanover Terrace and Harley Place (where his mother moved in 1856), and writing to his own friends from his newly-acquired lodgings, briefly in Howland Street and, for longer periods, in Albany Street, New Cavendish Street and Harley Street. This was the period when, as we have seen, his friendship with Dickens began to flourish, when he began to move in a much wider literary circle and to travel at will and when he first met Caroline Graves.

Shared accommodation with his mother was a convenience while his diversions, with Dickens and others, remained spontaneous and while such liaisons as he had were short-term. Yet these arrangements could hardly last and the turning point came with his growing relationship with Caroline.

When they met, who she was, where she came from have until now remained something of a mystery. The story of their meeting is mysterious enough. It is based on the memories of two close friends, John Millais, the son of Sir John Millais, Wilkie's contemporary, and Dickens's daughter Kate, who married Wilkie's brother Charles. First the story as told by John Millais in the biography of his father, published in 1895:

'One night in the fifties Millais was returning home to Gower Street from one of the many parties held under Mrs Collins's hospitable roof in Hanover Terrace, and, in accordance with the usual practice of the two brothers, Wilkie and Charles, they accompanied him on his home-ward walk through the dimly-lit, and in those days semi-rural, roads and lanes of North London. It was a beautiful moonlit night in the summer time, and as the three friends walked along chatting gaily together, they were suddenly arrested by a piercing scream coming from the garden of a villa close at hand. It was evidently the cry of a woman in distress; and while pausing to consider what they should do, the iron gate leading to the garden was dashed open, and from it came the figure of a young and very beautiful woman dressed in flowing white robes that shone in the moonlight. She seemed to float rather than to run in their direction, and, on coming up to the three young men, she paused for a moment in an attitude of supplication and terror. Then, seeming to recollect herself, she suddenly moved on and vanished in the shadows cast upon the road'[1].

All Millais could say was 'what a lovely woman'. Wilkie at least took some action. 'I must see who she is and what's the matter,' he exclaimed, as he dashed after her. He didn't return and even next day, when they all met again, he seemed reluctant to talk too much about it. But he told them that he had caught up with the lovely girl, who had explained the reason for her sudden flight as well as the story of her life.

She was, she evidently told Wilkie, a young lady of good birth and position, who had accidentally fallen into the hands of a man living in a villa in Regents Park. He had kept her prisoner there for many months 'under threats and mesmeric influence of so alarming a character' that she dared not attempt to escape, until in sheer desperation she fled from her captor who threatened to dash her brains out with a poker.

The story plainly improved in the re-telling and had a sequel, but John Millais was not prepared to tell it. 'Her subsequent history, interesting as it is,' he wrote tantalisingly, 'is not for these pages'. It was left to Kate Collins (or Kate Perugini as she eventually became after Charles Collins's death and her re-marriage) to breathe fresh life into the story in the late 1920s. S. M. Ellis[2] conjectured that the girl Wilkie had rescued was not only the inspiration for his subsequent *The Woman in White* but 'the same lady who henceforth lived with him,' and he said that Kate had virtually intimated as much. Gladys Storey[3] finally pinned Kate down in the 1930s and quoted her as saying that Wilkie Collins 'had a mistress called Caroline, a young woman of gentle birth, and the origin of the woman in white'.

At a stroke, Caroline became the Woman in White and the origin of Millais' story. Thus are legends born. The reality may have been slightly different, for both accounts were essentially second-hand, one forty years after the events described, one at least seventy years. Two questions need to be asked. Was Caroline the girl in question? Was she the origin of the Woman in White?

In sifting through the evidence, one finds it easier to accept the first than the full flavour of the second. That Wilkie met a girl in distress in such circumstances has a ring of truth about it, even if some of the details seem to reflect his own story-telling ability. Only Wilkie, of the three of them, would have taken such a romantic initiative with an unknown girl. And details of the friends and the place all seem authentic and, if true, can help put a reasonable date to his rather dramatic first meeting with Caroline.

Wilkie was still living in Hanover Terrace until the early part of 1856. John Millais, for his part, had left his rooms in Gower Street in late 1854[4]. We now know that Caroline was still married and living with her first husband in the summer of 1851. These facts narrow the date of the meeting in the Marylebone area to the summers of 1852, 1853 or 1854. If it was 1852, it would have been before June 8th of that year when Millais left London with Holman Hunt and Charles Collins. The following year seems to be ruled out since Wilkie was ill at the beginning of the summer, Millais was only in London from May 21st to June 21st (when he went to Scotland for fifteen weeks), and Wilkie was in Boulogne from July to September. Wilkie was again in Boulogne in 1854 from July 24th onwards, while Millais left London on May 23rd. Thus all three years are just possible; the early summers of 1852 and 1853 seem likely, and late May 1854, the most likely[5].

If Wilkie did meet Caroline in this dramatic fashion, who was she and where had she come from? Until now this has been difficult if not impossible to answer. But the appropriate census returns and the birth, death and marriage certificates of St Catherine's House have enabled us to clothe Caroline's past rather more fully. She was apparently christened Elizabeth Compton, and was probably born in 1830[6] and brought up in Toddington, a small village six or seven miles north-east of Cheltenham, quite close to Broadway. She was the eldest child of a large family in a rural village of some 250 souls, dominated by large family houses (Sudeley Castle, Toddington Manor and Dumbleton Hall).

Her parents were John Compton,[7] a carpenter, and his wife Sarah, hardly the well-to-do parents of independent means Caroline was to indicate in censuses and marriage certificates in later years. Towards the end of the 1840s she met George Robert Graves, an accountant's clerk from Clerkenwell in north London, while he was visiting the west country. A year older than Caroline, he was the son of a stone-mason and his wife, Lot and Mary Anne Graves. (He had been baptised at St Alphage's, Greenwich, not a quarter of a mile from where this is being written.)

They were married at the Parish Church in Walcot, Somerset, on the outskirts of Bath on March 30th, 1850. Caroline (or Elizabeth) was then twenty.

Less than a year after their marriage Caroline gave birth to a daughter, Elizabeth Harriet, who was born on February 3rd, 1851. George Graves had become a shorthand writer and they were living at 11 Cumming Street, Clerkenwell, not far from the Angel, with his mother Mary[8]. But life in London was soon to turn sour for Caroline. Later that year George Graves, who had by this time become a solicitor's clerk, caught tuberculosis and was taken to the west country by his mother in an effort to relieve his illness. But he died at the Moravian Cottages[9] in Weston, just outside Bath, on January 30th, 1852. Caroline was thus left in London, a widow with a young child of twelve months on her hands, at the age of twenty-two. She is next detected running a junk shop in Charlton Street, near Fitzroy Square.

Whether Wilkie Collins ran across her outside a villa in Regents Park or a house near Fitzroy Square will never be known. But that she may have begun to hide her past and fashion a new image to suit her good looks is quite possible. In later life she was to describe her first husband as a 'Captain in the Army'[10] and 'of independent means'[11] and her father as 'John Courtney, Gentleman'[12]. And there is a hint of the same theme in Millais' original story of a 'young lady of good birth and position'. Whether Wilkie himself ever penetrated Caroline's true background is far from clear. Even if he did, it was plainly in his interests to present her in the best possible light to his friends.

Caroline's real plight may never be discovered. Left a beautiful impoverished widow at twenty-two, she would be a natural prey for a determined unscrupulous benefactor. But her subsequent 'rescue' by Wilkie had one logical result. She was fully dependent on his support from the outset and could hardly be treated as just another casual acquaintance.

He was hardly a reluctant saviour. Added to the attractions of a lovely, vulnerable young girl, were the drama of their meeting and the whole panoply of surreptitious plotting which so far he had tended to devote to the romantic whims of his best friends. It became only a matter of time before he found it impossible to keep up the charade with his friends and, ultimately, with his mother.

It was a situation that could hardly have been contemplated in his father's lifetime. His mother too could hardly have approved, but, as so often in the future, she was forced to come to terms with Wilkie's growing fame and the liberal life-style that accompanied it. Pride and a reluctant tolerance became inevitably intertwined.

Wilkie's correspondence provides few clues about Caroline's whereabouts until several years after he met her.

Here and there a stray hint can occasionally be detected. His mother was beginning to look for a new house in the early part of 1856, and by the spring had found one at number 2, Harley Place, an individual terrace on New Road, which the following year became the present Marylebone Road. There was a gap of some three months between leaving one and moving into the other, during which she moved among her friends[13], Charley took temporary lodgings and Wilkie moved into rooms in Howland Street, following his visit to Dickens in Paris.

He had previously told his mother that he would probably stay with his friend Piggott in Richmond or a Mrs Dickenson at Farley Hill (or with 'lots of other friends if I like'). But his final choice of Howland Street may have been planned all along, for Caroline had plainly become a major influence. In any case it was in Howland Street that Dickens began to give the first hints of Wilkie's domestic arrangements with Caroline[14].

Just after Wilkie had left Paris, where he had stayed with Dickens's family, Dickens hinted to him in a letter that he had told his family that Wilkie had returned to London 'to consult his Doctor' and went on: 'I thought it best, in case of any contretemps hereafter with your mother on one hand or my people on the other'[15]. And he began to use the same shorthand for Caroline in subsequent letters that year: 'I am very anxious to know what your Doctor says,' he wrote shortly after Wilkie's arrival in Howland Street, 'if he should fail to set you up by the 3rd or 4th of May, for me, I shall consider him a Humbug'[16].

It is thus highly likely that Caroline was living temporarily in Howland Street with her young daughter Harriet. An extension of New Cavendish Street, where Wilkie was born, Howland Street was a street full of lodging houses and artists' rooms, and at one end a row of local shops. Wilkie may not have stayed there long but it made a deep impression on him, opening his eyes for virtually the first time to the way other people really lived and providing him with rich material both for his current articles and his later novels.

He had first been brought close to the servants in his parents' house when he and Charles were left alone for a few weeks, during his spell in the tea trade, and he had taken a condescending and less than sympathetic view of their habits ('knowing as I do what a set of apes the lower orders are in this country')[17]. But his stay in Howland Street, with its opportunity to witness the high turnover of servants and the heavy toil of their work, quickly began to spill out into the pages of *Household Words* with a completely different emphasis. 'Life means dirty work, small wages, hard words, no holidays, no social status, no future,' he wrote later[18]. Though he did not stay long in Howland Street, he was appalled by what he saw.

His mother's move from Hanover Terrace in the first half of 1856 was thus the beginning of a new pattern of life for Wilkie. When she moved later that year into number 2, Harley Place[19] (which two years later was re-numbered 11 Harley Place), he and Charles again took rooms with her. Their habits, however, had changed. Wilkie at least had tasted a new kind of freedom and Caroline was plainly not far away. Whether he joined her again in the next year or so is uncertain. Not until eighteen months later do we have firm evidence of where she was living with her daughter and confirmation that Wilkie was living with them.

Caroline moved into 124 Albany Street in 1858 and was immediately registered as the rate-payer[20]. It was a reasonably prosperous street on the east side of Regents Park and one can immediately surmise that Wilkie was helping out with the rent and rates, for it is not long after this that he is writing to his closest friends from this particular address. Throughout this period Caroline's name, as 'Mrs Graves', remained firmly in the local rate book. It was a habit that, as we shall see, continued on and off for most of their life together.

They stayed in Albany Street and in New Cavendish Street (where they had rooms from a local doctor for a similar short spell) little more than eighteen months each. While Wilkie wrote to his friends from Albany Street, it was only from 2a New Cavendish Street that he began openly to reveal the presence of Caroline. One gets the feeling that both places were temporary abodes, for Wilkie – sometimes with Caroline, sometimes without her – was easily persuaded in this period to stay for extended spells at Gad's Hill or Broadstairs, in order to write.

Once they moved into rooms in Harley Street, however, both their accommodation and their habits began to take on a more permanent aspect, even to the extent of appearing as man and wife. Not only did Wilkie fill in the Census return[21] in Harley Street as a married lodger, a barrister and as an author of works of fiction, but Caroline was described as his wife and Harriet, her daughter, was nicely disguised as Harriet Montague, a sixteen year old house servant (she was then ten years old).

At about the same time he was writing from Whitby to his landlord in Harley Street, a dentist named Gregson, passing on regards from 'Mrs Collins'[22]. Coming from the popular author of *The Woman in White*, it was a particularly fragile kind of respectability, and a fiction neither he nor Caroline attempted thereafter, except perhaps on their occasional travels abroad.

Wilkie's brother Charles had also begun to loosen his domestic ties. He was no longer pursuing a painting career. The dissatisfaction with his own work, begun in an over-critical mood, had ultimately ended in an inability to finish his canvasses. Shyness, indecision, disappointments in his relations with women – all had undermined his self-confidence. Unfinished canvasses piled up. The final straw came when he visited John Millais and his new wife Euphemia Gray (previously John Ruskin's wife) in Perthshire following their honeymoon. She agreed to let Charles paint her portrait and sat for him daily for a fortnight. 'Then seeing that the picture made very slow progress, and that she was presented as looking out of the window of a railway carriage – a setting that would have vulgarised Venus herself – she refused to sit any longer, and the picture was never finished'[23].

If anything turned his attention to writing rather than painting, this did. But he was also encouraged by the growing success of Wilkie and by the friendship of so many writers and editors. Like Wilkie he was a constant visitor to Gad's Hill, where he was quickly attracted to Dickens's younger daughter Kate. What she originally thought of the diffident, shy, rather delicate young man is difficult to fathom. According to Gladys Storey, Kate later told her that although she respected Charles and considered him the kindest and most sweet-tempered of men, she was 'not in the least in love with him'[24]. She had in any case hardly welcomed the replacement of her mother with her Aunt Georgina, following Charles Dickens's separation from his wife, and was no doubt inclined to look for a way out.

Her father was going through a difficult period, forcing his relations and friends to take sides in his marital problem. The children were no exception. This may have made it easier for Kate to look elsewhere for comfort and distraction and Wilkie's good looking brother was invariably on hand. Kate was soon receptive to Charles's romantic approaches, and they were eventually married at Gad's Hill in the summer of 1860 amid local celebrations and many celebrities from the artistic and literary worlds. Holman Hunt was best man. Dickens plainly believed that he had driven Kate into marriage. 'But for me,' he was heard to sob on Kate's wedding night, 'Kate would never have left home'. Yet Kate's letters to her mother-in-law from their honeymoon paint a picture of newly-wed bliss. 'Oh, he is so good and so dear', she wrote of Charles, 'I never knew of anyone so unselfish[25]. I am happier than I have ever been'[26].

Even before his marriage, Charles had taken separate lodgings for a spell, once when his mother was leasing Hanover Terrace. When his mother moved to Clarence Terrace he had joined her and, after their marriage, Kate and Charles shared part of the house with Harriet until she in turn left the place entirely to them, simply using her own room when she needed it on periodic visits to London from Tunbridge Wells. (This was the period when, as we have seen, Wilkie and Caroline were moving into Albany Street[27].)

Behind these arrangements was the crucial problem of money. While Wilkie was basking in his string of successes, culminating in the popularity of *The Woman in White*, and his mother had a regular income from investments, Charles had no reliable means of support. Moreover, even as late as 1860, when one was thirty-five and the other thirty, neither Wilkie nor Charles had a personal bank account. They simply relied on their mother to provide cash, through cheques from Coutts Bank, though Wilkie at least was in the habit of paying in large sums into his mother's account.

The Woman in White and no doubt the presence of Caroline as well as Charles's marriage soon changed these arrangements. Both brothers opened accounts of their own in 1860[28]. At the same time Harriet plainly came to an arrangement with Charles to support him with up to £200 a year[29], depending on his own earning power. Since Wilkie was occasionally giving money to his mother, both Wilkie and Harriet were in effect supporting Charles during this difficult period.

It explains why Charles and Kate stayed so long in France and Belgium on their honeymoon. He was busy writing sketches for *All the Year Round* based on their travels with a horse and cart. They were also discovering how cheap it was to live on the Continent, compared with London. Kate at least knew why they were living as they were and was careful not to reveal too much to her family. 'I have not even told any of them at home about the odd life we are leading,' she wrote to Harriet[30], 'for fear that they should fancy we were really frightfully badly off'. In fact they were doing their own shopping, wherever they stayed, and Kate, busy with the washing-up and bed-making, was able to report back to Harriet on one occasion 'we have lived for four weeks today on food of our own cooking'.

While Charles and Kate were economising on the Continent, Harriet was clearly anxious that she should not press too heavily on her own monetary resources in Clarence Terrace, for her mind began to turn to the possibility of letting out some of the rooms. She was soon persuaded otherwise by Charles, but the upshot was that when Charles and Kate eventually returned to London, they took over Clarence Terrace[31] and kept a room for Harriet when she visited London from her friends in the country. 'Whenever in winter at any rate you sleep in Clarence Terrace,' they promised her, 'that room is yours'.

Thus the two brothers, so different in appearance, in temperament and in capabilities, found romantic attachments in remarkably different circumstances. Wilkie, with few monetary anxieties, had moved permanently into a liaison with the unknown Caroline; Charles, with little earning capability, had married a rich man's daughter. What the rich man thought of them both has been preserved in a letter Dickens wrote to the daughter of a friend, Esther Elton[32]: 'There are no "Great Expectations" of prospective Collinses,' he confided, 'which I think a blessed thing, though I don't say so. Old Mrs Collins dined here . . . and contradicted everybody upon every subject for five hours and a half . . . so I was very glad when she tied her head in a bundle and took it home . . . Wilkie is in a popular and potential state and is beginning to think of a new book. He has made his rooms in Harley Street very handsome and comfortable. We never speak of the (female) skeleton in that house and I therefore have not the least idea of the state of his mind on that subject. I hope it does not run in any matrimonial groove. I *cannot* imagine any good coming of such an end in this instance'[33].

Before Wilkie and Caroline had even moved into Harley Street Dickens was a frequent visitor in London and elsewhere, as were Wilkie's other close friends such as Charles Ward, who was in the habit of dining with them, both before and after his own marriage. On one occasion Wilkie received a late ticket to a box at Covent Garden, which he felt obliged to accept, and showed no particular embarrassment at slipping off leaving Charles Ward with Caroline. 'You won't mind my going away at eight o'clock – will you? – and leaving the engagement between us two on every other respect *exactly the same*. Dine at six – cigar afterwards – tea – I slip off – Caroline keeps you company and makes your grog – and you stay as long as you feel inclined.'

Even after his marriage Charles Ward went round for the occasional dinner with Wilkie, in Caroline's presence, to talk about money matters and some of Wilkie's other needs such as books and wine. 'Has Caroline written to ask you to come here and take pot luck on Monday at six?' he wrote on one occasion. 'I shall be delighted to take the Lafite, if I can have it *without* the champagne. I say this, because I possess a year's consumption of champagne at least'[34]. Both Wilkie and Caroline sent their good wishes to his wife, Jane, on the birth of their first child. But there is no record of Jane herself going round for dinner.

Christmas, of course, being a family occasion was a particularly difficult time for Wilkie, but his bachelor friends rallied round and he made other arrangements with his married companions. 'I suppose you dine at home on Christmas day?' he wrote to his doctor, Frank Beard, one festive season. '*We* are going to dine at Verrey's at one o'clock (Piggott with us). As you are a "family man" I dare not say "come too". I shall be at home tomorrow if you are passing this way before three o'clock'[35].

If the proprieties were observed (that is, if their wives were not asked round), most of his friends seemed relaxed about Wilkie's liaison with Caroline. On one occasion Fred Lehmann wrote to Wilkie from Paris, inviting him to lunch with him at the Reform Club on his return to London. Wilkie agreed but Fred had overlooked the closing of the Club for the summer, and rushed round to Wilkie's to warn him. He need not have worried. Wilkie was still in bed at eleven-thirty, but he and Caroline insisted on Fred and his son Rudolf eating with them at home. 'She had cooked most of it herself I am sure,' Fred wrote to his wife Nina in the South of France, 'but you would not have guessed it from her very *décolleté* white silk gown. She seemed immensely taken with Rudolf. Wilkie was delightful as usual and sends you no end of love'[36].

The same habits were followed by most of Wilkie's friends, and their wives. Charles Dickens, separated from his wife, had no such difficulties. He often called at their rooms in Harley Street and enjoyed Caroline's company and the chance of teasing young Harriet, Caroline's daughter, in her childish imitations. 'I am charmed with the Butler,' he wrote to Wilkie following one of these episodes. 'O why was she stopped! Ask her flinty mother from me, why, why, didn't she let her convert somebody. And here the question arises – Did she secretly convert the Landlord?'[37] The nickname stuck, for a couple of years later Dickens was again passing on his love to the young Butler, 'from her ancient partner in the card-trade', and his kind regards to the 'Butler's Mama'[38].

'The Butler', or Harriet Elizabeth, was nine years old when *The Woman in White* was being written. She was a responsibility that Wilkie bore lightly. He was always fond of children, both other people's and later his own. In later life his friends' children remembered him with affection, entering into their games and their confidences and treating them as serious human beings. But

Harriet was something special and he treated her as such for the rest of his life. He gladly took on the expense of her education (paying bills of £16 at first, rising to £75 as Harriet reached seventeen)[39], and arranged insurance policies as a protection for the future. In the autumn of 1861 he took out a £400 whole life policy with Globe Insurance, and started a further £200 policy with National Provident[40] the following year. There were other burdens too. He suffered the usual parental anxieties and restrictions, and on one occasion was prevented from seeing Edward Ward because of an outbreak of measles and his concern for Harriet. Parental responsibilities were one thing; marriage quite another.

During the summer of 1859 Wilkie and Caroline took a quiet cottage on the Ramsgate Road outside Broadstairs, so that a new serialised novel could be started. Church Hill Cottage had nothing but downs between it and the sea and Charles Ward and Wilkie's brother Charles were frequent visitors. Once again in the throes of composition, Wilkie began to suffer from a variety of aches and pains. 'I am shut up at my desk every day from 10 till 2 or 3, slowly and painfully launching my new serial novel,' he explained to Charles Ward, before his visit. 'The story is the longest and the most complicated I have ever tried yet.' It was in fact *The Woman in White*. 'I have been suffering torments with a boil between my legs and write these lines with the agreeable prospect of the doctor coming to lance it. I seemed destined, God help us, never to be well'[41]. Wilkie and Caroline were in Broadstairs for nearly six weeks and Charles Dickens also joined them as a temporary visitor.

The results of these early efforts at Broadstairs began to appear in late November in *All the Year Round*[42], the new weekly magazine Dickens had started earlier that year, following his row with the publishers of *Household Words*, and which had contained his own serialisation of *A Tale of Two Cities*. The new serialisation was an immediate success, and by the New Year the weekly instalments of *The Woman in White* were eagerly awaited and being discussed at virtually every dinner party. The reviews were still to come, following the novel's publication in book form on August 15th 1860, but the public at least had responded with remarkable enthusiasm. *Woman in White* perfumes, bonnets and waltzes soon followed, along with the inevitable imitators, 'with stories of women in black, grey, green, yellow, blue and everything else'. The enthusiasts included the Prince Consort, Gladstone, Thackeray and Dickens.

By the time he came to lay down his pen on July 26th 1860, Wilkie was exhausted but exuberant, and in the mood for celebration. He threw caution and respectability to the winds and invited Augustus Egg, Edward

Ward, Henry Buller, Frederick Lehmann and Holman Hunt to a celebration dinner in his rooms in Harley Street. 'No evening dress – everything in the rough' were Wilkie's instructions: no wives either, for Caroline's presence always saw to that, though curiosity at least rarely kept his male companions away.

Caroline was Wilkie's closest companion throughout the writing of *The Woman in White*. But her role as the origin of *The Woman in White* is another matter. As Wilkie himself was to say many years later, he 'had not even thought of *The Woman in White* in 1855'[43] at least a year after his meeting with Caroline. Moreover the novel had its starting point in the plot, not the characters. 'The first step in the *Méthode Collins* is to find a central idea, the second to find the characters'[44]. By chance he received a letter asking him to take up some case of real or supposed wrongful incarceration in a lunatic asylum. And, by further chance, he came across an old French trial directly involved with a substitution of persons and 'it at once struck him that a substitution effected by the help of a lunatic asylum would prove a strong central idea'[45].

The source was Maurice Méjan's *Recueil des Causes Célèbres*[46], which he had picked up on a Paris bookstall two years before and which was still in his library when he died. 'I was in Paris wandering about the streets with Charles Dickens,' Wilkie later recalled, 'amusing ourselves by looking into the shops. We came to an old bookstall – half shop and half store and I found some dilapidated volumes of records of French crimes, a sort of French *Newgate Calendar*. I said to Dickens, "Here is a prize". So it turned out to be. In them I found some of my best plots. *The Woman in White* was one'[47].

Having worked out the basis of the plot, he now moved to the second phase of composition. As Edmund Yates, who discussed it with him, subsequently explained, the characters were quickly sketched in. 'The victim to be interesting must be a woman, to be very interesting she must be a lady, and as a foil to her, the person who is to represent her must be of inferior birth and station.' *The Woman in White* began to emerge, but whether the dramatic meeting in Avenue Road was written almost at once is still open to doubt. He told Edmund Yates that he hit upon the characters of the drawing master and Marion Halcombe 'with considerable trouble' and 'having made a beginning leapt at once to the third volume' and wrote the greater part of that before returning to the beginning. Thus the appearance of the 'solitary woman dressed from head to foot in white garments' may or may not have been introduced early in Wilkie's labours on his most famous novel.

It all strongly suggests that, as on so many other occasions, while he used personal incidents as important ingredients of his novels, the plot was paramount. His meeting with Caroline was certainly the basis for an important and dramatic incident in *The Woman in White*, but it did not prompt the novel. After all, even the title was an after-thought, coming on him in a flash while contemplating the North Foreland Lighthouse. In despair at finding a suitable title he was walking one afternoon along the cliffs near Broadstairs. He threw himself on the grass as the sun went down and looked up at the lighthouse. 'You are ugly and stiff and awkward,' he called out, 'you know you are as stiff and weird as my white woman – white woman – woman in white – the title, by Jove!'[48]

As the excitement, following the heavy demand for *The Woman in White*, calmed down, Wilkie left London for a while, first alone to friends in Yorkshire, then on a yachting trip down the Bristol Channel with his friend Piggott, and finally with Caroline to Paris, where they stayed at the Meurice, went to innumerable plays, dined at Les Trois Frères, one of Dickens' favourites, and had a pleasantly luxurious time, a striking contrast to the life Charles and Kate were leading not far away, and a remarkable change from Caroline's own environment of only a few years earlier.

The reviews of *The Woman in White*, when they did eventually emerge in the autumn of 1860, hardly supported the public acclaim. *The Times* quickly detected a major flaw in the timing of Anne Catherick's movements, volumes one and two implying a gap of two weeks in crucial dates, not a day or two as the author had suggested. Wilkie confessed that *The Times* was right, corrected it in later editions, but such were the complications of the plot that these later adjustments still put 'Anne Catherick in London sixteen days too early'. This anomaly still remains, and 'for more than a century no one seems to have been disturbed by the fact'[49]. While other reviews were less critical, *The Saturday Review* too struck a rather sour note, condemning with faint praise. 'Mr Wilkie Collins is an admirable story-teller, though he is not a great novelist . . . he is a very ingenious constructor; but ingenious construction is not high art just as cabinet making and joining is not high art'[50].

These were the reviews he faced on his return from abroad; but he had also received readers' letters, and the contrast between the grudging reviews and the enthusiastic correspondence taught him a lesson he rarely ignored thereafter. 'Either the public is right and the press wrong or the press is right and the public is wrong,' he concluded. 'Time will tell. If the public turns out to be right, I will never trust the press again'[51]. Sales confirmed the public's view and he henceforth acted accordingly.

This was also a period when illness began to dog him in a way that was hardly to leave him for the rest of his life. He had his first attack of rheumatic gout when he was still at home with his mother at Hanover Terrace; and it was not long before it attacked his eyes for the first time. Thereafter it was often, and increasingly, accompanied by other nervous disorders during periods of intensive writing. His dietary excesses hardly helped, though he tried hard to convince himself, and others, that the weather was often as much to blame as the food and drink he enjoyed. 'My digestion is out of order,' he told his mother on one occasion. 'It is not eating or drinking, but the horrible East wind.'

Some of his rheumatic troubles were severely crippling and put him out of action for weeks at a time. Even at Hanover Terrace, when he was little more than thirty years old, he spoke about not being strong enough to do more than 'toddle' out for half an hour at a time with a stick. 'My illness and long confinement', he told Edward Piggott, 'have muddled my brains dreadfully – I am still in very bad trim for anything that deserves the name of work'. Some years later he had the same symptoms, though far more severely. 'The gout,' he again confided to Piggott, 'has attacked my brain. My mind is perfectly clear – but the nervous misery is indescribable'. At the time he was in the middle of a monthly serialisation.

He had a similar nervous seizure when he was writing *No Name* at Broadstairs. On this occasion he rented Charles Dickens's favourite seaside residence, Fort House, a large house in its own garden, close to the sea, with 'plenty of bedrooms and a view of the sea from every one of them.' Wilkie and Caroline took it for several months during the summer of 1862 and Caroline packed accordingly. 'She has hardly done unpacking yet', he wrote to Piggott almost a week after their arrival. 'The quantity of luggage we have brought with us still makes my hair stand on end when I think of it.'

Piggott and Wilkie's other close friends, Charles Ward and Henry Buller, were frequent visitors. But the writing again brought on a nervous attack. 'Yesterday at 1 o'clock,' he wrote to his doctor, Frank Beard, 'I had to give up work with deadly "all overish" faintings which sent me to the brandy bottle. No confusion in my brains, but a sickness, faintness and universal tremblings – startled by the slightest noise – more nervous twitterings last night, little sleep – sick feeling and taste of coffee.'[52] The writing of *The Woman in White*, *Armadale*, and *The Moonstone* brought on similar nervous disorders.

His brother Charles seemed to be aware of part of the trouble. 'I am very sorry to hear an account of your nerves,' he wrote to Wilkie, when he was in the middle of *Armadale*. 'I believe that you are suffering far more from these than from anything else. Work and natural anxiety affect these dreadfully as you know. When you are doing nothing you are pretty well but directly that you begin to work again or cease to be moving about, have leisure to be anxious and think, you suffer. Your work is tiring work.' And ultimately Wilkie himself came to the same conclusion, noting how often he collapsed during or immediately after an intense spell of writing.

The solution was clearly to keep going as best he could and then get away to warmer, certainly drier, parts as quickly as possible. He did not always manage it, and he began to lean increasingly on regular doses of laudanum to ward off the incessant pain. Caroline was invariably on hand to see him through the worst attacks. 'Today the gout has seized on my left foot without leaving my right', Wilkie once reported to a friend. 'I am so utterly crippled that I cannot even get downstairs into the dining room. Both feet in pain, both feet nearly helpless . . . [The doctor] has prescribed simple "wormwood", the other medicine to be taken with it, if it agrees with me – to be left off if it does not. Caroline to mesmerise my feet, and to mesmerise me into sleeping so as to do without the opium'.

Caroline had her troubles too, though whether they were brought on by the anxieties of looking after Wilkie is difficult to say. At any event Wilkie was forced to seek Frank Beard's advice about her. 'She is apparently going to have another nervous hysterical attack' he told him. 'She was up all last night with the "palpitations"'. The attack did not last long and she was soon well enough to go round to see Frank Beard. Not long afterwards she was again busy organising Wilkie's visit to the baths at Wildbad and, a few months later, a three month visit to Rome, for the three of them.

The waters at Aix la Chapelle and Wildbad had been recommended by his doctor. Wilkie found the arrangements to his liking. Apart from the regular baths (a stream of hot sulphurous water on his back and legs, coupled with massage) and an accompanying tumbler of water from the local spring ('in taste like the worst London egg you ever had for breakfast in your life'), the local German doctor allowed Wilkie full dietary rein. He proposed no medicine and allowed all wines. He made only one condition: that they should be the best vintages and, as Wilkie wrote to his brother, his landlord had 'not a drop of liquor that was not excellent'[53]. Not surprisingly Wilkie regarded him as a 'model physician'. And, not surprisingly, the treatment did not cure him.

Three months later he was still trying to shake off what he described as 'a severe attack of rheumatic gout', this time by fleeing to the familiar climate of southern Italy, with Caroline and Harriet. It was Harriet's first trip to the Continent, and the first time they had travelled abroad as a family. Wilkie had already made detailed preparations for his next novel, *Armadale*, and, more important, had a promise of five thousand pounds for it in his pocket. Another Italian visit would enable him to sketch out the full structure of the story and, at the same time, escape from the rigours of an English winter which he was hardly fit enough to face.

The preliminary preparations for *Armadale*, in the Isle of Man and particularly Norfolk, were to lead to far more than another novel, as we shall soon see. But the work he was to do in Rome was an essential part of the way he went about novel-writing. He left little to chance. As he explained to an enquiring cleric two years later:

'In the story I am now writing (*Armadale*), the last number is to be published several months hence – and the whole close of the story is still unwritten. But I know at this moment who is to live and who is to die – and I see the main events which lead to the end as plainly as I see the pen now in my hand – as plainly as I see the ground laid, months since, in the published part of the story, for what (if I am spared to finish it) you will read months hence. *How* I shall lead you from one main event to the other – whether I shall dwell at length on certain details or pass them over rapidly – how I may yet develop my characters and make them clearer to you by new touches and traits – all this, I know no more than you do, till I take the pen in hand. But the characters themselves were all marshalled in their places, before a line of *Armadale* was written. And I knew the end two years ago in Rome, when I was recovering from a long illness, and was putting the story together'[54].

The three of them followed a familiar route to Rome, going by way of the South of France, Genoa and Pisa. All went well (with sunshine most of the way and a pleasant sea-trip between Genoa and Leghorn) until they reached Pisa. There the weather changed, the *sirocco* brought rain, fog and damp and, as Wilkie put it, 'the pangs of sciatica wrung me in both hands at once'. Caroline and Harriet (now known to Wilkie and his friends as 'Caroline junior' or 'little Carrie') were the next to suffer. As they boarded the boat again at Leghorn, for the last leg of their journey to Civita Vecchia, the wind got up and, according to Wilkie, 'the two Carolines suffered sea-martyrdom. Caroline junior had a comparatively easy time of it, and fell asleep in the intervals of retching – but Caroline senior was so ill that she could not be moved from the deck all night'. She had still not got over the voyage a day or so later in Rome and Wilkie, who actually felt the sea voyage had done him good, was by then beginning to suffer again from the rain and the north-east wind.

Before long, however, the weather improved, Caroline began to walk out and get some colour back into her cheeks, and Harriet, or 'young Carrie', made a quick recovery. 'We threw in a little pill and fired off a small explosion of Gregory's powder,' Wilkie reported, 'and she is now in higher spirits than ever and astonishes the Roman public by the essentially British plumpness of her cheeks and calves'. They were comfortably established in an apartment of five rooms on the first floor of the Hotel des Britanniques, with a good cook and a comfortable carriage to ride out in. And presumably they were neatly avoiding the embarrassment which could have arisen by regular visits to the more public *table d'hôte*.

Wilkie once again was enjoying showing a first visitor the delights of Rome and Caroline, like Dickens before her, no doubt had to hear the tales of the Collins's first stay there a quarter of a century before. 'This wonderful place,' he wrote to Charles Ward, echoing a similar letter to his brother Charles ten years earlier, 'is just what it has been ever since I can remember it – the ruins, the churches, the streets, the very house I lived in with my father and mother twenty-five years ago – all look as if I had left them yesterday. I see no change anywhere, except on the Pincian Hill – and there it is a change for the better, the public garden and park being greatly improved in the laying out'. As on his previous two visits he again ran across the Pope, this time in the Trastevere area, across the Tiber 'in a street about the width of Cranbourne Alley'. Once again Wilkie stood aside to let the Pope's outrider, the state church and members of the Papal Guard pass by. The Pope, who was followed by a guard 'with his legs bursting out of his blue breeches and his cheeks quivering like jelly as the horse shook him in the saddle', smiled out of the window of his coach, 'comforting himself with a pinch of snuff'.

Wilkie and the 'two Carolines' stayed on in Rome longer than they had originally intended, after a brief and unsuccessful foray to Naples. The weather eventually became dry enough to suit Wilkie's ailments and he had begun to make real progress in constructing the plot of *Armadale*. They decided to delay their visit to Florence. Wilkie loved Rome and they found much to amuse them. The opera was plainly a great success and cheap too. They regularly got the best box at the opera house – enough for six – for only one pound. Wilkie loved the informality of it all. 'No ticket delivered – the key of the box is handed to me by the box-keeper when I hand the money in the morning at the office – and we walk in at night when we like and open the box door for ourselves'.

Caroline and her daughter were enjoying a luxury they had still hardly grown used to. But after a couple of months Caroline began to get homesick. 'How like cats women are', Wilkie commented to Charles Ward, 'she bids me tell you with her kind regards that she wishes she was pouring you out a glass of dry sherry on a nice gloomy English Sunday afternoon'. They lingered on a little longer, however, and eventually returned to London in time for the spring weather. The trip had helped Wilkie through what might have been a particularly nasty winter in London in his state of health, and had enabled him to make further progress on his next novel, *Armadale*.

Caroline and her daughter Harriet had thus become part of the bachelor's whole existence. They shared his home, his work, his travel, his illnesses, his literary triumphs and even some of his friends, though their womenfolk kept themselves at a discreet distance. Some, like Nina Lehmann, were probably close enough to Wilkie to see something of Caroline privately and so, later on, did Laura Seymour, the actress friend of Charles Reade. Over these years, following the success of *The Woman in White*, Wilkie was at the peak of his writing ability – and of his earnings. *The Woman in White* was succeeded by *No Name* (for which he received three thousand pounds for the book publication alone and a total of over four thousand five hundred if serialisation in Britain and America was included)[55], and *Armadale* (for which he received the record amount of five thousand pounds before a word had been written). *The Moonstone* was still to come.

CHAPTER TEN

Martha

IN PREPARING FOR the detailed writing of *Armadale*, Wilkie decided to visit the Isle of Man and subsequently, the next summer, the coast and hinterland of Norfolk. He already knew the kind of atmosphere he was looking for and both spots promised him the sea air and sailing he loved. He was in fact to find another lifelong romantic attachment and the mother of his three children.

The crossing to the Isle of Man was calm but wet and Wilkie was plagued by a new breed of Englishman on holiday – Lancastrians. He met them on the boat and he met them on arrival in Douglas. They even made it impossible for him to book a hotel room ahead of his visit. 'All Lancashire,' he concluded, 'goes to the Isle of Man and all Lancashire is capable of improvement in looks and breeding'.

It was the most horribly crowded boat he ever sailed in. As he told his mother, in a graphic account of it all from the Fort Anne Hotel in Douglas, there was:

'. . . rain half the way across, and no room below, if I had been inclined to venture there. Tide out when we got here – disembarkation in boats – fearful noise and confusion – an old lady tumbled into the water and fished up again by her veritable heels. I waited as I always do in these capers until the hubbub was over – bribed a sailor – got myself and my baggage comfortably into a boat. Mounted a rock by a slippery path – barged through a staring line of Lancashire sailors – found myself here. Nothing that I wanted (in the literary way) at this place. Contacted the landlord – and drove off to a remote quarter of this island. Crowds here again – landlord distracted – and next day started in a boat for the place I wanted to see – the Calf of Man, separated from the island by a sound. Boat a little dirty fishing boat – crew a man for one oar, and two boys for the other. Pulled out of the bay and found a heavy sea and a smart south-west wind. Valiant crew just able to keep the boat's head to the sea and no more. I saw we should be wet through, and should take hours before we got to our destination. Ordered them to return and consulted the landlord.

"Can't do it, landlord."

"I thought not, sir."

"Can I get near the place by land?"

"Yes, sir."

"Have you got a carriage?"

"Got a jaunty cart, sir."

"And a horse?"

"Yes, sir."

"Put the horse to then."

Out came the cart with an Irish boy to drive. Set off at a gallop, mounted a hill, descended again by a road all rocks and ruts – I had to get down and walk from sheer inability to bear the jolting. At last we reached the place – wild and frightful, just what I wanted – everything made for my occult literary purposes'[1].

In fact he was telling his mother only half the story, for he was not alone. Caroline and her daughter Harriet were with him. And poor Caroline was once again sea-sick, though Wilkie himself pronounced the passage a reasonably calm one. What they thought of the Isle of Man, the weather or their fellow holiday-makers can hardly be imagined. Wilkie at least knew what he was seeking – and he used the Manx adventure to bring an eerie atmosphere to the haunted, derelict ship off the Calf of Man in one of the early chapters in *Armadale* and in the dream sequence which followed.

Most of the second half of the book, however, was to take place in and around Norfolk. And here he was on more familiar ground. His father had painted[2] the coastline fifty years earlier and had revisited it several times. Dickens had often visited Yarmouth and described it intimately in *David Copperfield* and in articles in *Household Words*. Friends of Wilkie's brother, Charley, knew the coast well and had sketched its churches. So he needed no persuasion to combine a little sailing with his friends, Edward Piggott and Charles Ward, with some useful exploration for his new novel. He was to find exactly what he wanted among the broads and meres of the low-lying countryside.

By the end of July, 1864, the three friends were comfortably booked into the Victoria Hotel at Yarmouth and quickly rented a boat and crew for what Wilkie described as their cruises up and down the coast. Yarmouth was a picturesque spot, with narrow streets, and even narrower 'rows' running at right angles. To Dickens, it was always the 'Norfolk Gridiron', and needed 'Harry-carriers', named after Henry VII, drawn by a horse and driver, to navigate the narrow lanes safely.

A large jetty, the Britannia jetty, provided a good landing place for boats and the fishermen's quarters had been a target for Dickens's nose (and pen) some years earlier. 'I smelt the fish and pitch and tar and oakum, and saw the sailors walking about and the carts jiggling up and down the stoney lanes between the hills of chips and little hillocks of sand: past gasworks, ropewalks, boatbuilders' yards, shipwrights' yards, caulkers' yards, riggers' lofts, smiths' forges and a great litter of such places until we came out upon a dull waste and a desolate flat.'

They sailed up the coast past Winterton Ness, 'the most dangerous headland on the coast' according to Walcott's *East Coast of England*, the latest guide[3] which Wilkie had taken with them. But the headland meant more to him than just another maritime hazard. As an avid reader of Daniel Defoe and a devotee of *Robinson Crusoe*, he recognised it not only as the most easterly spot on Britain's coastline, but precisely where Robinson Crusoe encountered his first shipwreck.

Defoe had done his own literary reconnaissance, along this coast, more than a century earlier. He too made his way north of Yarmouth[4] and 'was surprised to see, in all the way from Winterton, that the farmers and country people had scarce a barn or a shed, or a stable, nay, not the pales of their yards or gardens, not a hogstye, not a necessary-house', but what was built of old planks and timbers from the wrecks of ships.

Firm in the knowledge that fifty years earlier over two hundred sailing ships had been wrecked here, with the loss of over a thousand lives, Defoe deliberately planned Crusoe's first sea-trip, from Hull to London, to end in disaster as the boat 'passed the light-house at Winterton, where the shore falls off to the westward towards Cromer'. Wilkie knew his *Robinson Crusoe* and was still enthusing about it four years later through Gabriel Betteridge, the house steward in *The Moonstone*. 'When my spirits are bad,' says Betteridge, '*Robinson Crusoe*. When I want advice – *Robinson Crusoe*. In past times when my wife plagued me; in present times, when I have had a drop too much – *Robinson Crusoe*. I have worn out six stout *Robinson Crusoes* with hard work in my service'. And the allusions in *The Moonstone* did not stop there[5].

So it was hardly surprising that, between sailing excursions along the coast, he decided to follow in Defoe's footsteps and go up the coast road from Yarmouth towards Winterton, on his way to take a closer look at what are now known as 'the Broads'.

There is no direct evidence of where he went or what he did. But *Armadale* provides some indirect clues. In an appendix to the book he states that the Norfolk broads are described 'after personal investigation of them'. Moreover one of the most evocative of his descriptive passages, setting the mood of much of the later part of the novel, concerns a picnic visit by carriage and boat to what he calls Hurle Mere. The only broad with a similar name and with equally familiar features is Horsey Mere. It is close to Yarmouth and can be reached by a road north from Yarmouth through Winterton. Horsey Mere is no more than three miles from Winterton and it is possible to sail into the mere in a boat from the Broads and then take a short walk to the beach for a bathe in the sea.

Winterton had other attractions too. Norfolk is famous for its tall church towers and that at Winterton – the parish church of the Holy Trinity and All Saints – is one of the tallest, dominating the sand dunes and the countryside and, according to local custom, is 'a herring and a half higher than Cromer'. John Luard, an artist friend of Wilkie's brother Charley and of John Millais and a constant caller at Hanover Terrace when Wilkie was still at home with his mother, had done a well-known sketch of the bells[6].

It was the low-lying water of Horsey Mere, however, that captivated him and, as at the Calf of Man, provided him with the atmosphere he was seeking for *Armadale*:

> 'The reeds opened back on the right hand and the left, and the boat glided suddenly into the wide circle of a pool. Round the nearer half of the circle, the eternal reeds still fringed the margin of the water. Round the farther half the land appeared again here rolling back from the pool in desolate sandhills: there, rising above it in a sweep of grassy shore. . . . The sun was sinking in the cloudless western heaven. The waters of the Mere lay beneath, tinged red by the dying lights. The open country stretched away, darkening drearily already on the right hand and the left. And on the near margin of the pool, where all had been solitude before, there now stood, fronting the sunset, the figure of a woman. . . .'

With hindsight, it is tempting to believe that, as in *The Woman in White*, Wilkie Collins was again describing a dramatic first meeting with another woman who was to become of some importance in his life. The temptation grows a little stronger when it is realised that Martha Rudd, who was to bear him his first child five years later, was born only a few miles away from Horsey Mere at Winterton.

The truth is likely to have been rather more mundane. Martha was then aged nineteen[7], the daughter of a shepherd and his wife, James and Mary Rudd. There had been Rudds from Winterton in the herring fleet at Yarmouth for close on a century and Martha's father was one of the few exceptions.

How and where Wilkie actually met Martha it is impossible to say. Martha's (and Wilkie's) own grandchildren always put the meeting locally, probably at the Fishermen's Return in Winterton itself or one of the hotels in Yarmouth, where she may have been a servant. It is even possible that one of Martha's brothers was on Wilkie's hired boat in Yarmouth.

Martha was from a particularly poor family, her mother signing her birth certificate with a simple cross. The family found work on the land and from the sea, as so many still do today. Martha, like most of the women folk, must have had to find work in domestic service or at a local hostelry for she had already left her home in Winterton by the time she was sixteen[8], and with her dark good looks was striking enough to catch Wilkie's trained eye. One can hardly feel that they had much else in common: nor that the later episodes in *Armadale* owed much to their meeting.

His exploration of the Broads was interrupted by a brief trip to the Monckton-Milnes[9] at Fryston Hall in Yorkshire. Wilkie had known them for some years and was occasionally invited up for the weekend. He later described his host's house as 'delightfully comfortable, with palatial rooms, a fine park and perpetual company'. On one of his visits he met one of Garibaldi's sons: 'A remarkably stupid boy'. Before leaving Yarmouth Wilkie looked up his train connections in Bradshaw, changed trains at Peterborough and, no doubt after a stimulating weekend with the Monckton-Milnes' wide circle of literary and political friends (Algernon Swinburne was staying there at the time), returned to Norfolk where he planned to find 'some quiet seaside place on the east coast' to go on with his work. Such at least were his intentions when he wrote to his mother, prior to his visit farther north. Whether he found his patch of sand or simply returned to Winterton – and Martha – we shall probably never know[10].

The arrival of Martha in Wilkie's life should have caused few ripples, a casual encounter in a life apparently devoted to such casual encounters. Caroline was firmly established in Melcombe Place (they had moved from Harley Street in 1864, the year he probably met Martha)[11] and once again her name was down in the rate book[12] as well as in the London street guide. Her name had also begun to pass through Wilkie's bank account quite openly, starting with a payment of £20 to 'Mrs Graves' on August 23rd 1864 and going on thereafter until the year of his death.

Harriet's education was continuing, her school bills also moving through Wilkie's bank account and, as she reached eighteen, she too began to appear as a direct recipient of Wilkie's generosity[13]. But one wonders what might have been going through Caroline's mind, even before Martha's appearance. She had moved into a life she could hardly have contemplated, with a popular writer at the peak of his career. She was well-established as part of his household, presiding over Wilkie's table, entertaining such friends as would come to the house, and acting as an accomplished hostess. She plainly captivated both Wilkie and most of his friends. She had few immediate cares, save presumably one. Would Wilkie marry her and give her the basic reassurance she and Harriet still needed?

Even if she broached it openly the answer was no doubt always the same. Wilkie disliked the idea intensely. On John Millais' wedding day he confessed he could not resist jesting on the marriage of his friends. 'It is such a dreadfully serious thing afterwards, that one ought to joke about it as long as one can'[14]. And to one of his friends, on the birth of his second child, he observed 'I find married men look as if their feelings were hurt when you flatter them about large families'[15]. He was determined to avoid the condition as long as he could.

Following his encounter with Martha, he was soon back in the whirl of London. But Martha had clearly made a mark, for less than a year later, he was writing to his mother from Melcombe Place, where Caroline still presided, about another trip to Yarmouth, in spite of the fact that Piggott, as editor of the political weekly *The Leader*, was too tied to the country-wide elections to take a long yachting holiday. 'We can get the best boats,' he told his mother, in explaining his brief visit, 'and can be out on the sea all day. I want the sea badly – to freshen me after my work'.

How he kept in touch with Martha and how and why he eventually persuaded her to move to London – and when – is shrouded in mystery. But that she was in the background during Caroline's continued efforts to persuade Wilkie to marry her is hardly in doubt. One can only marvel at his stamina in keeping his two women reasonably content, living an intense social life (within the confines of his own peculiar habits) and working remarkably hard at his chosen profession.

Martha's move to London was inevitably one of the biggest decisions of her life. Throwing herself on the generosity of a well known novelist had its

William Collins R.A. and his wife Harriet, the parents of Wilkie Collins (from paintings by John Linnell).

top: Wilkie Collins as a child, by his father.
left: Charles Allston Collins, Wilkie's brother, on the steps of Gad's Hill, Dickens's home.
above: Gold locket to commemorate Collins's mother's death in 1868, during the writing of *The Moonstone*.

Four photographs of Wilkie Collins.

top: Caroline Graves in the early 1870s.
left: Harriet Graves, Caroline's daughter, on her wedding day, March 12, 1878.
right: Doris Beresford, Caroline's grand-daughter and Wilkie Collins's god-daughter, as a Gaiety Girl.

top: Wilkie Collins with Martha Rudd.
below: Martha.

Bought by ~ *Dawson Esq*

OF

HEWETSON AND THEXTON,

Manufacturers of Superior Household Furniture.

AND

BED FEATHER MERCHANTS, **UPHOLDERS** CARPET WAREHOUSEMEN &c.

200, 203 & 204, Tottenham Court Road, & 3 & 4, North Crescent, Bedford Square.

Painting, Paper Hanging, and Interior Decorating · DESIGNS, & ESTIMATES GIVEN · Foreign & Country Orders executed exactly & quickly

Terms. Cash on delivery of Goods & no Discount allowed

1873

Feb: 1st	5 ft 6 in Enclosed medieval Sideboard with cellaret drawers & trays		18. 10. 0
	4 Oak medieval chairs in green hard grained leather studded	45/-	9. 0. 0
	Large oak do Easy chair in do to match		10. 0. 0
	3 ft 6 in × 5 ft 4 in Oak Dining Table to match taking in one leaf		6. 0. 0
	Walnut wood inlaid Bureau Cabinet top & Glass		13. 10. 0
	Walnut wood spring stuffed right hand Couch enriched with gold in canvass		11. 10. 0
	Walnut carved devotional chair enriched with gold in canvass		4. 10. 0
	Rich Amboyna inlaid chair in canvass		3. 10. 0
	11 1/2 Yds of fine utrecht velvet for covering do	10/6	6. 0. 9
	16 Yds of ornamental pearl cord	9?	12. 0
	Buttons for do		4. 6
	Upholstery needlework covering Couch in velvet corded		15. 6
	Do do Devotional chair do in do &c		5. 6
	Do do Small chair in do &c		2. 6
	2 Rich Black & gold Chimney Glasses 7/7/-		15. 10. 0
		£	100. 0. 9

Recd payment for
Hewetson & Thexton.
4/2/73. W. Peat.

With best thanks ~

top: two photographs of Martha.
below: two photographs of William Charles
Collins-Dawson (Wilkie's son).

top left to right: Harriet Dawson, Florence Dawson, Marian Dawson.
below left to right: "Bobbie" Dawson, Lionel Dawson, Martha Rudd.

William Charles Collins-Dawson with his wife Florence and "Bobbie".

Lionel Dawson with his daughter Faith (the author's wife).

superficial attractions, but the kind of liaison she was inevitably forming cut her off for some time from her family in Winterton and other local friends. She was a working class girl from a poor family. Yet her attraction to Wilkie's roving eye is easily understood. She had the dark, strong features he admired and the frank openness he could respond to. She also lacked the acquired sophistication that Wilkie was coming to regret in Caroline. At nineteen she had the straightforward honesty he was beginning to miss.

When Martha was told of Caroline or when Caroline began to suspect the presence of another is also difficult to pinpoint, but the turning point in their joint relationships was to come four years later in 1868, a year of intense emotional shocks for the novelist. It is possible that Martha's move to London, whether encouraged by Wilkie or merely acquiesced in, came in the second half of 1867 or some part of 1868. He (and Caroline) had already moved into number 90, Gloucester Place, having been outbid in their effort to acquire a house in Cornwall Terrace.

He was hard at work on *The Moonstone* and, once again, under literary pressure, was suffering from an acute attack of rheumatic gout. This time he had to see it through the hard way and later described how his secretary could not put up with his involuntary screams of pain, as he dictated his weekly instalments, and his subsequent efforts to find one capable of ignoring his suffering.

Then came the biggest shock of all – his mother's death. He completed *The Moonstone* in a haze of pain and in utter grief:

'At the time when my mother lay dying in her little cottage in the country,' he was to explain later, 'I was struck prostrate, in London: crippled in every limb by the torture of rheumatic gout. Under the weight of this double calamity, I had my duty to the public still to bear in mind. . . . I held to the story – for my own sake, as well as for theirs. In the intervals of grief, in the occasional intervals of pain, I dictated from my bed that portion of *The Moonstone* which has since proved most successful[16] in amusing the public – "The Narrative of Miss Clack". . . I doubt if I should have lived to write another book, if the responsibility of the weekly publication of this story had not forced me to rally my sinking energies of body and mind – to dry my useless tears and to conquer my merciless pains'.

He and his brother Charles were with their mother in her last few days. 'The internal neuralgia which she has suffered so long,' he wrote as she neared the end, 'has broken her down – and at her great age, there is now no hope'. She died on March 19th 1868.

He got through this agonising period with the help of a new secretary, armed with a firm instruction 'to disregard my sufferings and attend solely to my words' and with increasing doses of laudanum. As he later told Mary Anderson, the actress, 'a young girl was found, who wrote on steadily in spite of my cries. To her I dictated much of the book: the last part largely under the effects of opium. When it was finished, I was not only pleased and astonished at the finale, but did not recognise it as my own'[17]. The girl may well have been Harriet, then aged seventeen[18].

As the summer approached he too was approaching the end of his weekly tasks. The queues outside the *All the Year Round* office in Wellington Street, which was publishing the instalments, soon indicated the success of all his efforts. Yet his worries were far from over. Hardly had he recovered from his mother's death, than Caroline dropped her bomb-shell: either Wilkie married her or she would leave him to marry a younger man. It has been widely assumed that his reluctance to do so may simply have been the fear of an unknown husband appearing from the past and of bigamous charges following in his wake. But we now know that Caroline had been a widow from the age of twenty-two and she may have felt that the time had come to provide her daughter Harriet, if not herself, with a much more assured future.

What brought things to a head, or when, it is impossible to say. Perhaps Caroline's meeting with Joseph Charles Clow, the son of a fairly well-to-do distiller in Avenue Road[19], just across Regents Park, and her feeling that the threat of marriage to a younger rival might finally persuade Wilkie. This was certainly Charles Dickens's suspicion. 'Wilkie's affairs defy all prediction,' he wrote to Georgina, his sister-in-law. 'For anything one knows, the whole matrimonial pretence may be a lie of that woman's intended to make him marry her, and (contrary to her expectations) breaking down at last'[20]. Perhaps it was the success of *The Moonstone* and Caroline's determination to share in the financial results. Perhaps the unexpected appearance of Martha in London. Perhaps just Caroline's love for Wilkie and her frustration in persuading him to legalise their relation-ship. Perhaps a combination of them all. But a few stray clues suggest that Caroline's ultimatum and Wilkie's abrupt refusal may already have been a sad fact by the early summer. She clearly moved out of Gloucester Place around that time.

For one thing, following his mother's death in February, Wilkie had a gold commemorative locket ordered to mark the sad occasion. In a personal diary[21], largely devoted to the completion dates of his instalments of *The Moonstone*, there is the simple entry for July 11th: 'locket finished', along with personal reminders for a new felt hat and repairs to his glasses. The gold locket, with his mother's photograph on one side and a lock of hair on the other, was never passed to Caroline, as would have been expected, but was given to Martha. Her great grand-daughter[22] wears it still.

There is other evidence of Caroline's absence that summer. He stayed with Fred Lehmann in July and by the end of the month was arranging to go to St Moritz with him in a state of growing strain. The exertions of finishing *The Moonstone* and his increasing reliance on drugs to lessen the pain of his recent illness were enough to explain his anxiety to get away from London. But Caroline played no part in his plans. He faced a last minute crisis when Fred was forced to postpone his departure and the child of another friend who promised to take Fred's place was taken desperately ill. Wilkie was at his wit's end: 'I hardly know what I shall do – except that I *must* get away – if Lehmann fails me'.

In the end they left for the Antwerp steamer together and reached Switzerland in early August. But even while he was away, Wilkie asked Charles Ward to look in at Gloucester Place to deal with the mail. Caroline was already elsewhere or not doing her normal chores. When Caroline actually left Gloucester Place is difficult to discern, though the last direct payment to her through Wilkie's bank account is February 26th[23]. This does not necessarily date her departure since these identified payments to Caroline were always irregular (in contrast to subsequent ones to Martha), for she plainly received cash payments, in addition, to run the house[24].

Finally came the most mysterious affair of all: Caroline's sudden marriage to Joseph Charles Clow, a young man eleven years her junior, in the presence of Wilkie's doctor, Francis Beard, Caroline's daughter, Harriet, and even Wilkie himself. Joseph Charles came from a reasonably wealthy family in the wine trade, living at number 2 Avenue Road, on the corner of Prince Albert Road, skirting Regents Park. It was only a few houses away from the place Wilkie had lived for three years as a schoolboy and within striking distance of the first appearance of the woman in white in his novel. Joseph Clow (Joseph Charles's father) and his wife, Frances, and two daughters lived there with their two servants and their coachman and his family[25].

Caroline and Joseph were married on October 29th, 1868, in the parish church of St Marylebone. The real oddity is why Wilkie Collins attended the wedding or indeed why Frank Beard, his doctor and one of his closest friends, was one of the two witnesses. We have Kate Collins's word[26] that Wilkie was there because he went round to see her and his brother Charles the same evening. Describing the events of that day some sixty years later to Gladys Storey, Kate (or Mrs Perugini as she became) is reported to have said that Wilkie 'told her all about it' and finished his explanation with the words 'I suppose you could not marry a man who had. . . .'

'No I couldn't' she broke in decisively. 'Poor Wilkie,' Mrs Perugini apparently continued, 'I liked him and my father was very fond of him and enjoyed his company more than that of any other of his friends – Forster was very jealous of his friendship. He had very high spirits and was a splendid companion, but he was as bad as he could be, yet the gentlest and most kind-hearted of men'.

What Wilkie could have gone on to say and what lay behind Caroline's sudden marriage remain a mystery. What is even odder, in retrospect, is the sequel. Within five months his close friends the Lehmanns were sympathising with him over a secret 'crisis' in his life and even offering monetary help. Within nine months Martha was to bear Wilkie his first child[27] not far away in Bolsover Street where she had lodgings. And within a couple of years or so Caroline was back with Wilkie and Martha was expecting his second child in Bolsover Street. The questions crowd in as rapidly as the events. Why did Caroline suddenly marry Joseph Clow with Wilkie's apparent blessing? When did he turn to Martha and learn of her first child? What kind of 'crisis' did he face? And what prompted Caroline's early return to Gloucester Place?

This, however, is running ahead too rapidly, for the symptoms of Wilkie's troubles developed slowly. By the autumn of 1868 – a year in which he had achieved one of his most enduring literary successes, launching what is still regarded as the first detective story[28], and had at the same time, been plunged into utter despair by the loss of his mother (quite apart from the departure of Caroline) – Wilkie was desperately bringing some order back into his life at Gloucester Place.

He had returned from Switzerland, after over six weeks' absence, in the middle of September and was quickly re-arranging his financial affairs, following the settlement of his mother's will. He and his brother Charles divided her investments equally, Wilkie receiving £8,344 in Consols and just under £1,000 in other stocks, to add to his existing capital of between £1,000 and £1,500. He immediately switched £1,500 into Russian and American bonds and Indian railways and paid £800 to Benham & Company[29]. Since he had been settled in Gloucester Place for nearly a year, and Caroline had left him, the assumption is that Martha may have been the indirect beneficiary.

Martha had moved into a house in Bolsover Street, not far from Gloucester Place. Her landlady was a Mrs Wells, who was living there with her three sons and two daughters[30]. It was a street not unfamiliar to the Collins family. Wilkie's grandfather had had a picture-dealing shop there fifty years earlier. Wilkie must have been a frequent visitor during these critical months of 1868 and, at some point between the last week of October (when Caroline was married) and Christmas, he must have been told that Martha was expecting his child.

It was the final straw in what had already been a momentous year. The sequence is quite staggering: the death of his mother; the completion of *The Moonstone*; the departure and marriage of Caroline; the news of his first child. Yet there is nothing to show that he ran away from his responsibilities. He already had Caroline's daughter, Harriet, and her mother-in-law, Mary Graves, with him in Gloucester Place. The extra responsibility would add to the pressures on his resources, and to the increasing complexity of his home life, but he seems to have borne it with equanimity, after the first shock.

As the New Year approached Wilkie seemed to have regained some of his poise. For New Year's Eve he was planning a dinner party at Gloucester Place for the Lehmanns, along with Charley and Kate and others, and a visit to the pantomime to cheer them all up. 'Depend on my not forgetting the gin,' he wrote to Nina just after Christmas. Soon he was busying himself trying to find Nina a cook, with Fechter's help, and then belatedly sharing in John Hollingshead's triumphant re-opening[31] of the Gaiety Theatre, taking friends along to what he described as 'the most comfortable, elegant and beautifully decorated theatre I have ever seen anywhere . . . I and my other friends walked into "box No. 8" wondering (with an experience of some other theatres) whether we were awake or dreaming'. And he did not forget the perennial needs of a theatre impressario. He told Hollingshead next day: 'I will certainly – as soon as my present dramatic occupations give me time – try and think of something for your stage. I fancy I know what you want, a nice little story, bright and lively, to begin at 8.00 or 8.30 and end at 10.00. If I find myself dropping salt on the tail of an idea, you shall hear from me again'.

He was in fact already hard at work on another play, suggested to him by his old friend Charles Fechter, to be called *Black and White*:

'Fechter's lively mind was, to use his own expression, "full of plots". He undertook to tell me stories enough for all the future novels and plays that I could possibly live to write. His power of invention was unquestionably remarkable: but his method of narration was so confused that it was not easy to follow him, and his respect for those terrible obstacles in the way of free imagination known as probabilities was, to say the least of it, in some need of improvement. One of his plots, however, he presented intelligibly in the form of a scenario. The story, as I thought and still think, was full of dramatic interest. Following Fechter's outline in the first two acts, and suggesting a new method of concluding the story, to which he agreed, I wrote the drama called *Black and White* being solely responsible for the conception and development of the characters, and for the dialogue attributed to them.'

Then came the casting, the subsequent rehearsals, and the usual theatrical mixture of enthusiasm and despair, shared in some detail, it seems, by Charles Dickens. Fechter was not in any case the easiest man to work with. He had, as Wilkie put it, no sense of pecuniary responsibilities. He had an ungovernable temper. And he suffered in a remarkable way from stage fright – even to the extent of being physically ill.

It was at some time in this period, however, that yet another cloud of anxiety began to settle round Wilkie's shoulders. Its precise shape is difficult to describe. While the rehearsals were still on he was writing to Nina Lehmann about his latest bout of rheumatism. 'I am all over pain today – obliged to shift the pen from my right hand to my left to get a dip of ink.' He reported that Fechter was 'improving' with only just over a fortnight to go to the first night on Easter Monday. But he added enigmatically: 'My troubles are much the same! – nothing settled yet'. It was the first outward indication of personal crisis.

Whatever it was, was pushed to the back of his mind by the first night at the Adelphi. Charles Dickens and his family were in one box and Wilkie's friends in another. Wilkie no doubt, in his usual nervous fashion, was presumably hiding himself backstage fearful of the outcome. He need not have been. When he was eventually persuaded to go on stage at the end he received an enthusiastic reception. Modestly, he put the audience's reaction down to Fechter's interpretation of the principal part which he felt had been 'even finer than his performance of Obenreizer in *No Thoroughfare'*. But the first night enthusiasm did not continue.

'As a play,' he explained later, '*Black and White* was considered by my literary brethren (and justly considered) to be a better work than *No Thoroughfare*. We left the theatre with the fairest prospect of another run of six months. But, after some few weeks the regular Adelphi audience reminded us gently, by means of vacant places in the theatre, of an objection to the play which had never once occurred to either of us. We had completely forgotten the popular mania of seventeen years before, satirised by the French as *Oncle Tommerie*. Almost every theatre in Great Britain had, in those days, provided an adaptation of *Uncle Tom's Cabin*. It mattered nothing that the scene of *Black and White* was laid far away from the United States, in the island of Trinidad, and that not one of the persons of the drama recalled the characters in Mrs Stowe's novel in the slightest degree. Mrs Stowe's subject was slavery and our subject was slavery; and even the long-suffering English public had had enough of it. . . . *We* had had enough of it, in our different way, after the piece had been performed about sixty nights'. So the play was taken off and given a provincial run before Fechter took it to the United States.

In the middle of the short run, however, Wilkie was writing a rather odd letter to Fred Lehmann. Thanking him for being such a kind friend, Wilkie quickly re-assured him that his head was 'well above water' and that he had no immediate monetary problems. 'I have few debts unpaid – I have three hundred pounds or so at my bankers – and a thousand pounds in Indian and Russian railways[32], which I can sell out (if the worst comes to the worst) at a gain instead of a loss. I may also, in a few months, sell another edition of *The Moonstone* (cheap edition) and get two or three hundred pounds in that way. So thus far, the money anxieties are not added to the other anxieties which are attacking me. If my health gives way and my prospects darken as this year goes on – you shall be the first man who knows it. Till then, thank you, most sincerely, once more'. And he confirmed that he would be going round to dine with them alone the following Monday evening. 'I am refusing all invitations on the plea of being "out of town". It is necessary to "lay the keel" of something new – after this disaster – and I am trying to keep myself as quiet as I can'. And he added, even more mysteriously, as a postscript, 'I shall pay the Arts. Damn the Arts!'

Coming within months of Caroline's wedding and, as we now know, Martha's pregnancy, Wilkie's 'troubles' could have had their origin in several different areas. The two letters to the Lehmanns are worth looking at closely, for between them they provide a few clues. They indicate that the difficulties mentioned in the first letter, dated March 11th 1869, were not new and had been around some time: These would almost certainly include the problem of what he should do about Martha Rudd and the child she was expecting. They would have to be cared for and their accommodation assured. He must also have had to consider, much more carefully than with Caroline, whether he should marry her.

It was ironic that his determination to avoid marrying Caroline should have led to her departure and to a more pressing reason for marrying Martha, all apparently within the space of a few months. His second letter, dated April 24th 1869, written after the play had been running over three weeks, refers to 'a disaster' and to monetary anxieties. Taken together the two letters strongly suggest that something specific had happened which had added to Wilkie's previous worries and that, whatever it was, it was related to money.

Leaving aside Caroline and Martha there seem to be three possibilities: there had been some unforeseen expense which had cost him dear; his relationship with Fechter and the play *Black and White* had developed into a crisis; or, once again, his health had suddenly worsened, brought on by the succession of shocks he had suffered in the previous twelve months.

Fred Lehmann at least concluded that whatever had happened would press on Wilkie's resources. And, for some reason, on February 16th Wilkie sold $3,000 of U.S. bonds, which he had inherited only five months earlier. He realised £528. There is no indication in his accounts of what it might have been spent on nor for whom it might have been intended, though on March 3rd he paid £100 to Charles Fechter.

It is at this point that conjecture begins to play a tempting role. Wilkie's second letter to the Lehmanns suggests that some payment must be made to 'the Arts' and that he intended to 'lay the keel' of something new, a strong hint of a new creative urge or story, presumably to replace a literary failure. One outside possibility is that the early termination of *Black and White* was likely to cost him and Fechter more than they expected and that, belatedly, Wilkie may have discovered that Fechter had borrowed heavily to get involved with the play in the first place. It is just possible. Earlier that year Fechter had written to Wilkie about a sum of £30 which Wilkie clearly owed him, but the letter[33] also reveals that Fechter already owed Wilkie (and Charles Dickens) £200.

Writing from his house in Park Road, St John's Wood, Fechter told Wilkie, 'It's £30 without "the humbug" of the guineas, but I must ask you not to send me the cheque for it. I must owe you £200 (Dickens as well as you) spent by Madame Fechter, and it is quite enough that you should have the goodness to give me credit in my present poverty and to ignore the unusual part of this payment without me having to take money from you. So let's just put it on the bill and do not talk of it again until I am in a position to pay you back'.

All this implies that Fechter, who already owed both of them £200, had suddenly added to the debt. It could have arisen directly from the problems of the play itself, but it was just as likely to have arisen from the liberal way in which Charles Fechter arranged his money affairs, generously lending large sums to needy friends and just as quickly having to lean heavily on other friends. As Wilkie put it later, 'I have met with many children who had a clearer idea than he possessed of pecuniary responsibilities. . . . When he had no money to spare, and he was asked for a loan of 'a few hundred pounds' he had no hesitation in borrowing the money from the friend who had it, and handing the sum over to the friend who had it not. When I remonstrated with him, he was always ready with his answer. "My dear Wilkie, you know I love you. Do you think I should love you if I didn't firmly believe that you would do just the same thing in my place?" '34

There is certainly enough evidence that at this time Fechter had just emerged from a particularly troublesome financial period and was far from out of the woods. The previous spring he had been pressed to repay £10,000 but stressed he had already 'repaid £6,000'35. Moreover, Charles Dickens had lent him £2,000 to meet promissory notes due in December 1868, and Fechter had at the same time been refuting a legal claim for some £2,700 on his assets in Paris. When Fechter left for the United States, towards the end of 1869, he was still said to owe Dickens 'several thousand pounds'36. (Georgina Hogarth later claimed that the money had all eventually been repaid. Dickens told her, 'I always told you Fechter would pay his money'. She asked: 'Has he paid all he owed you?' He answered: 'Everything'.)37 Whether Wilkie got caught up in some of these monetary difficulties in early 1869 remains conjectural. But Fechter repaid Wilkie £140 in June 1870.

Wilkie's health, however, may have been the real source of Fred's anxiety. It had deteriorated rapidly under the pressures of his mother's death, Caroline's departure and the necessity of writing *The Moonstone*, and he had only survived with the combination of his own determination and a growing dependence on laudanum. This was the period when, if ever, he became firmly addicted. How it eventually affected him is difficult to say but there is clear evidence that by the end of February 1869 he was making a valiant attempt to break himself of the habit, under doctor's instructions.

This is attested by a frank letter to Fred's sister, Elizabeth Benson, explaining why he could not accept an evening's invitation. 'My doctor,' he pointed out candidly, 'is trying to break me of the habit of drinking laudanum. I am stabbed every night at ten, with a sharp-pointed syringe which injects morphia under my skin and gets me a night's rest, without any of the drawbacks of taking opium internally. If I only persevere with this, I am told I shall be able, before long, gradually to diminish the quantity of morphine and the number of the nightly stabbings – and so emancipate myself from opium altogether'[38]. He was never subsequently cured of the habit, but his efforts suggest that something of a crisis must have arisen for him to consider such steps. And again, any impairment of his health had immediate monetary implications.

Somehow he got through this trying period and on July 4th Martha presented him with his first daughter, Marian, at her lodgings in Bolsover Street. Though there is no trace of his having registered the birth in the normal way[39], he had clearly come to terms with his new family. Once again marriage had been ruled out, as much no doubt by the contrast in their social background as by Wilkie's unwillingness to contemplate such ties. But he did what he must have thought best in the circumstances. He was careful to provide Martha with the outward appearance of a marriage, by discreetly turning himself into William Dawson[40], Barrister at Law, whenever necessary, thus conferring on Martha and her children the married name of Dawson.

When he had to use the name – whether in connection with household bills, holidays at Ramsgate, or even a later birth certificate – he never hesitated. He gave Martha and her children respectability. And also, from that year onwards, Martha (as Mrs Dawson) became the recipient of a regular monthly allowance from his bank account[41]. She was receiving close on £250 a year, quite apart from special payments for furniture and the like, sufficient to keep her comfortably off, not far from Gloucester Place.

CHAPTER ELEVEN

A Trois

WITH CAROLINE elsewhere, Martha quickly absorbed Wilkie's whole affections. But that did not imply any move to Gloucester Place. After the first shock of pregnancy, and the slow realisation that he was about to become a father, Wilkie's instincts quickly took hold. Unless he was careful, he might easily end up a middle-aged family man, trapped in Gloucester Place in a fashion he had so often despised in others. Yet he could not bring himself to abandon her; nor even contemplate it. Marriage was the trap; not parenthood.

Martha for her part may have hoped that Caroline's departure and the birth of Marian might persuade Wilkie to contemplate marriage. She can hardly have believed it. She had known him long enough to be sure of his love, his warmth and his kindness. But to try to push him further – towards marriage – was not in her nature. She had had ample time to realise what role she was destined to play. Nor was she the coaxing kind. She had moved to London with her candid eyes wide open and only in her secret heart did she occasionally wish things had been otherwise.

So Wilkie was soon in a new routine, slipping round to Bolsover Street to enjoy Martha's warmth and share the intimacies of parenthood. It was a role he adopted with enthusiasm. Caroline's child from an earlier marriage had always received his special attention. His own child brought out a latent warmth that only Martha could fully vouch for. Yet he rarely overlooked the champagne. Bolsover Street remained a love nest, as well as a home.

Even with a new family virtually round the corner, life without Caroline still left some miserable gaps in Wilkie's life. His close friends rallied round, however, and over the next year or so he spent far more time outside Gloucester Place than he had previously contemplated.

He had not realised, until Caroline vanished, how much his so-called bachelor life revolved around her. She and Harriet had become essential cogs in his routine: running the household, keeping his accounts, watching over his manuscripts, caring for his ailments, keeping his admirers at bay and his friends entertained.

While Harriet was able to replace Caroline with secretarial help and Martha could comfort him in other ways, his pattern of domestic entertainment, the informal dinner parties he and Caroline had loved to give to a small circle of close friends, was shattered overnight. He determined to fill the gap in a round of theatre and restaurant visits.

Work, too, provided an antidote and he quickly decided to throw his energies into the preparation of a new novel, on a theme not too far removed from his recent experiences: the problems of the marriage laws, and the legal rights of a husband over his wife.

At the beginning he shut himself away, working on the plot itself. 'I am in a state of penitential seclusion,' he told a close friend in the spring of 1869, 'building up the scaffolding of a new story (nothing to do, thank God, with the roof of the house) – dining with 'incidents' among the dishes, and going to bed with 'characters' in the flat candlestick – and fortifying myself against all social temptations behind one solid and changeless lie – namely that I am "out of town." '[1]

Although he kept in touch with Fred and Nina Lehmann, with Frank Beard, and with Charley and Kate and the Dickens family at Gad's Hill, he was deliberately lying low throughout the summer, as he began the arduous task of the writing itself – once again preparing for the inevitable start of serialisation, in London and New York, by the year end. In Fred Lehmann's absence on a round the world trip, he saw a good deal of Nina and, when he could, tried to keep Fred in touch with London. By the autumn, he was thanking Fred for a consignment of Stoughton bitters, newly arrived from Liverpool, which nicely interrupted his work on *Man and Wife*. 'I suspended an immortal work of Fiction,' he wrote to Fred, 'by going downstairs and tasting a second bottle properly combined with gin. Result delicious!' The first bottle had been sent to Frank Beard in return for a welcome parcel of country sausages.

Very shortly, however, having completed a third of the novel, he began to look around for a quiet spot to complete the rest, and his friends the Lehmanns soon provided him with all he needed – a private room, a bed and their understanding – at their home at The Woodlands in Highgate. Their family life revolved around him, thus providing him with distractions when he needed them and quiet when he was at his desk. Even his best friends were enjoined to creep past his room, when he was at work.

It was a period when he got to know the Lehmann children even better.

He had always been their favourite grown-up, treating them with all the seriousness children need and rarely get, involving himself in their schoolwork, dashing off couplets from Horace from a Latin crib, telling them stories of Tom Sayers, the famous prizefighter, and impressing himself on their memories in a way that lingered for close on half a century.

'I can see him now,' young Rudolf reminisced many years later, 'as I used to see him in those early, unforgotten days; a neat figure of a cheerful plumpness, very small feet and hands, a full brown beard, a high and rounded forehead, a small nose not naturally intended to support a pair of large spectacles behind which his eyes shone with humour and friendship; not by any means the sort of man imagination would have pictured as the creator of Count Fosco and the inventor of the terrors of *Armadale* and the absorbing mystery of *The Moonstone*'.

The Lehmann children noticed something else while Wilkie was at Woodlands: that he was 'a very hard and determined worker', a trait they could hardly have detected from his casual, social visits. And they saw how exhausted he was, as a result. 'I am nearly fagged to death,' he told another friend, as he came to the end of his efforts the following year, 'under the double stress of finishing *Man and Wife* as a novel, and as a play – and time fails me for everything but my work'[2]. He was going through the same sequence of hard work, exhaustion and the onset of another attack of gout.

Throughout these exertions and his attempts to fill in his yawning social gap, following Caroline's departure, he did not overlook those left behind. He still had Caroline's mother-in-law, Mary Graves, under his roof and Harriet's education was drawing to a close. He had paid her final school bill in the summer of 1868 and began to pay her casual sums the following spring, in the absence of her mother. Harriet had also probably begun to help Wilkie in his work, doing some of his clerical work, running errands, even preparing his writing for the printer. There is even reason to believe, as *The Globe* hinted after his death, that not only had Harriet long acted as his amanuensis when the affliction of the eyes prevented him from writing, but that 'the first book she copied was *The Moonstone* when she was fourteen years of age'[3].

One of his old friends who was conspicuously absent in this period was Charles Dickens. Though Wilkie was occasionally down at Gad's Hill, especially with Charley and Kate, their old relationship had gradually changed. No longer were they sharing their spare time with each other; and no longer were they collaborators in joint literary enterprises. Their last Christmas number for *All the Year Round* was *No Thoroughfare* in 1867.

To some extent, of course, their relationship was bound to change, as

Wilkie made his own reputation, with *Armadale*, *No Name* and *The Moonstone* following *The Woman in White*. Dickens had greeted them all with praise and appreciation, though his praise of *The Moonstone* was later modified by his oft-quoted comments to Wills about the construction of *The Moonstone* being 'wearisome beyond endurance' and 'the vein of obstinate conceit' in the novel making enemies of its readers. Dickens could hardly be jealous of his own protégé, but something seemed to have led to a cooling of their former companionship.

They had, of course, developed semi-permanent liaisons, one with Caroline Graves and Martha Rudd, the other, more tenuously, with Ellen Ternan, and thus their freedom to have a night on the town together had inevitably become more restricted, though this is more likely to have affected Dickens than Collins. Ellen Ternan had been introduced to the stage company producing *The Frozen Deep* as a professional actress, though she was only eighteen at the time. It coincided with a deep crisis in Dickens's relations with his wife and he was soon confessing to Wilkie: 'The domestic unhappiness remains so strong upon me that I can't write, and (waking) can't rest, one minute. I have never known a moment's peace or content since the last night of *The Frozen Deep*'.

How and when Dickens eventually installed Ellen in a house in Berners Street and, much later, a joint household in Slough (with his own pseudonym of Tringham[4]) and how he occasionally met her in a country hideaway at Condette, not far from Boulogne[5], is still in dispute among Dickens scholars, and particularly whether he had a child by her[6]. But it is all enough to explain why his enthusiasm for nightly escapades with Wilkie may have lost some of its ardour.

None of this should have affected their regard for each other. But something else did and there is good reason to believe that it concerned Dickens's attitude towards his son-in-law, Wilkie's young brother, Charles. For Dickens plainly nurtured a guilt complex from the conviction that, had it not been for his own selfishness following his separation from his wife, Kate would not have been thrown into Charles's arms and married him.

For a time all seemed well with the marriage and to the outside world Charles and Kate appeared to be an idyllic couple. Annie Fields, the wife of Dickens's American publisher, got such an impression on her early visits to London. 'If I could paint you a little picture with my pen,' she wrote to a friend[7], 'I would describe Mrs Collins, Mr Dickens's eldest daughter, as the most beautiful person we have met. She is like a fine piece of china . . . she has red hair which she wears very high in a loose coil. Altogether the effect is like some rare strange thing. . . .' The small house she and Charles had furnished tastefully, with rugs on the wooden floor, family pictures every-where 'and a broad window which is left open to let the trees wave across and to hear the voice of the birds', had a similar impact. Taste not money, Annie Fields concluded, was the secret. 'The Collins are quite poor which makes it all the better worthwhile to show how people in England manage when they are so.'

Charles Collins's growing inability to earn a living from writing and his continuing struggle with what was soon to prove a mortal illness, however, soon began to put pressure on their marriage and to exacerbate Dickens's anxieties. Charles and Kate had had a tight domestic budget to contend with from the beginning of their marriage. His mother began to top up his income between 1860 and 1863 with annual payments varying between £130 and £225. Wilkie, too, added the odd hundred pounds and occasionally offered more, when he clearly realised that Charles's writings were hardly fruitful[8].

Soon Harriet Collins was providing a regular £300 a year[9] partly, no doubt, to pay for the room Charles and Kate always kept for her in London, but in some years it made up between a third and a half of Charles's total income. Dickens also began to provide his share – £150 in 1867 and another £350 in 1868, before Harriet's death later that year gave Charles the capital he had always needed. Like Wilkie he received over £8,000 in Consols and a few other securities. But, from all accounts, this easing of the financial pressures on Charles and Kate did little to assuage Dickens's anxieties and his visible reactions to Charles's growing afflictions.

Beyond these monetary troubles, Dickens was naturally worried that Charles's frail health might leave Kate an early widow[10], and such a development was almost bound to come between Dickens and Collins. Dickens could see his daughter incapable of surviving without deep emotional damage. Wilkie could hardly bear to hear criticism of a brother who was both dear to him and in need of all the sympathy he could get.

As Annie Fields was to put it later, 'Dickens took a strange dislike to him [Charles Collins] during the last year or two of his life. I think it was his dreadful and continued sickness which neither exhausted his frame to death, nor ever ceased in order to allow a return to health. He could not understand the prolonged endurance of such an existence and in his passionate nature, which must snap when it yielded at all, it produced disgust. His mind was so bent upon the necessity of Charles Collins's death that Fechter says even at table he has seen him look at him as much as to say "astonishing you should be here today, but tomorrow you will be in your chamber never to come out again"'. Wilkie, she concluded, 'had been seriously estranged from Dickens because of his treatment of Charles'[11].

Evidence now strongly suggests that Dickens knew that Collins was not just ill but probably impotent as well, and should not have married Kate in the first place. He hinted at such a possibility in his assertion that there were 'no "Great Expectations" of prospective Collinses'[12]. And he apparently was told the truth by Kate and even asked whether she could get a separation[13]. Towards the end of her life, Kate confirmed that Charles 'ought never to have married'. Fred Lehmann too had hinted darkly that Charles was guilty of an 'infamy' in marrying at all[14].

Kate had growing difficulty in coping with the consequences and was soon gaining an unenviable reputation. John Lehmann, referring to his grandfather's letters of the time, speaks of Kate 'being intensely eager . . . to find other lovers' and quotes one letter from Fred to Nina describing the two Dickens girls, Kate and Mamie: 'Society is beginning to fight very shy of them, especially of Kitty C . . . Mamie may blaze up in a firework any day. Kitty is burning away both character, and I fear health, slowly but steadily'.

All this did not mean that Charles Dickens and Wilkie had stopped seeing each other or even writing. Wilkie was down at Gad's Hill from time to time and they were in correspondence at the beginning of 1870, when Wilkie's serialisation of *Man and Wife* had begun to run in *Cassell's Magazine* and Wilkie was still striving to finish the novel. It was, however, to prove the last time they wrote to each other and it ended on a sad note. 'I don't come to see you,' Dickens wrote to his old friend, 'because I don't want to bother you. Perhaps you may be glad to see me by and by. Who knows?'[15]

Five months later, in early June, Dickens had a seizure and died without regaining consciousness. As Wilkie later recalled: 'I finished *Man and Wife* yesterday – fell asleep from sheer fatigue – and was awakened to hear the news of Dickens's death'[16]. At the funeral a few days later, both he and his brother Charles rode with Frank Beard, their doctor and friend, in one of the three mourning coaches. His old links with Dickens had already been permanently damaged and Dickens's death simply confirmed yet another gap in Wilkie's life. By the end of the month, when *Man and Wife* was finally published, Wilkie was 'so utterly worn out' with all he had gone through that he and Frank Beard went off for a three day trip to Antwerp – 'simply for the voyage'[17].

Wilkie was once again reacting to the strains of authorship and later that summer he began to renew his acquaintance with Ramsgate. Broadstairs now had too many ghosts of his early holidays with Dickens and other friends. Ramsgate, on the other hand, had the advantage of a harbour where he could take a boat when he wanted it. It must also have prompted happy memories of his childhood visits and was to become the place he escaped to, with his family, for the rest of his life.

Whether Martha and her one year old daughter, Marian, accompanied him there in the autumn of 1870 is unclear, but they must have remained close during Caroline's continued absence. There is no evidence that Martha was ever a visitor to Gloucester Place. She herself might have felt uncomfortable there, and Wilkie would hardly encourage her, though her children were eventually to be treated quite differently. No letters to or from Martha have survived (perhaps there were few) and none have emerged even within her own family. She is not mentioned, even indirectly, in Wilkie's correspondence with his friends, as Caroline was, the main references being to his morganatic family rather rather than to Martha herself. Yet at some point in the late autumn – perhaps even when he was in Ramsgate – Martha must have told him that she was pregnant again. And, almost as if on cue, Caroline reappeared.

Wilkie's precise relations with Caroline baffled many of his friends and no episode was quite so baffling as her marriage to Joseph Clow and, then, within a matter of two years, her sudden reappearance in Gloucester Place. It is difficult to pinpoint precisely when she returned, but it could have been in the second half of 1870 or the early part of 1871[18]. Martha was almost certainly pregnant when she returned. Caroline had in any case re-established herself in Wilkie's household by April 3rd 1871. This was the day of the 1871 Census and in the return Wilkie put himself down as the head of the household and unmarried, while Caroline appeared as Caroline Graves 'a widow' and as 'housekeeper and domestic servant' – a nice contrast to their marital status in the Census of ten years earlier. The rest of the household consisted of Harriet, aged 20, Mary Graves, aged 70 and three household staff (a cook, a housemaid and a fifteen-year-old page)[19].

Joseph Clow seems to have vanished as swiftly as he appeared, leaving neither his name nor any detail of his whereabouts. We now know that Joseph was left £2,000 in his mother's will thirty years later and that he eventually died of influenza in 1927 in Paddington aged eighty-one[20]. The rest is silence, but he left a few puzzles behind him. Why had Caroline left him and why had Wilkie accepted her back and on what terms?

Why Caroline married Joseph Clow in the first place still remains uncertain, the readiest explanation at the time of her departure being her determination to provoke Wilkie. Her rather rapid return, however, prompted the idea that earlier, at the time of her marriage, she might have been pregnant and once the child had been born, Joseph Clow was no longer required. For a time it appeared that this might be the truth, particularly when one discovered that the birth of a child named Frances May Clow, carrying Joseph's mother's name, had been registered at Hertford Place on June 22nd 1869, and that the child's early death had also been registered thirteen months later. Was it Caroline's child? The truth was less dramatic. The baby turned out to be the daughter of Abraham Clow, a footman in Hertford Place, and his wife Jane[21].

Thus Caroline's return must be put down to disenchantment or incompatibility. The only reference Wilkie seems to have made to the episode is in a letter some six years later when he confesses to 'having met in real life with a woman who fell in love with a man utterly unworthy of her'[22]. That Joseph Clow continued to plague both Wilkie and Caroline is at least suggested by a letter he subsequently wrote to his solicitor. 'Look also at the enclosed note received a little while since. "Keates" is a nickname for Caroline (Mrs Graves). Is the fellow's brain softening? Of course no notice has been taken of his letter'[23].

The real question is why Caroline re-joined Wilkie and how Wilkie himself resolved his relations with both Caroline and Martha, especially since Martha was already expecting his second child in Bolsover Street. Caroline may have missed the security Wilkie undoubtedly offered and in any case both Harriet and Mary Graves were still in Gloucester Place. But her bluff had been called and she was now returning on Wilkie's terms.

He had clearly been restless in her absence, missing a woman to run his household, even to act as hostess to his male companions. This was a role that Martha, with her country background and simple ways, was unable to play or even aspire to. It is likely that, in filling in the Census, Wilkie was telling the truth. Caroline was to become simply his housekeeper, a housekeeper of a special kind, perhaps even a hostess, but basically a housekeeper, and no longer a mistress. It would help to explain Martha's role, the relationship between Caroline and Martha, and that between their two families for the rest of Wilkie's life. At almost forty, after a life as eventful as hers had already been, and with the prospect of every security and comfort, Caroline was at last willing to compromise, even though the terms were basically Wilkie's.

Caroline's return made little direct impact on Martha's habits. Wilkie was as attentive as ever, sharing the pains and joys of a growing family, leaving her in no doubt of his support and the strength of their affection for each other. Even the routine of his visits had invariably been governed by the pattern, and stress, of his writing, and his other distractions. Over the years Martha had grown used to such an intermittent relationship. When Caroline was in Gloucester Place, their entertainments inevitably deprived Martha of a regular visitor. And when Caroline was away, so did his habit of staying longer with close friends.

What Martha could not have bargained for was the return of her only rival for his affections in such bizarre circumstances. For close on two years she had had his exclusive attention at a time when she needed it most. She had had to come to terms with Wilkie's final word about marriage in the face of her first child, and had grown to accept it. The expectation of a second child had forged even closer links between them. Just when she had begun to feel secure in his love and his financial support, Caroline not only left Joseph Clow but was welcomed back in Gloucester Place.

How Wilkie broke the news is not recorded. But if his subsequent relations with Martha are anything to go by, he must have told her the whole affair. She may have shown her understanding, but she could hardly have relished what she now saw ahead of her.

She was entirely dependent on Wilkie, a simple, unsophisticated girl bringing up a famous novelist's family. Who can blame her for settling for a morganatic arrangement, which gave her the support and a little of the respectability she needed, and apparently insisted upon. Whether marriage ever crossed her mind as a real possibility is difficult to discern. To the end, she always insisted that, had she wanted, she could have married Wilkie Collins. Whether this was pride speaking or reality we shall never know. Had Wilkie felt the need to marry her, there were enough precedents to make it possible. But the combination of a loving mother of his children outside Gloucester Place, and a former mistress inside, plainly had a stronger appeal.

Caroline may have returned to Gloucester Place in the closing months of 1870, but it was in 1871 and 1872 that she began to settle more openly into a new pattern of life with Wilkie. How she coped with Wilkie's relations with Martha is difficult to imagine. Her own romantic attachment to Wilkie had plainly been broken and she had been replaced in Wilkie's affections by a girl at least fifteen years her junior. But she had her part to play and one to which she brought her own remarkable talents.

One picture of her at this time (it can be dated roughly by her hat and the outline of her dress), portrays a strikingly good looking woman, whose daughter one would find it difficult to believe was then over twenty. She had poise and presence and had grown used to life in a successful novelist's household. She was plainly treated on equal and affectionate terms by all of Wilkie's closest friends. Her own friendships developed alongside them. She, and her daughter, Harriet, gradually took over, once again, not only the running of Wilkie's house but also his literary needs and his correspondence with agents, printers and publishers, at home and abroad.

One particular relationship began to develop after Caroline's return, originally by Wilkie, later by Wilkie and Caroline together. Charles Reade had been an admirer of Collins since *The Woman in White* and, as fellow writers, they had grown to respect each other's talents and eventually, to depend on each other's criticisms. Whether Charles Reade provided the gem on which *The Moonstone* itself was based, is still open to conjecture. Walter de la Mare was the first to suggest it, and the moonstone in question, originally brought from India by Charles Reade's brother, is still in the possession of the Reade family near Reading. Wilkie himself always insisted that his sole knowledge at the time he wrote the novel was that two famous Indian diamonds – the *Sancy* diamond and the *Koh-i-Nor* – were originally ornaments found in idols worshipped by the Hindus[24]. ('These were the only *facts* known to me when I wrote *The Moonstone*'.) But whatever the truth of the story, Wilkie and Charles Reade were growing closer together as their writings progressed and as Wilkie found himself responding to Reade's reforming zeal.

In many ways Reade had replaced Dickens as Wilkie's main literary confidant. Socially, Reade had one interesting advantage. He too had an unconventional housekeeper, Mrs Seymour, a former actress. They had met some fifteen years earlier when she was at the peak of her career at the Haymarket Theatre and he was nursing ambitions as a playwright. They were an unlikely couple. She was 'well looking off the stage and could make up pretty'; he was a diffident, pale faced aspiring writer. They first met when he asked for an interview to read a scene from an unfinished drama. She hardly encouraged him. 'Yes,' she cried, when he had finished, 'that's good. That's plotting'. But with a laugh, 'Why don't you write novels?' He was hurt and quickly excused himself.

It was an unlikely beginning to a relationship which was to endure well over two decades, but she quickly realised that she had offended him and made amends and he, in turn, recognised an understanding spirit. Their friendship developed slowly and once her theatrical career was over, she slipped easily into the role of housekeeper and companion.

Even twenty years later she was still capable of saying, 'I hope Mr Reade will never ask me to marry him, as I should certainly refuse'[25]. What their true relationship was is difficult to understand, but Winwood Reade, Charles's nephew, always insisted it was purely platonic. It nevertheless raised sufficient eyebrows to keep them both at arms' length from formal society. Julian Hawthorne reported that although he was entertained by Reade and Mrs Seymour at Albert Gate, where 'their visitors were few, but all they wanted,' he 'never met either of them at society dinners or receptions'[26]. Wilkie and Caroline knew the problem though in Wilkie's case only Caroline seems to have suffered, for he was wined and dined without hesitation, provided that he went alone.

It was shortly after Caroline's return to Gloucester Place that the joint relationship with Reade and Mrs Seymour began to flourish. In May 1871, Reade's play, *Free Labour* (the dramatisation of his novel, *Put Yourself in His Place*) was in rehearsal at the Adelphi. Wilkie, for his part, had other things on his mind. Martha's second daughter was born and was promptly christened (after Wilkie's mother and, by chance, Caroline's daughter) Constance Harriet, later known as 'Hettie'. Just over a week later, however, Wilkie found time to go around to the Adelphi for the first night of *Free Labour*.

He had difficulty in finding Reade and the first he saw of him was when he stood up in his private box to take the acclaim of the audience. Even then Wilkie found it impossible to get up the stairs to congratulate his old friend because of the bustle and had to content himself by writing a congratulatory letter in bed next morning and sending it round to Reade's house with Caroline. He was still hard at work on his new book, *Poor Miss Finch*, and was again suffering agonies from gout, this time in the eyes, and he could hardly spare the time to call round himself. But this did not prevent him from sending Reade a detailed, and constructive, criticism of the play, as well as his delight at its success. 'My verdict is that . . . the play contains some of the most interesting and the most original scenes that I have beheld for many a long year past'[27].

This heady mixture of domestic bliss with Martha and social obligations with Caroline continued throughout the summer and autumn. Harriet clearly found life easier and more relaxed with the return of her mother and, increasingly, took on the burden of secretarial duties, especially when Wilkie was too ill to write himself. His friends were beginning to drift back into their old habits of dinner with Caroline and himself, Caroline issuing the invitations to his closest friends as often as Wilkie.

Charles Ward was an early caller. So were Charles Reade and Mrs Seymour. In their case the bait was the visiting editor of *Harper's Weekly* from New York. 'You and Mrs Seymour,' Wilkie wrote personally, 'are especially requested to dine here to taste the White Burgundy (which I mentioned the other day). . . . No evening dress, and no party. Choose which day will suit you both, please, and let me know by an early post'[28].

The relationship built up between Caroline and Charles Reade and her close assessment of his character was illustrated by an incident recorded by Wybert Reeve, the actor. On his first visit to Reade, he was accompanied by Wilkie and 'a lady friend', clearly Caroline. 'As we entered the room I saw a big, burly, carelessly dressed man, with a fine head, good features, rather long, straggling and uncut hair.' He was cutting the pictures out of various periodicals and sticking them in a large book open before him. 'You will see how I will please him,' Caroline whispered to Reeve and, turning to Reade, she exclaimed 'Oh, Mr Reade, pardon me, do forgive me', laughing and fixing her eyes upon him, 'I like looking at you; there is something in your face so good and so manly'. An open, coquettish approach, but Reade was plainly blinded. 'My dear Mrs _____' he replied. 'You flatter me. Upon my life, I should be angry if I did not know you were a woman of judgment' and he turned to the mirror, brushing his hair with his hands 'evidently as pleased as possible'[29].

Wilkie meanwhile was still involved in the next instalments of *Poor Miss Finch* for *Cassell's Magazine* and, at the same time, was preparing a dramatic version of *The Woman in White* for the London stage. It had been tried out in the provinces the year before, and was due to open at the Olympic Theatre in early October. The rehearsals were particularly trying, mainly due to the indecision of George Vining who was not only playing the part of Count Fosco but was also acting as producer. 'Endless arguments arose about crossing the stage, the position of the several characters, of a chair, a sofa or a table'.

As a result rehearsals went on interminably, from ten in the morning to five in the afternoon and sometimes from six or seven in the evening to one and two in the early morning. Wilkie was there often, looking 'perplexed in the extreme'[30], according to Wybert Reeve who was playing Walter Hartright and was later to play Fosco with great success both in London and New York. But he remained 'gentlemanly, patient and good tempered, always ready with a smile if a chance offered itself or a peaceful word kindly suggesting when a point was to be gained'.

His patience plainly paid off. The first night was a distinct success, and according to Wilkie, 'really took the audience by storm'[31]. Receipts in the first week reached £475 and went up steadily thereafter. A month later Wilkie was arranging a private box for Charles Reade and Mrs Seymour and again promising them a pleasant afternoon or evening to go with it. 'A new stock of Moselle is at this moment being put into the cellar. Come and draw a cork between 3 and 4, as soon as you get to town – or at 7.30 when there is dinner. The two Carolines[32] send you their love. . . .'

The play eventually had a run of nineteen weeks, and then had a further extended run in the provinces. While it was proving such a success, Wilkie himself was still completing the early publication of his latest novel in book form. Once again he was working under pressure and just managing to keep his head above water. By the beginning of December, as he neared the end, he confessed to a friend in breathless prose, 'I am feeling my work – heart reported to be weak – obliged to take tonics. Five weekly parts to do. And then Paris!' But it did not work out quite as he intended. With serialisation completed, *Poor Miss French* came out in a three volume edition at the end of January 1872. On publication day he was still planning his vacation. 'I am going to take a holiday – as long a one as I can,' he told his publisher, George Bentley. 'For I have been really working too hard this last year.' A week later he was still talking of getting out of the country by the end of February. In fact he got as far as Ramsgate, staying at the Granville Hotel, and only seems to have managed to obtain his passport by mid-March. He eventually reached Paris in July, before succumbing to gout once more.

Caroline's return to Gloucester Place and to Wilkie's social circle, coupled with Martha's second child, were seen in more mundane arrangements. Although Wilkie's name remained firmly in the Marylebone rate book (until they finally moved in 1888), Caroline's name once more replaced Wilkie's in the London street guide from 1872 onwards. Cheques, too began to appear in Caroline's name again (the first on February 17th 1872), and the regular £20 a month allotted to Martha was quickly raised to £25 to account for the extra mouth in Bolsover Street. Wilkie was well able to stand the expense. Apart from the year 1868–69, when he used capital from his mother's estate to add to his normal income, the years between 1871 and 1876 represented the period of his highest earnings – and expenditure. It was also the period when he began to receive a small but persistent income from his successes on the stage, starting with *The Woman in White* and going on to *Man and Wife*, *The New Magdalen* and others.

He was always convinced that sailing with his friends was the cure for all his ills. It undoubtedly helped to freshen him up and restore his general health. Whether it was always the best way to assuage rheumatism and gout is another matter. But, plagued once more with gout in the eye, he moved down to Ramsgate in mid-September to recuperate, to complete the first instalments of yet another novel and to sail when he wished. He found a suite of rooms in Nelson Crescent, one of the two handsome crescents on each side of the harbour overlooking the bay.

Rebecca Shrive was the landlady of number 14 and was to welcome Wilkie and Caroline along with his children and her grandchildren for the next decade and a half. When he was with Martha, as he often was, he arranged to stay on the other side of the bay in Wellington Crescent, where he immediately became William Dawson. On this occasion he stayed for five or six weeks, making some headway with *The New Magdalen*. This new novel was devoted to a reformed prostitute and the first chapters began to appear in *Temple Bar* while he was still there. He returned to London in late October 'much the better' for his stay in Ramsgate.

All the good he derived from his welcome break, however, was soon lost in his efforts to finish *The New Magdalen*, and his further efforts in the New Year, to get two of his plays ready for the West End Stage. Just as he was completing the novel and play versions of *The New Magdalen*, Squire and Marie Bancroft, who were running the Prince of Wales Theatre, decided to put on *Man and Wife*, which they had acquired from Wilkie eighteen months earlier. By the middle of January, he confessed to his publisher: 'I am so fagged with the double work of rehearsing my play and keeping the 'Magdalen' going at a very different part of the story, that I do not propose to write another long story for some little time – unless the dire necessity of making money drives me to it'.

The fact is he loved the theatre and always felt that he had a particular talent for it. 'When writing for the stage', he once explained during an interview in Gloucester Place, 'I act all the play over by myself in this large room repeating the speeches aloud, and striving to judge of their effect. Hard work, as you say, but still delightful enough in its way'. He was not always successful, but never lacked enthusiasm. He had begun the stage versions of both *Man and Wife* and *The New Magdalen* before the novels. And once the Bancrofts indicated their intention to put on *Man and Wife* in the early months of 1873, he entered into rehearsals, and even the re-shaping of the play, with characteristic enthusiasm. Squire Bancroft asked him to read the play to the full company. 'This he did with great effect and nervous force, giving all concerned a clear insight into his view of the characters; and indeed, acting the old Scotch waiter with rare ability to roars of laughter'[33].

While the rehearsals continued, Martha was not far from Wilkie's mind. As he went along Tottenham Court Road to the Prince of Wales theatre, in early February, he called in at Hewetson and Thexton, the furniture store, with Martha. They were evidently refurnishing Martha's new home in Marylebone Road, only a few streets away from the theatre and where she was to stay for just over a year. They bought a dining table, a sideboard, five dining chairs, an easy chair, a walnut bureau, a couch and an elegant devotional chair, with enough velvet to upholster the chairs and the couch. Wilkie also insisted on two rather expensive black and gold chimney glasses to lend richness to the decor. They cost him £30 and the whole bill came to just over £100[34]. The receipted bill was made out to Mr Dawson, Wilkie's morganatic pseudonym.

Just less than three weeks later came the first night at the Prince of Wales. It was, according to the Bancrofts, 'the most brilliant audience (so far as names then known throughout the world in every art and calling went) the theatre had as yet seen assembled within its limited walls'. But Wilkie was far from reassured. He passed almost all the evening in Squire Bancroft's dressing room 'in a state of nervous terror, painful to behold'. He was only partly encouraged by the occasional bursts of applause he could hear. He apparently had only one brief view of the stage during the whole evening until at the end he was 'summoned by the brilliant audience to show himself'.

Wilkie described his reception: 'The pit got on its legs and cheered with all its might the moment I showed myself in front of the curtain. The acting was really superb – the Bancrofts, Miss Foote, Hare, Coglan, surpassed themselves; not a mistake made by anybody'. But later the same evening he added doubtfully: 'The play was over at a quarter past eleven sharp. It remains to be seen whether I can fill the theatre with a new audience'[35]. He need not have worried. It turned out to be the hit of the season, running for twenty-three weeks. The Prince of Wales saw it twice; the Princess of Wales three times in just over a week; Wilkie spoke of hundreds being 'turned away for want of room'.

It was not his only theatrical triumph that year. *The New Magdalen*, already in rehearsal, was to attract similar public acclaim only three months later. But before he could enjoy it, he received one of the sharpest blows of his life. After years of struggle against cancer his brother, Charles, suddenly collapsed on Saturday, April 5th. He was tormented with increasing pain for the next few days until on the evening of the following Wednesday, he sank into unconsciousness. 'He fell into a sort of sleep on the morning of the day on which he died'[36]. Kate quickly sent for Wilkie. He was planning to dine at home with Wybert Reeve and take him to his private box to see *Man and Wife* that evening. When Reeve arrived he found Wilkie in extremely low spirits and preparing to hurry round to

Thurloe Place. He quickly arranged for 'a friend staying in the house' (presumably Caroline or Harriet) to accompany Reeve to the theatre, promising to meet them for supper after the play.

'When I got back,' Reeve later explained, 'his brother was dead and he had just returned, terribly broken down. The death seemed to have made a strong impression on him and led him to speak of a future state of existence, in which he had little belief. He was a Materialist, and urged that death meant a sleep of eternity; it was the natural end of all living things'. Wilkie called off an engagement with Squire Bancroft at the theatre next day and went down to Ramsgate to recover as best he could, before the funeral the following Monday[37].

Within a space of five years Wilkie had lost three people who, apart from his womenfolk, had been closest to his heart: his mother, Charles Dickens and his brother. The bond between the two brothers had always been close. They were utterly different in outlook, in appearance and in ability. Charles had inherited the striking good looks of his father as well as his religious eccentricities and, for a time, he seemed destined to follow his artistic footsteps. Wilkie had put up with his father's foibles, ignored his wishes and deliberately struck out on his own in another direction. But Charles's frustrations and Wilkie's growing success had never kept them apart. They had different interests, different friends and, not to put too fine a point on it, different morals. Their regard, even friendship for each other, however, remained firm to the end.

Throughout Charles's most difficult religious outbreaks Wilkie had protected him from the ridicule of his friends and the folly of his own actions. And Charles, in his turn, had instinctively known when Wilkie was driving himself too hard for his far from healthy body. Charles must have been disappointed, even shocked, at Wilkie's behaviour and the freedom with which he conducted parts of his private life. He knew more than most and at the crucial turning points in Wilkie's life was inevitably the first to be consulted. There is no evidence that he showed his disapproval publicly, though his private views were another matter. Kate, his wife, later spoke of Wilkie being 'as bad as he could be'. It was probably a view shared by Charles. If so, he remained steadfast to the end as an admirer of his brother's success. Wilkie, for his part, was eventually forced to choose between Charles Dickens and his brother. He never hesitated and supported his ailing brother, though it meant a growing estrangement from one of his oldest and dearest friends.

Wilkie was soon able to lose himself in the rehearsals for *The New Magdalen* at the Olympic Theatre, where Ada Cavendish was to play the leading role. A week after the funeral he spoke of other difficulties to John Millais. 'I have had some other trouble trying me since we met, but I stick to my rehearsals through it all'[38]. After his exertions earlier in the year and the shock of Charles's death, it was an exhausting period. 'Every day', he grumbled to his publisher, 'I have been occupied by the rehearsals of the dramatic *New Magdalen* – and when I got home again, there were the proofs of the reprint in two volumes waiting for me. After the double labour, I was fit for nothing but to go to bed'[39].

It was all worthwhile, however, for he soon had another theatrical success on his hands. The first night[40] reception was 'prodigious', Wilkie told a friend. 'The audience actually forced me to appear in front of the curtains before the play was half finished! I don't think I ever saw such enthusiasm in a theatre before'[41]. 'The acting took everyone by surprise' he enthused to another theatrical friend, 'and the second night's enthusiasm quite equalled the first . . . We have really hit the mark. Ferrari translates it for Italy, Regnier has two theatres ready for me in Paris and Lambe of Vienna has accepted it for his theatre'. It was also quickly destined for Berlin, The Hague and Moscow. For Ada Cavendish, who was to go on to other successes in Wilkie's plays, *The New Magdalen* proved to be her first money-making success[42].

It was a triumph that made up for all the pressure he had suffered in the early part of the year and ensured that he had two successes running simultaneously in the West End. It also meant that he was at last free to plan the full details of a lecture tour in the United States, which he had accepted in principle earlier in the year, before the death of his brother. It would give him the chance to earn substantial sums, he thought, just as Dickens had done at the height of his popularity. It would enable him to be present at the production of two of his plays on Broadway. And it would give him time to take stock of his complex private life. As we shall see, the extended break simply served to confirm him in the arrangements he had slowly worked out between Caroline and Martha.

CHAPTER TWELVE

America

THE RETURN of Caroline and the death of Charles were major turning points in Wilkie's life. He had borne them respectively with tolerance and fortitude and he now needed time to reassess the many complexities surrounding him. The possibility of a trip to the United States at last gave him the opportunity to get away.

He had looked forward to visiting the United States for some time. Although he had suffered from American pirating of his books and plays, his relations with his American publishers, Harper's, were remarkably cordial, and a lecture tour, in the style of Charles Dickens, had a compelling appeal.

By the spring of 1873, not long after the triumphant first night of *Man and Wife*, Wilkie was ready to accept the challenge and wrote accordingly to Harper's. By March 8th, *Harper's Weekly* was proudly announcing his decision to its American readers:

> 'Mr Collins has long cherished the intention of visiting this country, partly for the purpose of making an extended lecturing tour, and partly for the purpose of collecting materials for a new story, illustrative of life on the Western frontier. Ill health has prevented the accomplishment of this plan; but our readers will be glad to learn that rest and travel have so far restored his strength that he hopes to make the journey during the present year.'

Within the week, Wilkie was telling his London publisher of his intention to go to the States in the autumn[1] and writing with even more determination to his actor friend, Wybert Reeve. 'It would be very pleasant, and I should like it if we could go together.' Plans were made accordingly. Once Wilkie had successfully launched *The New Magdalen* on the London stage, he turned his attention to his proposed reading tour and how best to prepare for it. He finally decided to undertake a preliminary

series of readings in London and on Saturday, June 28th, he appeared at
the Olympic Theatre in the role of a solo performer reading his own story
The Terribly Strange Bed.

Reports of his performance varied considerably, as they were to do
again later in New York. Percy Fitzgerald, for a time a fellow contributor to
Household Words, dubbed Wilkie's performance 'singularly inefficient' and
went round to John Forster, who was clearly itching to hear the worst,
with chapter and verse. 'He had little or no voice, and scarcely attempted
to raise it. He seemed to think that the word "bedstead" was full of
meaning and we heard again this "bedstead" repeated till it became almost
comic. It seemed like an elderly gentleman of his club "boring" his neighbour with a long story of something "he had seen in the papers". He was
destitute of every qualification for his task'[2]. The *Pall Mall Gazette* thought
the same and hinted at a 'fiasco'.

The *Illustrated Review*, however, quickly came to Wilkie's defence. 'The
novelist was . . . cordially welcomed, was attentively (at times breathles-
sly) listened to throughout, was rewarded every now and then with
sudden bursts of laughter, and at the end with distinct rounds of applause
of the heartiest possible description . . . Wilkie Collins may cross the
Atlantic heartened on his way to his Reading Tour in the United States by
the recollection of the earnest applause accorded to him by a keenly
critical gathering of his own fellow countrymen'[3]. Wilkie took the rough
with the smooth, mentally inserted a necessary preface to his readings –
emphasising his lack of dramatic gifts and his intention to share a story
with friends – and went on with his plans for an autumn crossing.

Thoughts of the hazards of the Atlantic quickly concentrated his
thoughts on Caroline and Martha and their dependents. By the middle of
July he was reminding his solicitor that he needed to execute a new will
and to insure Martha's furniture in Marylebone Road. He eventually
signed the new will two days before departure and, for the first time, came
to the conclusion that Caroline and Harriet should get half of what he left
behind for their lifetime and that Martha and 'my two children' (his first
acknowledgement of parentage in print) should get the other half, and
should eventually inherit Caroline and Harriet's share. He left a final,
personal plea to William Tindall, his solicitor. 'I know you will give
personal as well as professional advice to those whom I leave to the care of
old friends like you – if they need it. Help them here [at Gloucester Place]
and at Marylebone Road, when they need help'[4]. Caroline and Martha
were inextricably linked together for the first time. There would be many
other occasions in the future.

Up to a few weeks before departure, Wybert Reeve was determined to accompany him, but within a week or so of departure had to cry off and Wilkie caught the *Algeria* from Liverpool on September 13th without him. Although Reeve caught up with him in New York, Wilkie had arranged for Francis Ward, Charles Ward's son and Wilkie's godson, to act as his secretary for part of the trip.

Wilkie was going to America with a touching faith in the Southern States, a high regard for some of its writers (fostered by the writings of Dana, Melville and Fenimore Cooper) and an open mind about the American people. He was not disappointed. He was soon noting their idiosyncracies, making new, and occasionally lasting, friends, basking in their quick hospitality and benefitting from their drier climate.

He arrived in New York on September 25th, and quickly settled in to a suite of rooms at the Westminster Hotel in Irving Place on East 16th Street. It was close to all the main theatres and had the advantage of having a separate restaurant where ladies could be entertained. Wilkie occupied the same suite Charles Dickens had used on his last visit, consisting of a sitting room, bedroom and bathroom, on the second floor, overlooking Irving Place. It was a warm-looking sitting room, upholstered in red satin, with an open grate and a handsome marble mantelpiece supporting some fine bronze ornaments. A combined sideboard and bookcase, with a series of books in paper covers, stood between the mantel and the window. The desk Dickens had used stood in front of the window and as soon as Wilkie realised who had used it, he was visibly overcome.

He kept himself to himself for a few days, plainly surprising the proprietor with his modest habits. 'Mr Collins is a queer sort of fellow. He takes most of his meals in his room, but I have seen him in the public restaurant a few times. He always wishes the servant to leave a plate of roast beef, so that he can take a snack of it when he comes in from his walk'[5].

Wilkie was clearly taking in all the local sights on foot. He hardly rivalled Dickens who managed to walk seven to ten miles a day when in the United States[6]. But he was determined to be more mobile than his new American friends. 'Nothing struck me so much,' he later declared, 'as the reluctance of the Americans to take walking exercise. I was a pretty good pedestrian in those days and thought nothing of a daily constitutional from my hotel in Union Square to Central Park and back. Half a dozen times on my way, friends in carriages would stop and beg me to jump in. I always declined, and I really believe that they regarded me as a piece of English eccentricity'[7].

Wilkie was hardly bereft of friends during these early days in New York.

His difficulty was that he was something of a celebrity, and though not on the Dickens scale, was certainly a household name. He had to find an agreeable compromise between the enthusiasm of the public and the warmth of his friends. His old friend Charles Fechter had been the first face he had seen at the dockside on arrival and they dined together at the hotel that evening, giving Wilkie an introduction to his first American dinner.

'You will find friends here wherever you go,' Fechter told Wilkie as he left the hotel. 'Don't forget that I was the friend who introduced you to soft shell crab'[8]. Wilkie found no difficulty in testing other new delicacies, even the habit in some American hotels of having several separate dishes set out at once. But the sweet champagne played havoc with his gout. And by the time his publishers, Harper's, had him round to dinner at their house on 22nd Street, Wilkie had the foresight to add a plea for extra dry champagne to his formal acceptance. 'I recall the difficulty we had to find the wine he required,' Henry Harper confessed afterwards[9].

In spite of the warmth of his reception in New York, Wilkie still had nagging doubts about his womenfolk at home. Martha in particular worried him. And a few weeks after his arrival in New York he was writing to his solicitor asking him 'to advise and help Martha, if she should want it'[10], in negotiating a new arrangement with her landlord at 55 Marylebone Road. And he added, in case his solicitor might conceivably forget his occasional pseudonym, 'You remember the name at 55? Mr and Mrs Dawson?'

Eight weeks later, from Boston, he again had occasion to seek help in relation to Martha's landlord who had offered Wilkie the lease and been refused. 'If by any chance,' he wrote to Tindall, 'he should let the house before I get back, Martha has by agreement a right to a quarter's notice to quit. If she is at all bothered I have told her to apply to you – but I do not anticipate this – as the landlord is a very respectable man'. And once more, the anxious reminder, 'You remember our name – Mr and Mrs Dawson'.

Wilkie was plainly overwhelmed by the hospitality he met on all sides. In New York, and later in Boston, he was wined and dined as a celebrity. He had begun with an official dinner at the Lotos Club[11], arranged by Whitelaw Reid, the American Ambassador in London, where Wilkie reminisced about his boyhood visit to Naples and Sorrento and his first introduction to American literature – and kindness – through a visiting American. Later he was the guest of the Union Club for breakfast and of the Arcadian Club for an evening reception and attended the annual dinner of the Mercantile Literary Association.

Within the first week, however, Wilkie found the personal invitations so great and the demands for 'readings' so numerous that Fechter had to rescue him. As the *Daily Graphic* put it, 'the only way he could escape from the manifold temptations of New York hospitality was to run away with Fechter, to his farm down in Pennsylvania. He intends to read up to New York from the country, as they read Hebrew, backwards'[12]. And this is exactly what he proceeded to do, starting his first reading in Albany and going on to Troy, Syracuse and Philadelphia before returning, briefly, to New York. A week later, at the end of October, he did a further reading in Boston.

As in his preliminary reading in London, he concentrated on a short story, this time *The Dream Woman*. And, as in London, the reception was mixed. The first reading in Albany was well received[13]. But the *Press* in Philadelphia found his voice too low and monotonous and there were serious doubts about the fitness of the subject. 'It was not pleasant to hear a famous Englishman describing before several hundred pure girls, how one wretched, fallen woman, after mysteriously killing her man, had captivated two more, and stabbed another to death in a drunken frenzy'[14]. On the other hand, the *Public Ledger*[15] said Wilkie delivered his 'parlour reading' before 'appreciative friends' and enlisted the 'full attention of the large audience', the plot 'being full of weird interest and ingeniously unravelled'.

By the time he got to Boston he was in need of some relaxation and friends of Dickens and the Lehmanns provided helpful protection. He managed to avoid a number of public dinners and was able to enjoy a night at the opera with James Fields, an old friend of Dickens, as well as several private dinner parties at the home of Sebastian Schlesinger, an old friend and business colleague of Fred Lehmann[16].

He appears to have relaxed considerably during his stay in Boston. The bustle and brittleness of New York were absent and the literary associations more agreeable. He might have had a different reaction, however, had he known what Dickens's friends, the Fields, were busy writing about him. Georgina, Dickens's sister-in-law, who had kept up a regular correspondence with Annie Fields since their visit to London, had hardly helped. When she first heard of a possible American visit a couple of years earlier she had quickly written to Annie Fields questioning Wilkie's reading abilities. 'I cannot imagine that he is fitted for the work in any way, nor can I conceive how his books could bear being cut up into portions for reading.' But she added that he was 'very agreeable and easy to get on with'[17]. The favourable report did not last, however, and within a few weeks of his departure for New York, Georgina was again stressing his unsuitability for the task ahead, and adding, more sourly, 'he has an unusual amount of conceit and self-satisfaction and I do not think anyone can think Wilkie Collins a greater man than Wilkie Collins thinks himself'[18].

Whatever the influence, both James and Annie Fields soon began to share some of the antipathy, at least privately. They looked after Wilkie well enough and he plainly thought himself among close friends. But James Fields had written to Longfellow before his visit, intimating his hope that Wilkie would not come to America ('he must be a strange fellow')[19]. And during his stay in Boston Annie confided to her diary her personal views of Wilkie. They were hardly flattering. Written up four days after his visit, her diary[20] describes Wilkie as 'a small man with an odd figure and forehead and shoulders much too large for the rest of him'. It goes on: 'His talk was rapid and pleasant, but not at all inspiring. He appears to be quick at adapting plays for the stage, a kind of superior Bouciacault. A man who has been much fêted and petted in London society who has overeaten and overdrunk, has been ill, is gouty and in short is no very wonderful specimen of a human being'.

Fortunately, Wilkie remained oblivious to it all and the reception to his readings in Boston was both warm and encouraging. The Music Hall contained the largest audience of the season, and was 'crowded to every part'. Once again he entreated his listeners to assume that he was reading a story among friends. The *Boston Transcript*[21] said he 'gave evidence of great power in facial expression and a good command over his voice'. The story, it thought, was 'one of thrilling interest' and was greeted 'by generous applause'. The *Boston Advertiser*[22] reported that his grey eyes were 'full of expression while reading' and his gestures 'free and animated'. His pleasant voice was 'neither full nor penetrating', but was 'well modulated and of excellent expressive power'.

The combination of outwardly warm friendship and an understanding reception to his readings left Wilkie with pleasant memories of Boston, and in later life he favourably compared it with Washington. 'May I confess it with all humility, in a whisper?' he told an American friend. 'I greatly preferred Boston. The prodigious streets and avenues at Washington depressed me indescribably and I never could get over the idea that the enormous cupola of the Capital was slowly squeezing the weak and attenuated building underneath, into the earth from which it had feebly risen'[23].

Throughout these initial journeys he had to put up with the constant demands of the press, which he found quite different from any he had experienced in London. Journalists pursued him everywhere. 'One day,' he reminisced later, 'I went to make a call at a quiet house, not at all a house where publicity is courted, and had hardly sat down when the door opened and in came a lady, little black dog in one hand and her card in the other. Could she have a few minutes' conversation; she was the representative of some paper or other, I forget which. It was too bad; I turned to my hostess to apologise for the impertinence, thinking she would resent it as I did, and she was actually laughing! And she implored me not to disappoint the poor, hungry lady. Remember, it is her daily bread, she murmured in my ear'.

After that he made a determined effort to get interviewers to turn up in groups. But this hardly solved his problem. Returning to the hotel one day, he found twelve female journalists awaiting him, sitting in a circle. 'They seemed to have formed a sort of alliance, for no sooner had I made my bow than the oldest and ugliest of them stood forth and, solemnly observing, "Let me embrace you for the company", offered me a chaste salute. However much I might have appreciated that same from a youthful beauty, I did not exactly court a repetition of it thus bestowed, and next day there were very moderate praises of my personal charms in consequence. I suppose I did look grim, for I felt it. Really they were not attractive. . . .'[24]

In spite of such pressures, he was enjoying the acclaim from friends and public alike. The Americans, he concluded, were 'the most enthusiastic, the most cordial and the most sincere people I have ever met with in my life. When an American says "come and see me" he *means* it. This is wonderful to an Englishman'[25]. 'A kinder, warmer-hearted set of people surely does not exist, only their ways *are* queer. . . .'[26] He was soon telling Fred Lehmann just how queer they were. 'Before I had been a week in the country I noted three national peculiarities which had never been mentioned to me by visitors to the States. (1) No American hums or whistles a tune either at home or in the street (2) Not one American in 500 has a dog (3) Not one American in 1,000 carries a walking stick. I who hum perpetually, who love dogs, who cannot live without a walking stick, am greatly distressed at finding my dear Americans deficient in the three social virtues just enumerated'[27].

It was soon time for Wilkie to leave his new-found friends in Boston and prepare himself for his major challenges back in New York – his first readings in the metropolis and the production of two of his plays on Broadway. His provincial reading tours had helped him to get a feel of an American audience and he decided to stick to his well rehearsed formula – a relaxed reading of one of his stories among friends. This also enabled him to devote some of his spare time to the rehearsals of his first play, *The New Magdalen*, in which the leading actress, Carlotta Leclerq, was to feature for the first time.

Both events followed each other in quick succession, the first night of *The New Magdalen* at Daly's Broadway Theatre on November 10th and his first New York reading of *The Dream Woman* at Association Hall on November 11th. Wilkie had every reason to feel satisfied with his reception. By the end of the fourth act of *The New Magdalen*, the audience was plainly impressed, and in answer to numerous calls of 'Collins, Collins', Wilkie was forced to take the full acclaim from his box[28]. He bowed his acknowledgements and sat down, but it was not enough. Again summoned, he was forced on to the stage, leading Carlotta Leclerq, to whom, with a graceful gesture, he tried to direct the applause. But the audience would not let go. Emerging for a third time, he made a simple acknowledgement:

'Ladies and Gentlemen. I venture respectfully to think that you have heard enough speeches of mine already. You have other speeches of mine to hear, in still another act. Permit me to make the briefest speech of all – I respectfully and cordially thank you'.[29]

The next evening he had more to say – from a reading desk on the platform of the Association Hall. He walked on stage around eight o'clock, to a large audience. Mingled with literary people, according to the *New York Times*[30], were 'a large number of young ladies who watched the reader with that steadfast fixity of gaze which only ladies can fasten on a gentleman of literary eminence, whose writings are to them like household words'. The rest of the audience was appreciative too. The *New York Times* said it never flagged in its attention and, towards the close of the reading, 'hung in breathless silence on the reader's words'. It found him a very practical speaker with excellent qualities and an ample fund of quiet humour. The paper reported hearty applause and said that Wilkie was 'twice recalled to the platform'.

The reports in the *New York Daily Tribune*[31] were equally favourable, remarking how well Collins read 'with perfect appreciation, with great clearness and distinction' and an adequate degree of dramatic expression. 'Interest was sustained until the close.' The *World* also approved, describing him as 'quiet and effective', and concluding: 'those present enjoyed an entertainment which they would not readily have missed'[32].

Only the *New York Herald*[33] hit a sour note. Though it regarded Wilkie as a clever reader, it did not like *The Dream Woman* ('a mixture of voluptuousness, cruelty and horror'), thought it a mistake for him to disclaim all intention of acting ('reading among friends', it felt, sat uneasily alongside his commercial intentions) and reported that some of the audience went to sleep and some left the hall. The trouble was that the *Herald* had fallen into a trap of its own construction two months earlier, when in a fit of misplaced enthusiasm, it had announced Wilkie as 'a reader of extraordinary dramatic power and fervour'[34]. As Wilkie began every reading in the United States with a disclaimer of any such attributes, one can feel a little sympathy for the literary editor of the paper.

Wilkie himself was evidently pleased with the receptions. As he told Fred Lehmann[35], he had succeeded basically by surprising his audiences. 'The story surprises them in the first place, being something the like of which they have not heard before. And my way of reading surprises them in the second place, because I don't flourish a paper knife and stamp about the platform, and thump the reading desk. I persist in keeping myself in the background and the story in front. The audience begins at each reading with silent astonishment and ends with a great burst of applause'.

He was also pleased with the ease he could make money from such readings, particularly at a time when Wall Street was going through one of its periodic panics[36], country banks were closing their doors and there was a flurry in the gold market. 'While others have suffered badly, I have always drawn audiences.' He was getting between £70 and £80 a night even outside the big cities and, if he 'read' five times in a week, could earn up to £350 weekly. But his health would not let him, and before long, in spite of the enthusiasm of a new manager, who was clearly determined to arrange a programme of readings stretching out as far as Salt Lake City, if not further, he was cutting down not only on his readings but on his travelling plans as well.

While the cold dry climate suited him admirably, he realised the limits of his endurance. Over the next few weeks he was busy enough, squeezing in visits to Baltimore and Washington, with the usual 'readings', between the two first nights of his play in New York. By early December he was closely involved in the rehearsals for the introduction of *The Woman in White* to the Broadway Theatre, and was relaxed enough to allow Wybert Reeve, who had now taken on the main part of Count Fosco, a reasonably free hand with the script. As Reeve later recalled, 'he willingly gave me permission to re-write and alter some part of the drama of *The Woman in White* – alterations which certainly appeared to greatly increase its effect on the public and its strength as a drama'[37].

Having successfully launched two of his plays on Broadway, Wilkie immediately turned his attention to his Canadian friends and arrived in Toronto in time for Christmas and his first reading on Boxing Day. He had already been introduced to the snowy delights of Montreal – a drive in a sledge – and to the advantages of such a dry climate. He had also had to put up with the hazards of icy streets and 'horrid stenches' in the hotel. But in Toronto he was among friends, especially his publishers, Rose and Hunter, who provided him and his godson, Francis Ward, with a delightful Christmas dinner. Then, with some trepidation, he was off to Niagara ('The lake here makes me feel rheumatic,' he complained, 'what will the waterfall do?'), and Buffalo (where he secured the Russian Grand Duke's bedroom at the hotel, a box at the theatre and the freedom of the club), and eventually began to move west along Lake Erie towards Chicago.

The travelling was a shattering experience to him. First came fifteen hours of agony to Toronto, made bearably acceptable by 'a compartment to ourselves, a faithful and attentive nigger to wait on us, dry champagne and a cold turkey'[38]. Then he faced the longer haul westwards, and his first experience of the latest sleeping car, in which he lay wide awake all night. 'Nothing will induce me,' he declared on arrival in Chicago, 'to repeat the experiment. I feel the "sleeping car" in the small of my back and on the drums of my ears'[39].

At the Sherman House Hotel, on the corner of Clark and Randolph Streets, he startled the landlord by his state of exhaustion. As Wilkie later explained, ' "What can I do for you?" that worthy man asked. I answered, "Let me have a bottle of the driest champagne you have got in your cellar – and then let me go to bed" '[40]. He went on: 'I drank the whole of it and informed him that though it was only noon, I was going at once to bed and that all visitors were to be told that I might possibly not get up for a week. I heard afterwards that after twenty-four hours some callers were allowed to come up and peep in at the door, which I had not locked, but all they saw was "Mr Collins still fast asleep" '[41].

His original plans to go farther west, to the Yosemite Valley and the Pacific, and to see his cousins, the Grays[42], in San Francisco, were quickly shelved. He was not up to it and he began to worry how he was to get back to Boston without utter exhaustion. Chicago in any case was hardly to his taste. He had no literary or publishing friends there, and the city he was seeing and experiencing was no ordinary city. It was still preoccupied with carving out a future for itself in an alien climate. Its frontier spirit was being tested for the second time in a generation.

Only two years before, all its earlier pioneering efforts had been wiped out in a night, as fire swept through its streets, fuelled by the gusts of wind from the lakes and as the explosion of the tar-works, the gas works and the armoury turned it into a fire storm that was ultimately quenched only by a combination of rain and exhaustion[43]. Whatever the cause – Mrs O'Leary's cow kicking over a lantern or, more likely, an explosive mixture of kerosene and petrol – the devastation had been catastrophic, with 18,000 buildings destroyed, 100,000 left homeless, 300 dead and property damage alone totalling over $200 million.

In the blaze had gone the Academy of Design, full of paintings for a forthcoming exhibition, and the Chicago Historical Society with Lincoln's own copy of the Emancipation Proclamation; so too had local interest in artistic, literary and cultural endeavours. Local citizens had other things on their mind and were mentally rebuilding their city as they cleared the rubble for survivors.

By the time Wilkie arrived, the rebuilding of Chicago was close to completion, but local talk was still of little else. He found it hard to take and was disturbingly out of tune with all he heard and saw. His prejudices were amply confirmed by an anniversary review of the Great Fire carried by the *Chicago Daily Tribune*[44], but originally published in London by the *London Saturday Review*. The paper was on his breakfast table the morning after his first reading.

'The peculiar state or temper of the human mind,' the *Tribune* reported from its London contemporary, 'in which material growth and extension are its only objects, and all its forces are concentrated with the utmost intensity on these, has never been so perfectly developed as in the United States; and if we were asked what city in that country showed that temper in its most energetic form, we might possibly think of Boston or New York, but should certainly relinquish them from Chicago. Just as the United States are the newest of great nations, so Chicago is the newest of great cities; and as the States look forward to an almost indefinite increase of wealth and population in the future, so Chicago expects in its own mind to become the BIGGEST AND RICHEST CITY ON EARTH'.

The *Saturday Review* had not left its patronising views in much doubt. 'We do not doubt that in a generation or two Chicago will become as cultivated as Manchester, ie there will be a cultivated group (plus library, museum and art gallery), but the bulk of the community will resist culture as it does in Manchester.'

Perhaps that explained why the auditorium of the newly built Music Hall in Chicago was only half full for Wilkie's first reading. The defective heating system, in the middle of a Mid-west winter, hardly helped. But the audience, full of local celebrities, gave him a warm reception. Wilkie paused in his walk to the platform to bow in acknowledgement. His quick, tiptoeing walk ('mincing' according to one observer) attracted attention, as did the depth and volume of his voice. Warned to expect a few defects in his delivery by east coast reports, the audience was happy to note that they had vanished.

In spite of the receptive mood of his listeners, however, Chicago clearly lacked the appeal of Boston and left Wilkie echoing the *London Saturday Review*. 'Don't tell anybody,' he wrote confidentially to his friends in the east[45], 'but the truth is I am not sorry to leave Chicago. The dull sameness of the great blocks of iron and brick overwhelm me. The whole city seems to be saying "see how rich I am after the fire and what a tremendous business I do!" and everybody I meet uses the same form of greeting. "Two years ago, Mr Collins, this place was a heap of ruins – are you not astonished when you see it now?" I am not a bit astonished. It is a mere question of raising money – the rebuilding follows as a matter of course'.

He slowly made his way back to Boston, for further readings in New England, breaking his journey in a fashion which astonished his friends but allowed him the sleep he needed. It took him several days to return to Boston with stops in Detroit and Rochester. Back among his friends, he was soon busy brushing up new material for his final readings, meeting new literary acquaintances and, as he soon admitted to himself, mentally preparing himself for his return to London.

He had taken earlier criticisms of his short story, *The Dream Woman*, seriously and, wanting to avoid offence where he had nothing to gain by obduracy, he began to prepare a shortened version of his play, *The Frozen Deep*, as his last contribution to his New England audiences. It was well received in Boston.

One person whom he clearly met, and had every reason to do so, was Augustin Daly, the American theatrical impresario, who had already produced an unauthorised version of *Man and Wife* on Broadway three years earlier. We now have clear evidence that they met because of the recent dramatic re-appearance of the manuscript of Wilkie's first unpublished novel, *Iolani*.

Until three years ago, the Polynesian manuscript seemed to have disappeared without trace. Then out of the blue, or rather from an office on East 44th Street in New York, came the dramatic news that the manuscript had at last come to light. Glen Horowitz, the well-known American book-dealer, announced that the manuscript was in his hands. Its full title, in Collins' own handwriting, was *Iolani; or, Tahiti as it was. A Romance*. The manuscript ran to 160 pages and had apparently emerged from the Fox family in Philadelphia. It had been in the family for most of this century, having been acquired at auction in 1903. The manuscript had in fact been auctioned originally in 1899, among the collection of Augustin Daly, following his death. The question, therefore, is how the manuscript got into Daly's hands. Glen Horowitz, who recently offered it for sale for $175,000 (compared with the $100 it changed hands for at the turn of the century), naturally believes that Collins gave it to Daly 'in gratitude' during his American visit. Just as likely it was loaned to him, in the hope of future publication, and never returned. No evidence either way has yet emerged, though the present true ownership of the manuscript clearly hangs on the distinction.

The rest of his stay in the United States was devoted to the usual round of dinners and banquets in Boston where he met (or re-met) Oliver Wendell Holmes, Mark Twain, Henry Longfellow and Josiah Quincy, and on a short visit to New York, to photographic sessions with Sarony and to a sad farewell dinner with Charles Fechter. They had met whenever they could, following Wilkie's first visit to Fechter's farm in Pennsylvania. Wilkie had quickly noticed a melancholy change in his old theatrical friend. 'Signs not to be mistaken,' Collins wrote later, 'told me that he was broody over his wasted opportunities and his doubtful future . . . When I left New York for the last time, he dined with me. The two or three other friends who were of the party remarked the depression of his spirits. We parted – not to meet again'.

It would be wrong to assert that melancholy had penetrated Collins too. But after his return from the mid-West, his mind increasingly turned to thoughts of home. His friends had kept in touch directly by letter or indirectly by contact with Caroline, again presiding in Gloucester Place. Before the end of February he was writing to his old friend Charles Ward from Boston, to thank him for his kindnesses to Caroline and to announce his return. 'I have decided on returning by the boat which leaves this port on the 7th of March. The times are bad. There is nothing very profitable to be done – and I want to be at home again'[46].

In turning his mind towards home and in particular to the hazards of the Atlantic lying before him once more, he decided to take out two separate policies with different insurance companies[47]. They were deliberately linked to his two daughters, Marian and Harriet. Both were for $5,000 or £1,000 each, 'in case I am drowned,' he told his solicitor. The premiums were for around $230 annually and were paid on his behalf from then on by Sebastian Schlesinger who put the policies in his office safe in Boston. Charles Ward, one of Wilkie's executors, was sent the original receipt. Wilkie later had trouble when one year he relied on a local Boston acquaintance to pay the premiums and was badly let down ('Was there ever such a doubly dyed and d . . . scoundrel???')[48]. But the premiums were maintained throughout Wilkie's life and, just before he died, he managed to introduce the girls to Schlesinger ('You will know why').

He sailed from Boston on March 7th on the Cunard liner *Parthia* and was given a friendly send-off. A party of friends went down to the harbour to say goodbye, one presenting him with a beautiful basket of flowers, and they were all invited to a farewell lunch on board by one of the Cunard officers[49].

He was returning with mixed feelings. He had been overwhelmed by hospitality and friendliness and he never forgot it. 'I leave America with feelings of sincere gratitude,' he wrote to an American friend when he was halfway across the Atlantic, 'and sincere respect. If all goes well with me my first visit to my kind friends in the United States shall not be my last'. He had made life-long friends and, on balance, he had had a welcome respite from gout. 'The climate suited me down to the ground,' he reminisced soon afterwards. 'I had heard so much about the dryness of the atmosphere and its effect upon English people, that I did not know what to expect. But I never was better in my life; I did not have an ache or a pain all the time. As for gout, it left me entirely for the time being, and you know how much I usually suffer from it. Oh, I shall certainly crack up America as *the* place for sufferers from rheumatic gout; and whatever else I can say in its favour I will'[50].

He had been stimulated as rarely before – perhaps never since his first visit to Italy as a boy. American acclaim, generosity and habits had also taken their toll and he later admitted that he felt himself 'torn in bits by the hospitality and loquacity which overwhelmed him at every turn'. It was, he said diplomatically, 'something to look back upon'. And he continued to do so, with pleasure, nostalgia and, eventually regret, when it became clear that ill-health would prevent a return to those shores.

He docked in Liverpool at 12.45 pm on Thursday, March 18th[51], and was in London a day later. He was soon enthralling his friends with his adventures first at a casual supper party with Mrs Walford[52], her cousin and their husbands, and a few days later at a dinner party at Gloucester Place with Frank Archer[53], the actor, his old friend, Henrietta Ward, and James Payne, the novelist and editor of *Chambers's Journal*. He had run into the Walfords while strolling in Hyde Park. They insisted on his joining them for dinner, if by a miracle he were disengaged for the following evening. He laughed outright. 'I haven't a single solitary engagement. I have only just come back from America, and have looked up nobody yet.'

That could hardly have applied to Martha who with the two girls was still in Marylebone Road and just around the corner from Gloucester Place. That he called round there rather early after his return was adequately confirmed nine months later with the birth of their third child, a son, William Charles, on Christmas Day.

CHAPTER THIRTEEN

Illness

HE RETURNED from the United States exhausted, exhilarated and probably fitter than he had been for years. The dry climate had suited him. He had had theatrical triumphs on Broadway, made money in the middle of a financial panic and had managed to pack what seemed to be a lifetime's acclaim from an unknown continent into a hectic few months.

Yet within months of his return, he was again suffering agonies from gout, an affliction that increased in intensity over the next decade and a half, and ultimately sapped his strength and undermined his writing ability. He had just turned fifty. He had, it has been widely assumed, reached his peak, as a writer and as a man. It was to be downhill from now on, with the occasional recovery in health and in writing, but essentially a decline into becoming something of a recluse.

It is a tempting scenario. Yet some of his happiest moments were still to come; not, it must be admitted, the heady pleasures and surprises of his youth, but the calmer, deeper rewards of a settled family life and the certainties of stable relationships among a few well chosen friends.

His was no ordinary family. Caroline and Martha had already slipped into their new, somewhat unorthodox, relationships. Caroline, once his mistress, was again running Gloucester Place, paying the bills, planning his meals, and, at forty, playing the attractive hostess to a well-known novelist. Harriet, her daughter, was still transcribing his writings, answering his correspondence and keeping in touch with his publishers, solicitors, bankers and financial advisers. She had become, in all but name, an attractive secretary in her early twenties.

Martha, only a few years older and still in her twenties, remained the most vulnerable of his womenfolk. She met his emotional needs in a way that the livelier, more vivacious and more unpredictable Caroline had always found difficult. Both mistress and mother of his children, Martha brought a calmness to his life he had always wanted but rarely attracted, and Wilkie's love of children was allowed full rein over the coming years. The austere bachelor household his friends saw was continually invaded with the screams and laughter of children, first his own and later Harriet's.

Martha, discreetly round the corner from Gloucester Place, had coped with the uncertainties of her rented accommodation in Marylebone Road during Wilkie's absence in America. But, as he feared, the decision to move had come nearer, and by the time of his return, she had already begun to look around for another house. How far Caroline and his solicitor were also pressed into Martha's service while Wilkie was away, is difficult to discern. But most of the decisions had clearly been made before he got back[1] and Martha and her two young girls moved into Taunton Place on or around Lady Day, 25th March, only a week after Wilkie's boat docked in Liverpool.

Wilkie's extended absence cannot have been pleasant for Martha. The return of her rival for Wilkie's affections to Gloucester Place, and the obvious re-opening of his purse-strings to Caroline, must have come as a shock to the unsophisticated Martha. It was bad enough to accept that Wilkie had no immediate intention of marrying her; how much more painful it was to know that the father of her children, after his regular visits, was returning to the company, if no longer the arms, of his former mistress. And even in his absence the pain was hardly assuaged.

On top of the anxiety of wondering whether her landlord would evict her (in spite of all Wilkie's undoubted assurances before departure for New York), there came the growing realisation that Caroline was to be an essential part of the new leasing arrangements. Then came the final humiliation: the writing of Caroline's own name on the new rate book in Martha's new lodgings in Taunton Place[2], and the knowledge that Caroline was paying the rates for the next three years. Not until 1877 did Martha's own name finally appear in the rate book. Even then, the local authority found it difficult to accept the truth, for she was recorded as 'Caroline Dawson' until she moved a year after Wilkie's death. A fitting commentary perhaps to a rather unusual relationship. And throughout it all, Martha remained 'Mrs Dawson' in the Post Office Street Directory, the respectable wife of a respectable, though often absent, barrister. At Wilkie's insistence the public niceties remained paramount.

On his return a new pattern was quickly established. Martha was sharing accommodation in Taunton Place, in an attractive row of cottages not far from Regents Park and within walking distance of Gloucester Place. It was a walk he was to know well over the next fifteen years as, in the guise of William Dawson, he 'joined' his family and shared their hopes and fears. As he put it to Fred Lehmann, 'work, walk, visit to my morganatic family, such is life'.

The cottage in Taunton Place was a house he was to regard as the source of much love and contentment; and it was there, in late April or early May, that Martha told him she was pregnant again. He could hardly have been surprised and, judging from his subsequent remarks about his family, was probably as delighted as any normal father. But it coincided with yet another bout of illness and his visits to Taunton Place – and elsewhere too – were soon curtailed. 'I have got the gout flying about me,' he confided to an old friend later that month, 'and keeping me nervous and unfit for work'[3].

He was hardly to throw the pangs of rheumatic gout off for very long for the rest of his life and the swiftness with which he changed from an active traveller in North America, in its dry climate, to an intermittent invalid in London plainly astonished him on his return. Rheumatism was virtually always with him except, as he reminded an American friend, when the weather was dry. 'And when is it dry for three days together in England? Never! In *your* country I felt five and twenty years old. In *my* country I (not infrequently) feel five and ninety'[4].

Whether illness, or the ease with which he had been able to make money in the United States, undermined his literary energy, his literary output was somewhat reduced over the next year or two. He had already arranged the publication of the North American story, *The Dead Alive*, in Boston during his stay there and, on his return, he polished up the narrative of *The Frozen Deep* for serialisation in *Temple Bar*. Both were to appear in book form, along with his 'reading', *The Dream Woman*, towards the end of 1874. Thereafter his energies were plunged into a series of cheap editions, under a new agreement with Andrew Chatto, and into dramatic versions of *Armadale* and *The Moonstone*. The upshot of his continual pressure to persuade a publisher to support his enthusiasm for sixpenny or shilling copies was that Chatto and Windus began to issue his existing novels at two shillings apiece (and even cheaper) and thereafter became his main publishers, acquiring all his previous copyrights.

Although he remained determined to get his worth in the market place, he was under no compelling financial pressures. His income continued at a highly satisfactory level throughout the early 1870s and was still running between £3,500 and £4,500 a year after his return from North America[5] and was to remain over £3,000 a year for the next few years. It was a propitious time for Martha to present him with their third child. The baby was due in the last week of December and as the time approached, he began to realise that his normal Christmas festivities were likely to be severely interrupted, whether in Gloucester Place or Taunton Place. It had not been his favourite season (more 'cant' than goodwill, he felt), but, with a four-year-old and a six-year-old to consider, his Christmases had inevitably become much more family affairs than in the past, when he and Caroline would slip out to their favourite restaurant with a few friends. On this occasion the interruption was complete, for the new baby made his appearance under Frank Beard's care, on Christmas Day itself.

Wilkie was delighted. He was soon writing to his solicitor telling him of his 'Christmas box in the shape of a big boy' and reminding him to add William Charles to his will so that he would have 'his share with the two girls'[6]. Neither of his daughters, Marian and Harriet, had had their births registered, but a change in the law evidently persuaded him to register his son in the normal way and he was subsequently registered as William Charles Collins Dawson, nicely commemorating his father and brother and their family name. But it was a decision he clearly brooded over, for the birth was not registered until the following February[7].

After completing the revision of *The Dream Woman* and *The Frozen Deep* after his return, he began to prepare a further novel, *The Law and the Lady*. It was, in effect, another legal mystery, stressing the unfortunate impact of Scottish law on a second marriage, and began to appear in serial form in early 1875 and was quickly followed by a three-volume hardback edition. *The Saturday Review* reluctantly acknowledged Collins's story-telling skill ('he can tie knots that are almost as ingenious as the knot of Gorius, and can form a puzzle that would be no discredit to a Chinaman'), but wondered whether it was all worthwhile. 'The secret fills three whole volumes. We doubt, however, if it altogether repays the trouble of getting at it.' Yet sales were better than the reviews indicated. Collins still knew his reading public.

So it was the following year, with *The Two Destinies* in which Collins explored the mysteries of telepathy and the supernatural. Once again the *Saturday Review* took him to task. 'This is an amazingly silly book,' it told its readers. 'Indeed it is almost silly enough to be amusing through its very absurdity. It records, if we have counted rightly, three attempts at suicide, two plots to murder, one case of bigamy, two bankruptcies, one sanguinary attack by Indians, three visions, numberless dreams, and one shipwreck'. Once again, however, sales were not unduly disappointing.

Though still troubled by illness, this was plainly a stimulating time for Collins. As an author his name was still on everyone's lips, his books were selling well (whatever the critics were inclined to say), his income remained remarkably high and he seemed to have a succession of plays on in the West End.

After the revival of *The Magdalen*, came a particularly successful revival of

Miss Gwilt (the dramatic version of *Armadale*), with Ada Cavendish and Sir Arthur Pinero, then at the beginning of his career, and a revival of *No Thoroughfare*. Yet his dramatic luck was about to run out, for the reception of *The Moonstone*, as a play, was very different from its original impact as a novel.

He had a natural difficulty in adapting the complexities of the plot for the simpler needs of the stage and, with hindsight, plainly overdid the simplicity. He cut down the action to twenty-four hours, confined it to 'the inner hall of Miss Verinder's country-house', and then combined this with a few daring innovations insisting that the first act should end without the fall of the curtain, 'low music from the orchestra' marking the lapse of time 'until the action of the piece renewed'[8]. He had persuaded Neville, the manager, to allow him some say in the choice of the cast and was delighted that Laura Seymour had agreed to take the part of Miss Clack. Although he was still making major changes to the text a matter of weeks before the play opened at the Olympic, sending them round with Caroline to Laura Seymour, he remained optimistic throughout the rehearsals. 'The complete performance', he assured her, would be 'really remarkable'.

It was not to be; the public thought otherwise and the play lasted only nine weeks. It was a particularly sad occasion for Laura Seymour for, within weeks of the close of the play, she was taken ill with cancer of the liver and never managed to go on the stage again. She died two years later.

The second half of the 1870s marked Collins's final burst of foreign travel. Although he continually hoped to go back to North America (almost promising to do so in 1877), he eventually reconciled himself to the notion that perhaps he would be wise to confine himself to the Continent, which was still strenuous enough for such a recurrent invalid. France inevitably called and within six months of his return from Boston, he was relaxing for a week in Boulogne. Another six months and he was off to France again, through Paris and as far as Marseilles and Nice, in the company of William Frith, the artist, and his two daughters and one or two other friends.

Collins's continental visits were invariably prompted by his need for a fresh stimulus and a periodic escape from the rigours of London's unpredictable climate. Six months after his return from Nice, he was again feeling the damp of his native shores in his back and shoulders (partly brought on by an extended sailing holiday off the East Coast) and was looking for a quiet spot to begin his latest serialisation. By the early October of 1875 he had decided 'to pay in a stock of health for the coming winter', first in Brussels, later in Berlin and Dresden. A year later he was off again, this time to France and Switzerland.

It may seem odd that neither Caroline nor Martha accompanied him on these intermittent trips. Martha's absence was understandable. The social gap was perhaps too wide and she had three small children to look after. Caroline was another matter. Both she and Harriet had accompanied him in the past, but on each occasion had suffered agonies from sea-sickness. His short continental visits, they probably decided, were not worth the suffering. In any case there were plainly occasions when Caroline's presence might not have been appropriate.

His planned visit to Venice towards the end of 1877 was in a different category. He intended to gather material leisurely for his next novel and was to be away long enough to make any suffering Caroline might face in crossing the Channel reasonably worthwhile. A two or three month visit to Italy meant that she would have time to readjust after the strains of the journey and, in the leisurely pursuits he contemplated, provide him with the help and company he needed.

Once he had launched *The Moonstone* at the Olympic in mid-September, he and Caroline began to make preparations for an early departure. In Caroline's absence from Gloucester Place, Harriet, who was now twenty-six, was put in charge not only of Wilkie's literary affairs but also the domestic needs of the household. Her grandmother had died earlier that year and by now Harriet herself was already undertaking all Wilkie's secretarial chores, and had taken over some of the regular household payments, using Wilkie's bank account for the purpose. Before they departed Wilkie also made sure that Martha had her weekly allowance raised from £5 to £10 a week[9] and made arrangements for other items to be debited to his account on her behalf. Then he took £200 for travelling expenses and they were off.

Following the modern route of the Grand Tour, Wilkie and Caroline went via Brussels through Southern Germany into the Tyrol and down to Venice where, no doubt, they followed Wilkie's earlier habits, staying at the Danieli (as Wilkie and Charles Dickens had done), breakfasting at Florian's and lunching at Quadri's, Caroline enjoying the rich flavour of a city that would readily accept her, whatever her role, and Wilkie finding once more the sadness, the bizarre and other essential ingredients for his next novel. Whether the Danieli was the inspiration for *The Haunted Hotel*, which began to appear in serial form in *Belgravia* the following summer, Wilkie never divulged, but it crept into the pages of the novel and fitted the plot admirably.

A former Palazzo built by Doge Andrea Dandolo, with the ceiling of one of the principal guest-rooms attributed to Veronese, the Danieli had been transformed into a modern hotel with all the latest services, just as the 'Palace Hotel Company of Venice (Limited)' proceeded to do with its own palazzo in the novel. Wilkie even contrived to link Caroline's name with Florian's in one episode, where Maraschino punch was introduced to the startled waiter by Countess Narona. 'The wonderful city of the waters,' as he called Venice, enchanted them both and the warmer weather began to restore his vitality in the way he had hoped.

Harriet was soon receiving favourable reports of them, passing them on to his literary friends at home and abroad, adding her own asides about her 'godfather', and signing the occasional letter as 'Harriette E.L. Graves', a perhaps understandable embellishment that Caroline would have approved of.

Wilkie at least felt the need to return to London for Christmas – his young son's birthday – and to be close to Martha and her family. They returned at a leisurely pace through Paris and he resisted the temptation to join his friends Nina and Fred Lehmann at their villa in Cannes. He had a book to write too.

Though he didn't realise it at the time, he had just completed his last trip to the continent; and so had Caroline. His escape from the early pangs of an English winter had put him back on his feet, but only temporarily. The relentless return of his old enemy, rheumatic gout, was not long delayed and, coupled with his other growing disabilities in the heart, stomach and even kidneys, and the continuing need for the soothing balm of laudanum, continental trips soon began to lose their attractions. From now on his holidays increasingly revolved around his sailing, basically from Ramsgate, and the family gatherings which accompanied him.

There may have been another reason for curtailing his continental trips. Martha can hardly have been unmoved at the thought of Caroline and Wilkie moving at leisure through Europe's finest tourist spots while she was confined to Taunton Place. Her own lot, admittedly, had been a reasonably comfortable one. She had a happy family and had re-established the strained relations with her own family in Winterton. But the father of her children was inevitably an absent one and she may have delicately reminded him that there was little to be gained from extending such absences even further in the company of Caroline. Ramsgate offered a compromise for them all.

His reception in Taunton Place, with Christmas only a week or so away, was nonetheless heart-warming. William Charles would be three on Christmas day and Marian and Harriet were growing into tall, attractive schoolgirls of nine and seven. Their health, education and happiness were already part of his life and Christmas brought them together in a way that Caroline could never achieve. Martha had some compensations.

As he faced the rest of the English winter on New Year's Eve, 1877, only a couple of weeks after their return from Venice, he told his friends how very much better he felt for his travels abroad and how he was emboldened 'to face the English winter'[10]. His hopes were soon dashed. Less than six weeks later he was again suffering from the perennial rheumatic pains. And as he busied himself with *The Haunted Hotel*, preparing it for serialisation in *Belgravia* in the early summer, the rheumatism rarely left him. By August, his eyes were again badly affected and he was confined to the inevitable dark room.

This was to be the pattern for the rest of his life – a combination of writing, family life and almost perpetual pain. His letters to friends and acquaintances are scattered with unhappy references to his suffering, though he rarely allowed it to dominate him for long. 'Adverse fate,' he wrote to an old friend in the early 1880s, 'has tortured me with rheumatic gout for weeks past and my recovery is so slow (or rather my weakness so great) that I can only crawl up and down the sunny side of the way for half an hour, and return to the sofa with legs that tremble as if I was ninety years old'[11]. Sometimes it was his legs, sometimes his hands, invariably his eyes.

Both Caroline and Martha had shared his sufferings over the years and, in their different ways, had helped him to cope with his afflictions. Work brought on tension and anxieties, and these in turn revived old ailments, some inherited, some peculiarly his own. He often ate the wrong things and possibly drank too much. And, on top of these excesses, was added a fatal, though soothing, ingredient – laudanum.

How far his eating habits contributed to his troubles is a moot point. The problem was a simple one: he had grown to appreciate French food at an early age – eagerly awaiting the arrival of *foie gras* in Paris when still an apprentice in the tea-trade – and had simply indulged his taste-buds thereafter. On one early occasion, when staying with Dickens in Boulogne, frustrated by Dickens's spartan dictum that anyone not down for breakfast by nine should 'go without', Wilkie was later discovered breakfasting in solitary state at the Casino on *pâté de foie gras*.

His appreciation grew with age and opportunity and over the years his letters are full of culinary asides. At one moment he is regretting the retirement of a cook 'whose lark pudding was one of the four great works which are produced in the present age'; at another he stresses that nothing can beat 'a well-made, well-cooked apple pudding'; at yet another he congratulates himself on finding a Parisian cook who encourages his 'natural gluttony'. His friends clearly knew what would please him and his thanks for glorious pâté, sweet lobsters, dry champagne, oysters, asparagus, eggs, from his closest friends are not only evidence of a 'bachelor's' needs but a testimony to his preferences.

He was hardly passive either, for he had clear views about how things should be done. 'I look on meat simply as a material for *sauces*' he told Nina Lehmann. He liked asparagus 'cold with salad oil'. He would sometimes take bread soaked in meat gravy only. At night his preference turned to cold soup and champagne[12]. He also had an inordinate liking for black pepper. 'It is seldom provided at dinner tables to which I repair,' he once explained, 'and therefore I take care to provide it myself'[13]. In general he insisted that nothing that the palate relished could be hurtful to the system and that nothing that the palate disliked could be wholesome[14]. But, occasionally, these decided culinary views had disastrous consequences.

His enthusiasm for 'Don Pedro pie', for example, full of garlic, led to a joint experiment in Frank Beard's kitchen. As Frank's son reported later: 'They returned to the upper regions, flushed but victorious, and the dish was the dinner. . . for the evening. It was a glorious success, but there was just one little drawback. The garlic had predominated so strongly that no one save the two *chefs* themselves could venture upon tasting it. The upshot of it all was that Wilkie went home and took to his bed, while my father remained at home and took to his. They were both very ill for several days, with a horrible gastric attack, and garlic was never more mentioned in the house'[15]. He had in any case some strange recuperative remedies. 'I was foolish enough to eat slices of plain joints two days following,' he once told Nina Lehmann. 'The bilious miseries that followed proved obstinate until I most fortunately ate some *pâté de foie gras*. The cure was instantaneous – and lasting.'

His physical troubles had started in his thirties and he occasionally hinted that they had been inherited from his father and grandfather. He told Frank Archer[16] that he suspected that his grandfather was to blame for his gout. And his father had succumbed to a bad bout of rheumatism in Italy and was plagued with inflammation in the eyes for the rest of his life[17]. Another trait, which plainly ran in the family, was Wilkie's nervous concentration on the work in hand. As we have already seen, his brother Charles had put his finger on this characteristic of his working life earlier in his career[18] and it was to recur regularly thereafter.

William's nervous concentration, during the completion of his paintings, is mentioned in Joseph Farrington's diaries[19], and Wilkie was well aware of a similar failing. He often described the sequence in his letters. On the completion of *Heart and Science*, he confessed: 'I am so weary after finishing my story that a sinking of the soul (and body) comes over me at the sight of a pen . . . Is there any fatigue in this weary world which is equal to the fatigue that comes of daily working of the brains for hours together? Georges Sand thought all other fatigues unimportant by comparison – and I agree with Georges'[20]. Putting the effects more precisely in a letter to Nina Lehmann, he added: 'For six months, while I was writing furiously – without exception, one part sane and three parts mad – I had no gout; I finished my story, discovered one day that I was half dead with fatigue and the next day that the gout was in my right eye.'

Eighteen months later he was making the same complaint to another friend: 'The last ten or twelve chapters of *I Say No* were written without rest or intermission (except when I was eating or sleeping). Now when the effort was over, a most prostrate wretch could hardly have been found'[21]. *The Guilty River* led to identical results three years later as he explained again to his old friend, Nina Lehmann: 'You know well what a fool I am or shall I put it mildly and say how indiscreet. For the last week, while I was finishing the story, I worked along without feeling it, like the old post horses, while I was hot. Do you remember how the fore-legs of those poor horses quivered, and how their heads drooped, when they came to journey's end? That's me, padrona – that's me'[22].

His compulsion to drive himself on was eventually curbed to some extent by the onset of what he called 'certain symptoms in the neighbourhood of the heart', basically angina, which continued to plague him over the last years of his life. But it is remarkable how, in these later years and even in the years of his main triumphs, especially *The Moonstone*, he managed to keep up such a regular pattern of writing. The answer, of course, was increasing doses of laudanum. When he began the habit is difficult to discern. He was already 'toddling out' with the aid of a stick and suffering from inflammation of the eyes in his early thirties, when living at home with his mother in Hanover Terrace.

Whether this led him to contemplate the use of laudanum is not known. But from the early 1860s onwards, the application of laudanum became a prominent feature of several of his novels – *No Name*, *Armadale* and, particularly, *The Moonstone*. It was not, however, until the crisis brought on by his mother's death, in the middle of writing *The Moonstone*, that his afflictions plainly led to regular doses of laudanum and to something of an addiction. As we have seen he tried to break himself of the habit by a series of injections in the following year[23], without any ultimate success and, over the years, the dose necessary for his comfort increased inexorably.

It is not difficult to understand why he turned to laudanum. It was a familiar form of medicine and he had come across its effects from an early age. He always recalled from his boyhood days his mother's advice to

Coleridge[24] when he was in tears about his addiction to opium, and both he and his father were keenly aware of the effects of the drug. William Collins's friend Owen, the portrait painter, had died from drinking a bottle of laudanum by mistake; William himself during his last illness had been administered a variety of drugs – what he described as 'opiates' and 'Battley's Drops'[25], a form of opium; and their friend Sir Walter Scott had used laudanum when writing *The Bride of Lammermoor*. Wilkie himself often spoke of Walter Scott's experiences, as well as those of De Quincey and Bulwer Lytton[26].

Familiarity need not lead to addiction, and it is difficult to know exactly when the regular habit of taking laudanum was established, but in 1888, the year before he died, Collins admitted to having taken the drug for twenty years, nicely confirming the year of *The Moonstone*, 1868, as the turning point. The amount he was taking regularly by the end of his life is not in doubt. In the presence of Hall Caine[27] he took down a bottle full of laudanum, poured himself a wine-glass full and admitted that he took the same quantity 'more than once a day'. De Quincey, too, he reminded Hall Caine, had drunk laudanum out of a jug. He was in effect taking enough to kill any ordinary person, and he illustrated the point by confirming that one of his servants had done just that when, in an ill-considered fit of emulation, he too had knocked back a wine glass full of laudanum. In fact over dinner one evening Sir William Fergusson, the eminent surgeon, gave the opinion that Wilkie's nightly dose alone was enough to kill everyone round the table[28].

While it is clear that Wilkie was eventually able to sustain large, regular doses, enabling him to cope with the irregular bouts of rheumatic pain, it would be idle to pretend that the costs were not high. He was soon dependent on such doses and the distress caused when his supplies ran out on a trip through Switzerland was graphically described by Fred Lehmann, shortly after they left St Moritz.

'Fred,' Wilkie confessed one morning[29], 'I am in terrible trouble, I have only just discovered that my laudanum has come to an end. I know, however, that there are six chemists at Coire; and if you and I pretend, separately, to be physicians, and each chemist consents to give to each of us the maximum of opium he may by Swiss law, which is very strict, given to one person, I shall just have enough to get through the night. Afterwards we must go through the same thing at Basle. If we fail, heaven help me!' Their efforts, though trying, were successful, but the shock, and consequent fear of running out of supplies, must have severely reduced his inclination to travel very far without adequate preparation.

The impact, of course, went well beyond the obvious addiction; and he spoke openly to his friends of ghosts standing behind him, and of a green woman with teeth like tusks who appeared on the stairs, along with other ghosts, 'trying to push him down'[30]. He also spoke of 'another Wilkie Collins' appearing before him if and when he worked into the night. As the story goes, 'the second Wilkie Collins sat at the same table with him and tried to monopolise the writing pad. Then there was a struggle, and the inkstand was upset; anyhow, when the true Wilkie awoke, the inkstand had been upset and the ink was running over the writing table. After that Wilkie Collins gave up writing of nights'[31].

These were the outward manifestations of laudanum. What else was it likely to have done? He himself was convinced that it cleared and stimulated the brain and soothed the nerves. Bulwer Lytton said the same. On one rare occasion (when Collins had reluctantly recommended laudanum to one of his friends and it had not had the desired effect) he wrote: 'Your report is a disappointment to your medical adviser. . . Laudanum has a two fold action on the brain and nervous system – a stimulating and a sedative action. It seems but *too* plain to me that *your* nerves are so strongly affected by the stimulating action that they are incapable of feeling the sedative action which ought to follow. Whether a considerably larger dose than any you have taken would have the right effect I dare not ask. Such a risk is not to be run except under a competent medical adviser'[32].

It may have clarified his mind and held the pain at bay, but there can be little doubt that, after *The Moonstone*, there was an appreciable change in the quality of his writings. Literary judgments vary, but with a few exceptions, such as *Heart and Science*, *The Haunted Hotel* and *The Black Robe*, it seems to be generally accepted that his sustained grip on plot and atmosphere was only rarely seen in the seventies and eighties. It is easy to put this down to the impact of laudanum alone. Its main influence may have been, as Alethea Hayter has demonstrated[33] (from the work of Coleridge and others, as well as Collins), in blocking his ability to convey landscape descriptions in pictorial terms.

In *The Moonstone*, for example, the shivering quicksand not far from the country house had, in her view, become, under the opiate influence, a symbolic landscape rather than a pictorial one. And she concluded: 'Wilkie Collins wrote many more novels after *The Moonstone*, but none of them contained distinctly visualised landscapes like the ones in *The Woman in White* and *No Name*. He travelled in France, Italy, Germany, America, but their scenery did not find a way into his later books, which convey almost no sense of place or of external nature. His murder story *The Haunted Hotel* has an ingenious plot, which again makes use of the premonitory dream;

but though it is supposed to take place in a Venetian palace, and though Wilkie Collins had been in Venice shortly before he wrote it, there is no Venetian atmosphere; most of the story might as well be taking place in a station hotel in Wigan . . . This is perhaps one of the most distinct before-and-after signs of opium's effect on the imagination – that it alters a writer's power to convey the visual impact of landscape'. And she added that laudanum not only calmed his nervous susceptibilities; in the end it atrophied them. 'The most obvious damage to his literary achievement which the opium habit inflicted was its impairment of the power of sustained concentration needed for the tightly-constructed plots which were his greatest excellence.'

It is a persuasive diagnosis. His first interest in writing had been aroused through the visual, stretching from his childhood visit to Italy to his own later continental visits, stimulated throughout by his parents' artistic approach. The use of descriptive passages to heighten tension and to provide the atmosphere for his intricate plots became a major ingredient in his best work. That it was undermined by laudanum in dulling his ability to convey a sense of place, and that the drug prevented him from developing the plots on which his first novels depended is hardly in dispute. What remains at issue is whether the decline in his abilities as a sensational novelist came not only from his excessive and increasing reliance on drugs but also from the absence in his later years, particularly after *The Moonstone*, of the curbing hand of Dickens. Its replacement by a temptation to take up causes, egged on by his developing friendship with Charles Reade, hardly helped. All plainly took their toll. But it was ill health and his efforts to cope with it that settled the pattern of his life in his later years.

Those later years, especially after his final visit to Venice, were taken up with family life. He had already begun to share the anxieties of parenthood through his children's illnesses and had suffered agonies when Marian had broken her leg, at a time when he himself was laid up with gout in the eyes and legs[34].

He was in effect beginning to experience with his own children what he had already suffered and enjoyed in helping to bring up Harriet, Caroline's daughter. To his satisfaction she had emerged as a capable secretary and a particularly good looking girl in her mid-twenties, inheriting all her mother's attractiveness. She was articulate, hardworking and meticulous, watching his correspondence, taking his dictation, seeing his proofs through to publication and liaising with all his professional advisers.

How Wilkie came to change his solicitor in 1877 is not recorded, but Harriet's influence is easily inferred. She had been acting as courier between his solicitor, William Frederick Tindall, and himself for some time. How and where she first met Henry Powell Bartley, who was to become his new solicitor, is not completely clear. But it is known[35] that the Bartleys regularly took a house for the summer in Ramsgate and it is more than likely that Harriet and Henry first ran across each other on holiday. In any case Henry had been admitted as a solicitor in August, 1877[36], and had immediately set up on his own account at 30 Somerset Street, Portman Square, just round the corner from Gloucester Place. He was certainly nearer than William Tindall in Essex Street, close to the Strand, a point Harriet no doubt made to Wilkie. But a young eligible solicitor clearly had other attractions too, and before the end of the year, Wilkie had wound up his affairs with William Tindall and transferred them to Henry Bartley.

By the time Wilkie and Caroline returned from Venice, Harriet and Henry Bartley were already in regular touch on Wilkie's legal affairs, and their closeness quickly blossomed into friendship, love and thoughts of marriage, which neither Wilkie nor Caroline were inclined to discourage. The Bartleys were all that Wilkie and Caroline could have wished for Harriet. They were a well-to-do middle class professional family from Kensington, who claimed they were descended from an Italian count named Bartoloni. Henry's parents had been married in October 1849[37], a few months after his father had qualified as a solicitor, and he was born in Lansdowne Crescent, Kensington, just over five years later. He was thus three years younger than Harriet.

Wilkie and Caroline threw themselves into the wedding celebrations with some gusto. The ceremony took place at St Mary's church, Marylebone, on 12th March, 1878. Harriet, like her mother before her, felt obliged to cover up her father's modest background and, no doubt with her 'in-laws' in mind, put him down as a former 'Captain in the Army' on the marriage certificate. When they got back to Gloucester Place for the wedding breakfast, the tables groaned under the weight of Wilkie's French and English cuisine – truffles, lobster, salmon, ham, chicken, pâté and a galaxy of sweet dishes of all kinds[38].

'Bride cake', as Wilkie put it, firmly in English on the French menu, was given pride of place, as the two families made their first assessment of each other. The Bartleys were obviously delighted to be moving into a literary world of which they knew very little and to be meeting celebrities of all kinds. Their uneasiness at what they found in Gloucester Place can be readily understood. Caroline's position in the household, as his recent continental travelling companion and rather more than a housekeeper, must have been the source of much comment back in Kensington, as it was to be over the years to come. But Harriet was warmly welcomed as a natural part of the Bartley family and a worthy wife of Henry.

They settled down in a pleasant house close to Swiss Cottage[39] and not much more than a stone's throw from the spot where Wilkie may have met her mother in such dramatic circumstances a quarter of a century earlier. And in the following years it was to be the birthplace of Harriet's first three children – all girls, and all with distinct red hair.

CHAPTER FOURTEEN

Family

BY THE LATE 1870s and early 1880s, Wilkie was thus nicely distracted by two young families – Harriet's and his own – growing up in separate households within a mile of Gloucester Place; and it was hardly surprising that Gloucester Place should have become the focal point of their lives. Harriet's mother was still there and she herself continued to help Wilkie, when she could, in his literary affairs. As for Martha's children, Wilkie remained their main supporter and, at one remove, as much a father as he could manage in the circumstances.

All the evidence suggests that he took his responsibilities seriously and that he gained enormous pleasure from his regular visits to Taunton Place. The crates of sherry, even champagne, he occasionally had delivered to Martha certainly suggest that he did not stint on the cost of running two homes. Nor did he ignore their educational needs, arranging a governess for the two girls, Marian and Harriet, as soon as he felt they needed it and Miss Strong, the person chosen, was paid directly by him[1]. By 1883, when Harriet's third child, Evelyn, was born, the six children of Martha and Harriet ranged from fourteen down to the newborn and the nicknames of 'Charley' (William Charles), 'Hettie' (Harriet), 'Dah' (Doris Edith), 'Cissie' or 'Cissey' (Cecile Marguerite) and 'Bollie' (Evelyn Beatrice) began to reverberate through Gloucester Place[2]. Only Marian, the eldest, seems to have escaped such familiarity.

It was, of course, not just in Gloucester Place that the two families would see Wilkie. The habit of going down to Ramsgate, which had begun as a convenient base for his sailing, became even more ingrained as Wilkie realised that his continental visits were perhaps over. He had always loved the place since being taken there as a small boy for his first swim. It also avoided the painful memories of lost friends, so quickly evoked in Broadstairs.

He had begun to stay in Nelson Crescent with Caroline in the early 1870s and had, from time to time, rented virtually the whole house from the landlady, Rebecca Shrive. It was a habit that continued almost until his death and by the late 1870s it had become an annual affair, both of them taking over number 14, or a good part of it, for two or three months at a time. Rebecca Shrive remained in charge of their visit for over a decade and a half[3].

What began with Wilkie and Caroline quickly grew into a succession of visits from Harriet and Henry and their children, as well as Wilkie's own children. It was here, above all, that Harriet's and Martha's families grew to know each other. All stayed at 14 Nelson Crescent or, if Harriet and Henry visited too, they would stay a couple of doors away. Martha's visits were another matter. Her children, when unaccompanied by her, would stay with Wilkie and Caroline. But Wilkie always watched the proprieties carefully where Martha was concerned. When she was in Ramsgate, he quickly became William Dawson, barrister at law, and they stayed in an identical Crescent across the bay, at 27 Wellington Crescent, only a few yards from the house his mother had taken him to fifty years earlier.

His days in Ramsgate were easily organised. He often devoted time to his writing – even taking his specially constructed 'desk' down for the purpose – but walking, fishing and sailing gave him the relaxation he needed. He would be at sea two or three hours at a time during the periods when he had writing to undertake. At other times he would cruise up and down the coast, using Ramsgate as a base, for two or three weeks or even longer.

His love of the sea and sailing went deep. It was, if anything, his main hobby and distraction. And it is strange how many of his literary friends remained unaware of it. Seeing him in Gloucester Place, they had every excuse in assuming that he rarely strayed outside. Take Julian Hawthorne. He came to see Wilkie in Gloucester Place and promptly wrote an unflattering portrait of what he saw. 'Though the England of his prime had been a cricketing, athletic, outdoor England, Wilkie had ever slumped at his desk, and breathed only indoor air. He was soft, plump and pale. Suffered from various ailments, his liver was wrong, his heart weak, his lungs faint, his stomach incompetent, he ate too much and the wrong things'[4]. The medical diagnosis was near the mark but if anyone was determined to breathe huge quantities of sea air and under virtually any conditions, it was Wilkie.

His enthusiasm was simply expressed. 'The perfection of enjoyment is only to be obtained when you are at sea, in a luxurious, well-appointed steam yacht in lovely summer weather'[5]. A typical Collins combination: sea air and luxury. Though he did not always achieve it, he contrived to do so whenever he could. Edward Piggott's father, who had a yacht, helped on occasions. For a time, when he was flush with money in his early days as a novelist he seriously toyed with the idea of buying a boat of his own, but his mother was less than enthusiastic.

Thereafter he and Edward Piggott rented a boat and crew and got what they could afford, Wilkie invariably insisting on being in charge of the food. In his clearly autobiographical story for *Household Words*, as early as 1855, he and his fellow sailor ('Jollins' and 'Miggott' nicely disguising himself and Piggott) were bound for the Scilly Isles with a crew of three. 'Miggott' could clearly be in charge of lowering the foresail or double reefing the main sail, but 'when grog is to be made or sauces are to be prepared, Mr Jollins becomes in his turn the monarch of all he surveys'[6]. In real life too Wilkie was apt to insist on Fortnum & Mason's provisions to take aboard.

Wilkie continued to believe that the sea air did him good. It plainly toned him up, after his strenuous and exhausting bouts of intensive writing. Whether it helped or hindered his efforts to assuage the pains of rheumatism is more doubtful, but he remained optimistic almost to the end of his life about its therapeutic effects. 'Neuralgia and nervous exhaustion generally have sent me to the sea to be patched up and the sea is justifying my confidence in it'[7], he once told an old friend. His father had felt the same fifty years earlier, when he went to Brighton to cure rheumatic inflammation of the eyes by trying 'the effect of the sea air'[8]. In neither case was the confidence fully justified. His father's treatment was a disappointment and so, at the crucial moments, was Wilkie's.

On one occasion, suffering acutely from a rheumatic back, he went off with Piggott from Cowes for a lengthy cruise along the southern coast. 'All my nervous pains and susceptibilities to changes in the temperature', he reported to his mother[9], 'increased as soon as I left the shore. For ten days and nights I stuck to the vessel in spite of them. But time did nothing to acclimatise me to the penetrative dampness of the sea air. . . . A better yacht of her size I never sailed in. All accommodations below perfectly comfortable – high winds and high seas now and then, but not a drop of rain – an excellent captain and crew – in short, everything right and good, except my obstinate beast of a back, which registered (in pain) every shift of the wind to North or East all through the voyage'.

The experiment hardly stopped him going to sea nor apparently damaged his optimism. Over twenty years later he was again reporting a similar failure. Writing to an American poet in 1885[10], he explained: 'Look here, Paul Hamilton Hayne! The less you say about your friend Wilkie Collins the better. His stars, for the last three months, have given him up as a bad job. He went to sea with the ridiculous idea (at his age!) of restoring his youth. He left his ship with the animal spirits of five and twenty, and the splendid complexion of the days when he was a truly beautiful baby – he returned to London – and the next morning, when he approached the looking glass to brush his beard, he perceived a red streak in his left eye. In three days more, his eye was the colour of a (cooked) lobster. The Gout-Fiend had got him. The Gout-Fiend bored holes in his eye with a red-hot needle. Calomel and Colchium knocked him down, and said (through the medium of the Doctor): "Wilkie, it's all for your good". Laudanum – divine laudanum – was his only friend. He got better – then worse again – then better – then worse once more'.

A sad, though familiar, end to one of his sailing expeditions, but it did not prevent him from going out to sea again and again. Nor from taking his annual, sometimes semi-annual, visit to Ramsgate. In fact his visits to Ramsgate became so much a part of his life that some of his friends increasingly assumed that he would eventually settle down there. But, with a sideways glance at his outgoings in London, he instinctively knew otherwise. As he wrote to Edward Piggott, he was convinced that Ramsgate air kept him in a state of preservation. 'Beard seems to think that my destiny is to *live* at Ramsgate. With two houses to keep going in London, I don't quite see how I am to accommodate myself to this future'.

The cost of continually cruising along the coast was not negligible either. He shared the costs for many years with Edward, both of them joining the local yacht club. Before long the sailing bug had been passed on to both Harriet and, particularly, Henry Bartley, and within the Bartley family there was much discussion about the extravagant tastes Henry had begun to acquire within the Collins household. Whether Wilkie himself ever acquired a yacht of his own is far from clear. He certainly answered correspondence from aboard the Yacht Phyllis in the harbour at Ramsgate, but the only evidence of a yacht being owned there related to Henry Bartley, not Wilkie.

When Harriet had her first children, she and Henry would be invited to stay with Wilkie and Caroline at 14 Nelson Crescent[11]. 'Come, the sooner the better and bring *all* the children,' he wrote to Harriet. 'Good heavens! Don't I like Dah, and the quiet little curly head. I wish I was a baby again – with nothing to do but to suck and sleep'[12]. Later they all overflowed into neighbouring houses. 'The Bartleys', he told Frank Beard on one occasion, 'are within two doors of us, and the children are in and out a dozen times a day'[13]. Martha's children too joined the throng, Charley occasionally staying with Wilkie and Caroline as this particularly revealing letter to Doris (or 'Dah'), Harriet's six year old, brings out. Wilkie wrote it on his return to Gloucester Place after a spell in Ramsgate[14]:

My dear Doris,

I was very glad to receive your letter at Ramsgate and to see how nicely it was written. We had some very fine weather and the sea air has done me a great deal of good. Charley[15] was with us. He rowed in a boat in the harbour – and he went to a place called Sandwich on a tricycle – and he ate good dinners – and he enjoyed himself very much. We came home yesterday – and a man ran after our omnibus all the way from the railway station to this house. He was poor and he wanted to get a little money by carrying our luggage upstairs and he did it very well, being a strong young man. He was pleased when I paid him and I think he went away and got some beer. We hope you will come and see us soon. We send our love to you and to Cissey and to Bolly and to your Mamma.

Your affectionate godpapa . . .

They had probably arrived at London Bridge station (London's oldest) from Ramsgate and the amateur porter must have run all of four miles to Gloucester Place.

It was not simply in Ramsgate that the two families got to know each other. Gloucester Place was a similar magnet for Harriet's and Martha's children. Marian and Hettie often reminisced in later years about the mews at Gloucester Place and the carriages they could recall seeing there[16]. In the Census of 1881 Marian, then aged twelve, was plainly staying in Gloucester Place, since she is registered as part of the household[17]. Both she and her young sister Harriet ('Hettie') were not unfamiliar with either Gloucester Place or Wimpole Street, where Wilkie was to spend the last eighteen months of his life. And the familiarity between the two families resulted in a copy of a first edition of *The Dead Secret* with the inscription 'Lizzie Graves from the author', in Wilkie's handwriting, being handed down through Martha's children to the Dawson family, covered in childish crayoning[18].

These were happy years in Collins's life. Racked with pain, which kept him away from the round of dinner parties he once thrived on, and often from the theatre he adored, he nonetheless had another side of his life which his acquaintances could only guess at. He never hid his private life, nor its irregularities, from any of his closest friends, nor deliberately dissembled with his regular literary contacts. But few of them would be aware of the pleasures he derived from his two families. On one occasion, dropping a quick line to Harriet about the children, he adds 'I have given Doris and Cissie a pencil each. They are writing books, as good as gold'. He was a family man in all but name. It may all go some way to explain not exactly why he continued to produce a regular series of novels in the last decade of his life, but perhaps how he managed to keep going.

Although Collins spoke continuously about the physical pressure of writing, of the intensity of concentration it required and, above all, of the toll it took on his health, it remained a compulsion as well as an obvious satisfaction to him. In spite of all his ailments he continued to devote the greater part of each year to a major project and throughout the eighties, when neuralgia and angina were added to his endemic gout and rheumatism, and laudanum was a regular companion, he managed to complete seven major novels, two volumes of short stories, two plays (one new, one revised) and a variety of short articles.

He brought a combination of patient preparation and bouts of intense continuous writing to all his novels. His method of work rarely changed throughout his life. First came the central idea, the quirks of the plot and the characters. He never lost his fascination with the essentials of this necessary scaffolding and with the intricacies of keeping the reader alert, interested and avid to know 'what next'. In a word 'story-telling' of the highest order was what he was after. His modest quip[19] to a friend, 'I am only an old fellow who has a liking for story-telling, no more,' hid an intense professionalism which his contemporaries found hard to match. It was a professionalism that required a deliberate discipline.

He explained more than once both his aims and his methods. 'I have always held the old-fashioned opinion that the primary object of a work of fiction should be to tell a story.' Plot, character and dialogue were all part of the process. 'When I sit down to write a novel,' Anthony Trollope once explained, 'I do not at all know, and I do not very much care, how it is to end. Wilkie Collins seems so to construct his that he not only, before writing, plans everything on, down to the minutest detail, from the beginning to the end; but then plots it all back again, to see that there is no piece of necessary dove-tailing which does not dove-tail with absolute accuracy. The construction is most minute and most wonderful'[20].

Wilkie had himself confirmed his writing habits in explaining his detailed preparation for *The Woman in White*, and the disciplines imposed on him by weekly serialisation. 'When I set down to write the seventh weekly part of *The Woman in White*, the first weekly part was being published simultaneously in *All the Year Round*, and in *Harpers Weekly*. No after-thoughts, in connection with the first part, were possible under these circumstances – the same rule applied of course week after week to the rest of the story. I had no choice but to know what to do beforehand throughout the whole story – and months before a line of it was written for the press, I was accumulating that knowledge in a mass of "notes" which contained a complete outline of the story and the characters. I knew what Sir Percival Glyde was going to do with the marriage register and how Count Fosco's night at the opera was to be spoilt by the appearance of Professor Pesca, before a line of the book was in the printer's hands'[21].

Walter Besant, who took over Collins's last novel *Blind Love*, found the same minute preparations when he received Collins's notes. 'I found that these were not merely notes, such as I had expected,' he eventually wrote in the preface, 'simple indications of the plot and the development of events, but an actual detailed scenario in which every incident, however trivial, was carefully laid down: there were also fragments of dialogue inserted at those places where dialogue was wanted to emphasise the situation, and make it real. I was much struck with the writer's perception of the vast importance of dialogue in making the reader seize the scene. Description requires attention: dialogue rivets attention'. Trollope in fact hardly approved of such preparations, complaining that he could never lose the taste of the construction, thus echoing a criticism Dickens had earlier made about *The Moonstone*.

Our main concern, however, is not to make a literary judgment, but rather to assess how his methods of writing impinged on his health. The preparations, he felt, were essential to his success as a 'story-teller'. They often took several months, even years. The final writing, however, became, as a direct result, a much more concentrated effort. With the scaffolding, including even essential dialogue, in place, he could simply start to write within the guidelines he had already set for himself. Given the deadlines also imposed by serialisation, and his own impulses, the feverish bouts of writing he so often described were the inevitable result.

He wrote *Guilty River* in a month, writing twelve hours a day. On another occasion he described himself as 'a wretched worn-out man with spectacles on his nose and a grey beard on his chin, prostrate in an arm chair, looking at a pen often after eight hours use of it in the process of invention called novel-writing'[22]. And in spite of all his ailments, he never changed his writing habits, even as he got older. If anything he seems to have driven himself with increasing intensity.

Of the novels of the eighties three stand out for different reasons: *The Black Robe*, *Heart and Science* and *Blind Love*. *The Black Robe* was an attempt to combine a religious theme with one of his normal mixtures of plot and character, contrasting the wiles of an ambitious mother with those of a Jesuit priest. Although, through Father Benwell, he managed to express all his latent antipathy towards the power structure of the Vatican, the message remained subsidiary to the plot.

This could hardly be said of his next novel *Heart and Science*, for anxiety about the growing role of vivisection dominated the plot. It struck a ready chord with some. *The World* thought it 'a thoroughly fine romance' and went on: 'There is no man living, in this country at any rate, who could have produced its superior or its equal'. But it was generally felt to be out of tune with his normal readers' expectations and not entirely satisfying at an intellectual level either. It roused controversy rather than sales, and provided further ample justification for Swinburne's jibe:

'What brought good Wilkie's genius nigh perdition? Some demon whispered – "Wilkie! Have a mission" '.

Blind Love was his last, unfinished, novel. Completed by his old friend Walter Besant, it was based on a true situation recounted to him by a friend of the Lehmanns. Once again, and for the last time, his imagination had been caught by the possibilities of fraud – this time in the insurance world. Two thirds of the writing was Wilkie's but as Walter Besant was quick to acknowledge, the whole of the outline, the complexities of the plot and even parts of the dialogue in the final third of the book, completed by Besant, were Wilkie's own work. He had returned, in the end, to what he knew best and what he liked most in a story, well plotted and well told. He had lost, in this final decade, much of his cutting edge both in the writing and in the handling of complex material. But at least his original driving force, his fascination for the unexpected in real life, remained to the end.

Throughout these later years he somehow maintained his links with the stage. His theatrical successes were behind him – only a major disaster and a few helpful revivals ahead. But he continued to go to the theatre whenever he could and managed to keep in touch with all his old, even some new, theatrical friends as time went on.

Regular theatre going had probably started when he was on *The Leader*, receiving first night review tickets, but he had been an enthusiast and devotee much longer, stretching back to his first visits to Paris, where he was surprised at the way French dramatists were more highly regarded – and rewarded – than in London. In later years he and Dickens had followed their theatrical instincts whenever they were in Paris and his habit in London was to invite groups of friends to share a box whenever the fancy took him. His own stage successes in London, New York and Paris had brought even further theatrical friendships which he cultivated until his death.

His final effort to write something special for the theatre produced a result he was hardly ever to forget. *Rank and Riches*, a four-act melodrama, was apparently written in the early 1880s and simply awaited a suitable theatre and a strong cast. By the early part of 1883, the *Adelphi* had agreed to take it on and Alice Lingood, who had impressed him in *Camille*, George Alexander, George Anson and Charles Hawtrey were all set for what they and the producer Edgar Bruce assumed would be another success in early June. It all turned out rather differently.

Sir Arthur Pinero was, by chance, standing beside Wilkie at the back of the dress circle on the first night. 'We exchanged greetings,' he recalled later[23], 'and I noticed that, expecting a call at the fall of the curtain, he wore a large camellia in his button-hole. Everything went wrong. The audience, amused by some awkwardly phrased expressions, tittered; then, as the play advanced, broke into unrestrained laughter; and finally, enraged by an indignant protest from one of the actors, hooted the thing unmercifully'. George Anson had ill-advisedly lectured the audience at the interval, shaken his fist and called the first-nighters 'a lot of damned cads', which not only failed to stem the flood of cat-calls in the later acts, but brought him similar treatment at most of his subsequent first-nights. He eventually emigrated to Australia.

Wilkie could hardly endure first nights when he had a success on his hands. How he coped with such a hostile, unexpected reception is not recorded. But he soon had other distractions – obligations to write short stories, preparations for his next novel and the inevitable bouts of sailing. And within six months he was discussing the revival of one of his greatest triumphs, *The New Magdalen*, at the Novelty Theatre in Great Queen Street.

Frank Archer and Ada Cavendish headed a strong cast, but Wilkie, perhaps still unnerved by his recent setback, continued to worry whether people would even find the theatre. He was unable to get along himself to the first night – whether from neuralgia (as he claimed) or nerves is difficult to say – but the reception was as warm and enthusiastic as ever. He eventually went along to see for himself and was plainly delighted with Frank Archer's performance. A week later the Prince and Princess of Wales turned up and it ran for over sixty performances.

Thereafter, though he had no more stage performances of his own, he continued to go when he could and his love for the theatre and those who attended it remained undiminished. He rarely tired of discussing what he had seen – sometimes about events the week before (recalling Caroline and Harriet's surprise that Bulwer Lytton's *Lady of Lyons* was partly in blank verse)[24]; sometimes about events thirty years earlier (reminiscing over stage giants of the past – Keble, Mrs Siddons, Macready, and the elder

Farren in London; Regnier, Coquelin, la Font and Lemaitre in Paris). He kept in touch with all his old theatrical friends – Ada Cavendish, Squire and Marie Bancroft, Arthur Pinero, Fred Archer, and Wybert Reeve.

They continued to call on him; he wrote to them; and he occasionally gave advice. He made new friends, among them Lillie Langtry (to whom he also offered encouraging advice) and Oscar Wilde. Even within a few months of his death, he was still going over old theatrical ground with his friend Frank Archer, recalling one of the finest theatrical performances he and Dickens had seen in Paris. Frederic Lemaitre, he felt, had given the greatest performance he had ever seen in *Thirty Years of a Gambler's Life*. 'Dickens and I saw the play together, and at the end of one of the acts we were so utterly overcome that we both sat for a time perfectly silent'[25].

Meanwhile, throughout those last years of his life his family was growing up. Marian and Hettie were becoming old enough to go to school and to dispense with the services of a governess. Casting around for a suitable place nearby, his eye fell on the Maria Grey College in Fitzroy Square, not far from Gloucester Place and Taunton Place and only a few streets from where the girls had been born. It was a combined kindergarten and school, with a good exam record, and had a leaning towards equipping its pupils to become teachers. One had become Instructress General of Female Schools in the Punjab. Wilkie plainly had his eye on their future and both girls in fact were to become governesses for a time in their early twenties. Their brother Charley was eventually sent to a day school in the City.

While all the children were regular visitors to Gloucester Place, Martha herself remained in Taunton Place. She was hardly neglected. Wilkie was round there regularly and his orders to his wine merchants invariably included cases of champagne for her. 'The pints of champagne have disappeared,' he once wrote plaintively to Beechene Yaxley[26]. 'Will you send me six dozen more of some *Vin Brut* in half bottles? The sherry is also reported to be on its last legs. Please let me have a three dozen case (as before) and send another three dozen case, addressed to Mrs Dawson'. Martha had her own friends too and, although her unorthodox life raised a few eyebrows in Winterton at the outset, she remained in close touch with her sisters. One of her older sisters, Alice, lived with her as a servant in Taunton Place for a time[27]. Others visited her and the Winterton contacts were maintained until she died.

The family in Gloucester Place would hardly be complete without Wilkie's constant companion, his dog Tommie. He loved animals and had a particularly soft spot for his brown and white Scotch terrier, invariably by his side as he wrote or as he convalesced. Tommie featured in many of his letters and even crept into one of his books, *My Lady's Money*, as one of the 'Persons of the Story: Tommie (Lady Lydiord's Dog)'. But lest he lost him to posterity, Wilkie quietly reclaimed him at the end of the book, when unravelling the future of the main characters: 'And last, not least, good-bye to Tommie? No, the writer gave Tommie his dinner not half an hour since, and is too fond of him to say good-bye.' The household clearly revolved round the friendly animal. As Wilkie himself wrote to his American correspondent Mrs Bigelow: 'When evening comes, I sit and think – and smoke when I am tired of thinking – and wish I was on my way again to my dear United States. When I can neither smoke nor think any longer, then my dear old dog comes, looks at me, wags his tail and groans. This means, in *his* language "Now Wilkie, it's time to go to bed!" So the evening closes'[28]. Wilkie's daughters were still recalling similar stories up to thirty-five years ago[29]. Wilkie only realised how ingrained Tommie had become in all their lives when he died. 'How closely that poor little dog had associated himself with every act of my life at home,' he told Frank Beard, 'I know only now. I can go nowhere and do nothing – without missing Tommie'[30]. And within four months he had recognised it by sending a cheque for £5 to the Dogs' Home[31].

His love and involvement with children had always extended beyond his own family and went back at least to the romps on the grass at the Boulogne fêtes which he so loved during his early friendship with Dickens. One particular friendship, which has only recently come to light, covered these last few years of his life from 1885 onwards. It is a remarkable, warming episode, both teasing and revealing.

'Nannie' Wynne had been christened Anne Elizabeth Le poer Wynne, and was the daughter of Mrs Henry Wynne, a friend of Wilkie's closest friends, Edward Piggott and his doctor, Frank Beard. Her husband, an ex-India civil servant, had died young. They lived not far away in Delamere Gardens, and, like so many of his friends' children, Nannie was immediately struck by the way Wilkie took her seriously. Soon she was asking how he wrote his stories and bringing him flowers from the country. And he was promising her a specially written ghost story. (It was in fact *The Ghost's Touch*[32].)

His letters to Nannie span a period of three years (1885–1888)[33] and cover all his enthusiasms and topical thoughts from California to gambling and from the Jubilee to her account of an earthquake on the Riviera. But they are remarkable for one teasing thread: within weeks of the first letters he is treating and addressing her as his loving wife. 'Dear and Admirable Mrs Collins,' he begins, and soon he is her 'devoted husband' asking about their children. Even her mother is dragged in. 'Love to my mother-in-law and don't show her these lines or she will regret our marriage. Tear up. Tear up.'

His enthusiasm for the role is allowed full rein. 'Si carissima sposa mia. Let me say goodnight and waft you a kiss in this way till we meet again.' And: 'Most ungrateful of husbands if I failed to present myself to my dear little Mrs Wilkie while she has her holidays.' And again: 'I am proud of my wife. Her account of the earthquake is the best that I have read yet. She is also a little angel who thinks of her husband and sends him a nice box of flowers.'

After a lifetime of avoiding the marital state he finally lives it through a twelve-year-old, and a friendship which her mother clearly found surprising but not disturbing.

Real family life went on too. Once Harriet's three girls had grown old enough to be left in other people's care, she again took up the secretarial tasks he had relied on for so long. Several of his later novels were copied in her handwriting and his letters to her, in these later years, are full of drafting instructions and advice to the printer, as well as enquiries about her family.

One particular episode hit them all hard. Soon after Harriet, Henry and the girls had moved into a house on the Finchley Road, Harriet realised she was about to have a fourth child. Wilkie was preparing *The Legacy of Cain* and Harriet continued to copy parts of it for him as long as she could. As the New Year came and went the crucial day drew nearer and, on 3rd January 1888[34], a week before Wilkie's sixty-fourth birthday, Harriet gave birth to her fourth daughter, later christened Violet Clara.

Everyone was delighted. But within a few weeks, the new baby's health showed signs of weakness and by the middle of February, a new anxiety had arisen: whooping cough was diagnosed. They all watched with growing concern as the baby literally fought for its life; but on 5th March[35] the struggle came to an end. Wilkie was as devastated as anyone, and only allowed himself to write to Harriet ten days after the baby's death. 'I only venture to write to you when the worst that affliction can do has been done – and even now, I ask myself what I can write to you that is worth reading . . . No *man*, let him feel for you as he may (and I have felt for you with all my heart) is capable of understanding what a mother must suffer who is tried as you have been tried. The fate of that poor little child – after making such a gallant fight for its life – is something which I must not trust myself to write about. My sorrow is yours and my sympathy is yours. For the rest time is the only consoler'[36].

He invited Harriet round to Gloucester Place as soon as she felt able to leave the other girls (now nine, seven and five). But he reminded her that if she left it too long, she would have to wait a while: he had a troublesome removal facing him.

He eventually moved out of Gloucester Place to 82 Wimpole Street on Saturday, 24th March. He had been forced out, he told his friends, by the 'exorbitant terms' asked for the renewal of the lease by the agent of his landlord ('an enormously rich nobleman named Lord Portman'). He had been asked for no less than £1,200 for the new lease, 'to say nothing of other merciless stipulations'[37]. He quickly decided 'to see him damned first' and after twenty happy years in Gloucester Place, he had to contemplate moving to new quarters, in the middle of serialising a new story for weeklies in Britain, Canada, Australia and the United States.

The confusions of the removal haunted him for weeks. With half the furniture gone, he lived in one of his dressing rooms at Gloucester Place, until the rooms in Wimpole Street were fit for occupation. Six weeks after his arrival in Wimpole Street he still had no carpet down in the dining room. As for the removal itself, he shuddered at the thought for weeks afterwards. Everyone, except Martha, seems to have been involved in helping him out. As he wrote, evocatively, to his friend Quilter[38]:

'If you please, Sir, I don't think the looking glass will fit in above the bookcase in this house.'

'Your Father's lovely little picture can't go above the chimney piece. The heat will spoil it.'

'Take down the picture in the next room and try it there.'

'But that is the portrait of your grandmother.'

'Damn my grandmother.'

'If the side-board is put in the front dining room, too, I don't know where the cabinets are to go.'

'How will you have your bed put? Against the side of the wall, or standing out from the wall?'

'I say, Wilkie, when you told Marian and Harriet that they might help to put the books in their places, did you know that Faublas and Casanova's Memoirs were left out on the drawing room table?'

'I beg your pardon, Sir, did I understand that you wanted a lamp in the water-closet?'

'Dear Sir, we are sorry to notice irregularity in the supply of copy lately. Please excuse our writing to you on this subject. We must not keep the colonial newspaper waiting for their proofs.'

'My dear Quilter, do the domestic circumstances reported above excuse me for not having written sooner. Oh. Surely, Yes?'

Not only were Marian and Harriet (Hettie) helping with the books; they were also occasionally looking after his correspondence and even a month after the official removal date, Marian was writing from Wimpole Street to Wilkie's wine-merchants, thanking them for their 'liberal decision' not to charge him the new tax on the champagne they held in reserve for him[39] and still referring to the 'worry and confusion' of the removal.

It had been a particularly trying year for Wilkie – a mixture of excessive work, ill-health, a troublesome move and the tragedy of Harriet's baby. Other difficulties too seemed to be emerging in the Bartley family which were to throw a shadow over the years to come. Whatever the reason, Wilkie's free-spending habits had clearly begun to be reflected in the Bartley household too. Henry's growing extravagances were already beginning to be seen in several areas, especially in his enthusiasm for sailing and his expenditure on a yacht in Ramsgate Harbour. Harriet shared his enthusiasm and delighted in preparing curtains and other fittings for their comfort on board. Wilkie, of course, could afford the odd extravagance. Whether Henry could so easily do so on the income of a young solicitor, with a family of three girls to bring up, is more doubtful.

Henry's parents blamed Harriet and indirectly Wilkie for Henry's expensive tastes. There were, of course, other contrasts between the Bartley family and the habits they witnessed in Gloucester Place. Wilkie and Caroline's habit of throwing oranges to the terrier, Tommie, during dinner was unlikely to appeal to a conservative middle-class family[40]. And they must have wondered what influence such an atmosphere must eventually have on their grand-daughters. Yet, as we shall soon see, it was Henry, and not Wilkie or Caroline, who was eventually to run counter to the Bartley family, and to bring such unhappiness to Harriet. It is easy, with hindsight, to detect the seeds of these future troubles in the last years of Wilkie's life. It is also easy to draw wrong conclusions from certain financial transactions. But they still remain puzzling.

In June 1888, three months after Wilkie moved to Wimpole Street, he made a payment of £200 to Henry Bartley[41]. No other similar payments had been made over the previous ten or more years. This was followed by further payments totalling nearly £300 before the end of the year. And in 1889, still more payments amounting to close on £300 were made to Henry. All this added up to something like £800 in just over twelve months. Although they could hardly be the usual solicitor's bills, they could, of course, have an innocent explanation. But in view of the tensions and troubles which were to follow within the Bartley family, shortly after Wilkie's death, it seems reasonable to ask whether, even at this stage, Henry was beginning to run into financial difficulties and was in need of monetary help.

If this was the case, it must have added a further strain to Wilkie's other anxieties, as he grappled with ill-health and his self-imposed pattern of work. In what was destined to be his last normal summer, however, he remained remarkably resilient, bouncing back from another bout of illness in sufficient shape ('like a well trained pugilist' he felt) to take Martha and his family to Ramsgate. As he put it to Sebastian Schlesinger, who was now living in London, 'Wilkie Collins of 82 Wimpole Street had disappeared from this mortal sphere of action and is replaced by William Dawson, 27 Wellington Crescent, Ramsgate. In plain English I am here with my "morganatic family" – and must travel (like the Royal personages) under an alias – or not be admitted into this respectable house now occupied by my children and their mother'[42].

He was in fact still involved in the preparations for his next novel. 'It is a tough job this time,' he told Schlesinger. 'I have been nowhere and have seen nobody and am nothing better than the slave of my pen – the most agreeable slavery that I am acquainted with.' Since *The Legacy of Cain* had been completed a couple of months earlier, this was presumably the early stages of what was to prove his last, unfinished, novel, *Blind Love*.

They were all in Ramsgate for close on two months, while he once again put up the scaffolding of the novel. Marian and Hettie, now nineteen and seventeen, were probably intermittent visitors, with Wilkie, Martha and Charley, still a schoolboy of fourteen, in continuous residence in Wellington Crescent. Wilkie, as vigilant as ever over propriety where Martha was concerned, had arranged for Caroline to remain in Wimpole Street. The intermingling of the children of the households was one thing: the womenfolk quite another.

The sea air braced him for the winter ahead, but the treatment, as so often in the past, did not last long and only a month or so after his return to London he was again grappling with his old enemies. 'The infernal fog and damp has completely unnerved me and neuralgia has nailed me again,' he was writing in early November. The winter plainly took its toll and, to add to the pressures on his weak frame, he had the misfortune to be virtually thrown out of a cab late one evening on returning from a dinner party with Sebastian Schlesinger.

Turning into Knightsbridge, his four-wheel cab collided with another vehicle. He later described it all graphically[43]. 'A frightful moment of broken glass – a turning round of cab and horse – a twist over of the cab just as I jumped out of it. My coat covered with broken glass – but my face and hands untouched. I did not feel it much at the time – but I fancy it has given me a shake, and stirred up the gout. But there are no bad symptoms, so far. . . .'

It cannot have helped. A month later he was taken ill again and was confined to the house for at least six weeks. By the end of March he was still far from recovered. He described himself as 'saturated with bile – racked by neuralgia (in the face this time)'. 'This morning,' he wrote to a friend, 'there is a cloudless sky – a splendid sun – and I have as much chance of "finding the longitude" or "squaring the circle" as I have of going out for a drive. And with a pretty woman too! A handkerchief covers my right cheek – an abscess is forming in my mouth, which contains hot laudanum and water, and is dumb to the utterance of Love'.

He was hardly in a state to work at his promised serialised novel – due to begin in mid-summer in *The Illustrated London News* – and he was still grappling with the sale of his outstanding copyrights to Chatto and Windus. It was presumably about this time that he took the decision to merge two of his proposed novels into one. He was still talking of 'two novels' at the end of March. Between then and June he must have finally decided how to merge the two ideas into one, combining his earlier efforts on *Iris* with his later preparations for *The Lord Harry* (incorporating details of a recent insurance fraud, told to him over dinner by a friend of the Lehmann's, Horace Pym, at their house in Berkeley Square) to become *Blind Love* [44]. But his body was being pushed too far. In mid-June, in a brief period of relaxation, the inevitable happened. He had a severe stroke.

Wilkie's condition was described by Harriet next day: 'Yesterday about 10 o'clock a.m. he had a bad attack of pain in the heart and paralysis of the left side. Mr Beard remained with him at night – and his condition is very sad – but we hope he is not in pain. He is conscious at intervals, but the oppression on his chest seems suffocating' [45].

The rest we know. Serialisation of *Blind Love* began in July. Shortly afterwards Wilkie persuaded Walter Besant to finish off the serialisation for him. In August and September he perked up a little and began to see a few close friends. An old friend of Harriet's later recalled seeing him at this time [46]. 'I thought then he would pull through, he was so strong and intellectually quite himself, so far as it went. He said as he grasped my hand with all his old warmth, "You see, I'm all right. Feel my arm!" But I had hard work to hide my eyes lest he should see what I really dreaded. Then he said in the most cheery terms, "Let's have a cigar" – a small one – and Caroline held the box and we each took one and then lighted them and so enjoyed this last smoke together'.

Even as late as the first week of September he was writing to Sebastian Schlesinger reporting himself (in a decidedly shaky hand) 'on the way to recovery'. He was, he said, well looked after. 'Two good nurses, the doctor who is nursing and my two daughters to see it and help. I want you to see my children – why, you will easily guess.' Two weeks later he was dead. But his family, and their financial future, had been in his thoughts to the end.

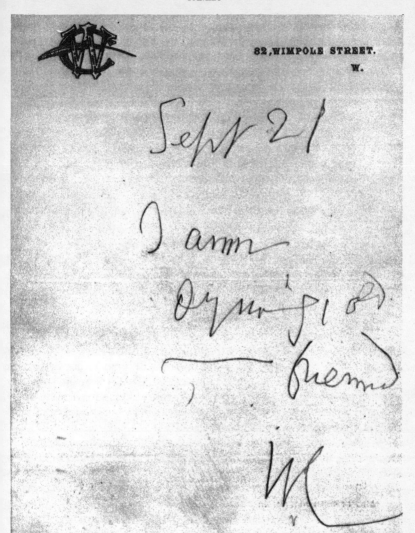

'I am dying old friend.'

Wilkie Collins's last note to his old friend and doctor, Frank Beard,
September 21st 1889

[185]

CHAPTER FIFTEEN

What Went Wrong

LIFE WENT on without him. Of Wilkie's close dependents, Caroline's way of life was the only one immediately affected by his death. Her primary role in the household had vanished overnight and her allowance in his will, generous though it was, would not allow her to stay long in such a large house in Wimpole Street. She moved out within a matter of weeks. Martha, running a more modest house in Taunton Place, remained there for well over a year after his death and even then simply moved because that particular row of houses was being demolished. Harriet was still with Henry and her children in St John's Wood.

Martha felt the material change in her life quite slowly. Her two girls seemed reasonably well provided for and William Charles, at fifteen, was still at school. Their needs were small, and their income secure. Whether Marian and Hettie received the £2,000 insurance money Wilkie had begun in Boston fifteen years earlier is still unclear[1]. Even if they did not, they seemed certain to inherit it, and much more, following the death of Caroline and her daughter, Harriet. (Or at least William Charles would and their income would benefit accordingly.)

Wilkie had ensured that his children would be given a good education and had protected them as well as he could from the scandal of his own actions. He had helped them to escape from Martha's working class background into the atmosphere, and the assumptions, of a respectable middle class family. Yet, for all his efforts, they never lost the consciousness of who they were and why they were different. Although they had had the privilege of a governess and the advantage of a liberal education at the Maria Grey School in Fitzroy Square, they were still unwilling to get too close to their school friends. Just as Harriet, when travelling abroad with Caroline and Wilkie ten years earlier, had felt the strange opprobrium of other children's parents, so Marian and Hettie found it difficult to be accepted for similar reasons.

They were quite dissimilar. Marian, the older of the two sisters, was extremely good-looking, bright and lively; Hettie was plainer, more subdued, and the more easily resigned to her position. Hettie became a governess for a time, but until the First World War opened up other opportunities, neither settled down to a particular occupation. Like the daughters of any middle class Victorian family, they had been brought up with the gentle accomplishments of needlework, music and household responsibilities but were in no way fitted to cultivate a normal social life. The combination of a strict upbringing and a consciousness of their fundamental unacceptability brought with it a growing resignation, even frustration, with their lot. And it was soon to take on a sourer note as the realisation of their financial vulnerability dawned on them.

Their brother, William Charles, 'Charley' to the family, was eventually to meet similar frustrations. But he had had a happy childhood and had found it easier to make friends at school and in later life. Like his sisters, he had been brought up in a modest house, but with forays into another more opulent world, in both Gloucester Place and Ramsgate. One of his closest schoolfriends was Charles Howell Thomas, who was the same age. Like other schoolboys of the time they thrilled to the stories of the British soldiers in India, on the Afghan frontier and in Africa. 'Jingoism' had been encouraged long before the Boer War and tales of military courage and bravery against the tribesmen on the North-west frontier and the Zulus in Natal abounded in the cheaper magazines of the day.

One particular episode seemed to strike a chord with both boys[2]: the bravery of the small British garrison at Rorke's Drift where, for the best part of a day, a handful of a hundred soldiers had held a force of three to four thousand Zulus at bay. The award of eleven VCs in one engagement made it certain that the story of one day's glory by the second battalion of the 23rd Regiment, soon known as the South Wales Borderers, would live on[3]. So it did in the minds of Victorian schoolboys and particularly Charley Dawson and his friend Charles Thomas.

After Wilkie's death, Martha ensured that Charley continued his schooling and later got a job in a London office as a clerk. She was playing safe, but Charley had other ideas and by the time he was nineteen (when they had just moved into a new house in Plympton Road, Brondesbury, just off the Edgware Road and not far from Wilkie's first school) he suddenly announced that he was joining the South Wales Borderers with his old school friend Charles Thomas. Both went off to Hounslow for their medical and within a couple of days had signed up with their favourite regiment and were in uniform at the Borderers' main depot in a beautiful Welsh valley in

Brecon. The glamour of Rorke's Drift was still exerting its influence.

Charley's military records show him to have been a healthy nineteen-year-old, with dark brown hair, brown eyes, a scar on his left knee, and of above average height. What they could not say was that, in contrast to his father, he was strikingly handsome and seemed to have inherited all the upright, strong features of Wilkie's father and brother. He differed from his father in other ways too. Quick to learn and grasp new ideas, his interests were towards the practical rather than the literary. While his mother and sisters lived quietly on the inner edge of London[4], he was slowly acquiring more than the usual Army training, deliberately seeking out educational courses, a teachers' training course and instructors' courses in signalling, musketry and gymnastics. He soon rose to the rank of sergeant.

Then came the Boer War which was eventually to turn his mind in other directions. He sailed for South Africa early in 1900 with the second battalion and was quickly in action[5]. His battalion was in time to help Lord Roberts' efforts to relieve Kimberley in February and March and was in action at Jacobsdal, prior to the taking of Bloemfontein. Then came further action as the Boers were pressed along the railway line up towards Brandford, Charley's battalion moving 'very steadily, advancing and lying down under fire like an Aldershot field-day'.

Whether these 'engagements with the enemy' lived up to his schoolboy visions is unclear and he soon succumbed, like so many compatriots, to dysentery and was on a boat returning to England within five months of his departure. But he had been 'under fire' and had received the Queen's South Africa Medal, with Cape Colony and Orange Free State clasps.

On his return, his efforts at self-improvement continued. He became a riding instructor to the mounted infantry and was secretly enthused at the possibilities of the internal combustion engine. His hopes fastened on the possibility of a commission, but deep disappointment lay ahead and it gradually became clear to him that promotion to the rank of officer was unlikely. Not so for his friend Charles Thomas, who was duly commissioned in the First Glamorganshire Royal Garrison Artillery in 1904 and appointed Captain little more than a year later. He eventually reached Colonel, rose to Second Permanent Secretary at the Ministry of Agriculture, and retired as Sir Charles Howell Thomas, an honorary fellow of Queen's College, Cambridge, and a governor of the London School of Economics and the University of Wales.

The contrast between their immediate prospects was, on the face of it, difficult to understand. They had had a similar education, had shared similar enthusiasms and had given good accounts of themselves during their service careers. Only one difference apparently separated them – parentage. Whether his basic illegitimacy was a factor in his not obtaining a commission is difficult to confirm; that Charley might suspect so was a further example of the legacy Wilkie had bequeathed, unwittingly, to his morganatic family.

Charley left the Army in July 1902 and was soon indulging his new-found interest in motorised vehicles. He had naturally learned to drive and, apparently out of the blue, came an offer to become the chauffeur of the Earl of Orkney. This may have been the result of a chance meeting, but it is far more likely that one of Harriet's girls had a hand in the affair. All four had been attracted to the stage and the eldest and Wilkie's favourite, 'Dah', now known as Doris Beresford, had become a well-known 'Gaiety Girl'. So by chance was the Countess of Orkney, formerly Constance Gilchrist. Hence, no doubt, the introduction.

Whatever the reason, Charley was soon driving one of the latest French models, a *Vinot-Déguingard*, subjecting it to detailed analysis and inspection and maintaining it on the road. In return for his expert services, rare in those early days of motoring, he was occasionally invited to a local shoot on the Earl's land.

His mother Martha, along with his two sisters, had by this time moved out of London and had gone to live in a modest house in Southend. The sea air, it was felt, would help her bronchitis and the cheaper rents available outside London were plainly an added attraction to three women whose only additional income came from the occasional job of governess taken on by Hettie. They were all still assuming that on Harriet's death the other half of Wilkie's capital would revert to them, though some of the news from the Bartley side of the family must have raised increasing doubts in their minds over the years.

The realisation of the full truth, however, only came on Harriet's death in 1905, in theatrical 'digs' in Richmond, where her eldest daughter Doris was living. Harriet, it became immediately clear, had no money to pass on and had been virtually bereft of Wilkie's promised support for years. Marian, Hettie and Charley were left to realise that Wilkie's unorthodoxies had not only deprived them of a true name but, in some way, had led to their unexpected impoverishment as well.

Prospects seemed to be far worse for Marian and Hettie than for Charley, who had far more opportunities opening up before him. And for a time this was borne out by events. Charley married a sea-captain's daughter a few months after the shock of Harriet's death, and started his own motor business in Ramsgate, even registering an invention for a new style variable gearbox in the name of 'William Charles Collins-Dawson, motor engineer'. This was the only occasion on which Charley appears to have used the name of Collins in this way. The invention itself may now appear somewhat cumbersome, but in 1907 it put him in the vanguard of motoring experts and enthusiasts. He was soon embracing motor boats within his expertise. He and his new wife, Florence, settled down in a house in Ramsgate within yards of the house his father had been taken to on holiday seventy years earlier and just round the corner from Wellington Crescent where he and his father and mother had subsequently spent several happy holidays.

Not long afterwards their first child Helen Martha (later known as 'Bobbie') was born. Life at last seemed to be moving his way. His motoring expertise was in demand and very soon he was tempted to move back to London to exploit it further. Motoring organisations were being set up to represent chauffeurs and owner-drivers, and before long Charley became one of the early organisers of the Society of Automobile Mechanic Drivers. He slipped into the essentially administrative role with ease. Their second child, Lionel Charles, was born, and the small family at last seemed secure when tragedy struck.

Within five months of the birth of their son, Charley caught 'flu', went to recuperate with Martha in Southend, and died suddenly from a cerebral haemorrhage at the age of thirty-eight.

It was to take the Dawson family over a quarter of a century to recover their financial balance. Charley's children were split up and had to be cared for by his widow and other members of the family; Martha and her daughters survived as well as they could in Southend and, following Martha's death there in 1919, Marian and Hettie needed continual support from Charley's children until they too died in Southend, within a few months of each other, in 1955. Over their last few decades Wilkie's remaining capital slowly disappeared as a combination of inflation, trustee-imposed investment mistakes and sheer day-to-day needs took their toll.

Wilkie's well arranged plans had slowly gone awry. At the heart of the problem was the disappearance of a large amount of the bequeathed money on Caroline's side. Martha's family were always convinced that a solicitor was in some way connected with the mystery but neither Marian nor Hettie ever spelt out their true suspicions.

There is now, however, enough evidence to suggest where the weak link in the chain was and what may have happened to undermine Wilkie's intentions.

Of Wilkie's closest acquaintances, Caroline suffered most from his death. She had to move out of Wimpole Street and find somewhere more modest to live. She had to cope with the oblique references to herself in the press. And she must have felt that a relationship of close on forty years, which had excited her, comforted her, and even rescued her from her own marital folly, had snapped all too swiftly and cruelly for her to cope with in her mid-fifties.

Harriet, on the other hand, had a settled family to fall back on, a solicitor's home to look after and 'in-laws' who had grown to accept her for what she was, a lively and worthy wife for Henry. Henry, too, was immediately involved in the aftermath of Wilkie's will both as his solicitor and, with Frank Beard and Sebastian Schlesinger, as one of his executors. Over the next nine months they were concerned with the sale of his most treasured possessions. Although a few items were returned to individual friends, four separate auctions disposed of his original manuscripts, his library and his paintings and drawings. They took place in the months of October, January, February and June following his death[6].

Henry showed more interest in the family pictures than in Wilkie's books, most of which were taken up by the London dealers. He eventually spent over £150 at the picture auction, acquiring several pictures by William and Charles Collins, as well as the study of Wilkie undertaken forty years earlier by John Millais. Several of the pictures of Wilkie's family, by John Linnell and Alexander Geddes, which had graced the walls of Wilkie's study, were acquired by another old friend, Horace Pym[7].

The last traces of Wilkie's occupancy of 82 Wimpole Street vanished on 24th October when all the furniture there (including the mahogany writing table of his father's on which Wilkie had written so many of his novels) was finally put under the hammer. Thereafter Caroline was forced to find separate lodgings, while Henry and Harriet devoted themselves to their growing family.

Relations with Henry's parents and his brothers had remained close, in spite of the Bohemian atmosphere the Bartleys always detected in Wimpole Street. This fascination with Wilkie's household rarely flagged and different members of the Bartley family, as they returned from the occasional meal in Gloucester Place or Wimpole Street, kept Margaret Bartley, Henry's mother, well briefed on Wilkie's unorthodoxies. She was also not averse to sending someone round to Gloucester Place to see how things were developing.

Henry and Harriet inevitably shared in some of the latent criticism within the Bartley family, and the expensive yacht, *Doris*, which Henry kept in Ramsgate harbour had hardly helped. Nonetheless both Henry and Harriet ('Harry' and 'Mite' to their relations) were still warmly accepted within the family and, on the retirement of his father, Henry was given full control of the family firm. It came as no surprise, therefore, when Henry's younger brother Richard, who had been admitted as a solicitor in the summer of 1890, joined him in the partnership in Portman Square, extending the firm's name to H.P. and R.E. Bartley.

A year later Harriet gave birth to her fifth child, Iris Dora. They now had four girls, with a gap of twelve years between the eldest, Doris, and the new baby. Henry's extravagance and heavy spending, however, had hardly abated, even with the added burdens of a growing family and the absence of Wilkie's occasionally helping hand; and, within a year of Iris's birth, Harriet's domestic happiness and the stable environment she had known so long slowly began to disintegrate.

It is difficult to know how she herself saw or felt the changes, but over the next three years the drama unfolded year by year. It was seen first within the Bartley family itself, as Henry and Richard dissolved their legal partnership[8], with each brother going his own way. Within a year, Henry's own firm of solicitors in Portman Square was wound up[9].

Henry's basic troubles, though they included romantic distractions, were plainly financial. He lost a considerable amount of money and, in the year in which his firm was wound up, he approached the National Portrait Gallery to enquire whether they would wish to buy two portraits of Wilkie, especially the one by Sir John Millais. The Gallery was clearly determined to keep Henry's bargaining under control for at the outset he asked for double the price he had paid at auction only a few years earlier. Once the Gallery was satisfied with the picture's authenticity, they offered Henry the price he had paid originally. He eventually agreed, with some reluctance. In confirming the picture's origin, Henry produced a strange letter from Sir John Millais, in which the artist had expressed surprise that the portrait had come up at auction at all, since he was under the impression that Wilkie had intended it for the Piggott family[10].

Shortly afterwards Caroline, who had no doubt been told of Henry's offer to the National Portrait Gallery, wrote to ask whether they would be interested in *her* pictures of the Collins family[11]. She was politely declined. The underlying assumption must be that she too had begun to feel the pinch and her sudden death the following year in lodgings above a cabinetmaker's shop in Newman Street, from a heart attack, following an attack of acute bronchitis, confirmed the sad decline in her fortunes.

She died in circumstances far from those Wilkie had planned for her and in the clear knowledge that all the high hopes she and Wilkie had entertained for Harriet's future in encouraging her marriage had come to nought. Henry had not only broken with his own family, the Bartleys, but he had finally left Harriet and the four girls and gone to live with another woman in a pub on the Thames.

Caroline was appropriately buried beside Wilkie in Kensal Green Cemetery on 14th June 1895, in a grave arranged originally by Frank Beard and Henry Bartley. Frank Beard was by this time dead and Henry was elsewhere. From then until she left London to go to Southend, Martha continued to tend the grave and, the following year, she even arranged to have it transferred to her own name. She is still in the records at Kensal Green as the owner.

To their credit, the Bartley family rallied round Harriet. Henry's mother helped her to find a smaller, though adequate, house in Kilburn Priory, just off Maida Vale, and not far from their own house in Hamilton Terrace. More important, she arranged a regular monthly allowance for Harriet which was to continue until Henry's mother died five years later[12].

Henry, having cut himself off from the Bartleys and from Harriet and, in some way, severed the flow of money from Wilkie's inheritance to Caroline and Harriet, vanishes from the story for a couple of years, only to re-emerge again in Guildford in the summer of 1897, sadly dying of cancer. He died in August, after a painful illness of close on nine months[13], in the presence of a nurse. At the end of the week a small paragraph in the local *Surrey Advertiser* briefly recorded his death and who he was and stressed his 'great suffering'. No will has been traced.

That Henry was instrumental in the disappearance of virtually half of Wilkie's wealth, within five or six years of his death, is hardly in dispute. Exactly what happened to it is more difficult to spell out, without detailed knowledge of the administration of the estate and the yearly trust account, which should have been prepared by Henry and his ultimate successor. The circumstantial evidence, however, covering the period between Wilkie's death in 1889 and Harriet's death in 1905, strongly suggests that Henry's personal difficulties, whether self-generated or otherwise, had in some way reduced the regular annual income which both Caroline and Harriet should have been able to rely upon.

Caroline's death in lodgings in Newman Street, Henry's clear need to sell off Wilkie's pictures, Harriet's reliance on Henry's mother for an allowance and the absence of any residue of the original £5,000 capital on Harriet's death all point in the same direction; that is, to a confirmation of the hearsay evidence passed down to the present generation, within both the Dawson and Bartley families, that Wilkie's solicitor had in some way deprived his dependents of their rightful inheritance.

Harriet managed to bring up her four daughters on her own, with the financial and moral support of the Bartleys. The relationship was not an easy one. Harriet trailed with her all the memories of the Collins household, and Richard's family in particular, which had taken the brunt of the break-up of the joint partnership, could hardly be expected to switch all their sympathy to a family whose background and upbringing had tended to be so different from their own. Harriet's girls were in any case turning out to be not only outstandingly beautiful but, through Wilkie's old theatrical friends, considerably attracted to the stage. Doris in particular had inherited all her grandmother's and her mother's good looks and, at eighteen, was remarkably poised for her age.

Her first social success came from the initiative of Henry's younger brother Frank. He had shared their sailing enthusiasms in Ramsgate and clearly had a soft spot for the four girls. Though a bachelor, he delighted in giving dinner parties for his friends and, on one occasion, which evidently caused much talk among the Bartleys, he asked Doris along to fill up an unexpected cancellation. The Bartleys hoped (and no doubt politely insisted) that Harriet would see that Doris was correctly dressed and would behave accordingly.

Their anxieties were groundless. Doris's first public appearance had the impact she was to have at the stage door of the Gaiety Theatre over the ensuing decade. She captivated everyone, and Frank had an unexpected social success on his hands. Within a couple of years she had been engaged by a touring company and a year later she had taken on a major role and attracted the attention of George Edwardes at the Gaiety.

It was precisely at this point, at the beginning of 1900, that Henry's mother, Margaret Bartley, who was still living close to Harriet and the girls, died. And the regular allowance Harriet had relied on ceased immediately. She received £50 in the will 'to give her a reasonable time for making arrangements for herself and her children that may become necessary'.

The 'arrangements' quickly included a further removal to an even more modest house. But Doris at least had made her first theatrical foray and was on the verge of a glamorous, though still financially precarious, career. Her sisters, then aged nineteen, seventeen and nine, were all to be attracted by similar footlights over the coming years. Glamour rather than security was to be the touchstone of all their lives, with Harriet making ends meet as best she could with their help. It is remarkable that they coped as well as they did.

Doris's first tentative step to fame, if not fortune, was with John Le Haye and Dalton Somers' touring company in light comedies and musical comedies. Her real opportunity came when she took over the leading role from Katie Seymour in *My Girl* in 1899. She was just twenty. George Edwardes, who was then running the Gaiety Theatre, was constantly on the look out for new talent and regularly visited the provincial theatres in his quest. He saw Doris, was impressed and offered her an immediate contract.

Doris joined the Gaiety at the time when John Hollingshead's original policy of 'legs, short skirts and French adaptations' (which, in spite of his earlier friendship with Wilkie and Charles Dickens, had got him a black-ball to his application for membership of the Reform Club) had already been replaced by George Edwardes' more sophisticated musical comedies, and when the 'Gaiety Girl' herself had been transformed from a girl in tights to a beautiful elegant creature, clothed in expensive Parisian fashions. 'The new Gaiety Girl's greatest attraction,' one critic later explained, 'was her face, brilliantly lit by the new electric lamps, and shown off to perfection in the elegant setting provided by Edwardes'[14].

Doris was an ideal recruit. One of her later notices described her as having 'remarkably beautiful blue eyes, real golden hair that owes none of its sheen to anything approaching "applied arts" and a neck and arms – well you can judge for yourself, can't you?'[15]

Her first full Gaiety production was *The Messenger Boy* in which Katie Seymour, whose part she had taken in the earlier touring company, starred alongside Edmund Payne. It opened in February 1900, in the middle of the Boer War (just after Charley Dawson's arrival in South Africa), and ran for over a year. Then came *The Toreador*, in which Doris at last got her name in the programme and was rubbing shoulders with Olive May (soon to become the Countess of Drogheda) and the new star of the show, Gertie Millar, who was to dominate the Gaiety, along with the music of Lionel Monckton, for almost a decade, and to become the Countess of Dudley. The show had the longest run known at the Gaiety.

After the last night of *The Toreador* the old theatre succumbed to the extensive rebuilding of the whole area. Yet within four months, the 'new' Gaiety Theatre arose on a site only fifty yards from the old, alongside the new London thoroughfare, the Aldwych; and in the early autumn of 1903, Doris, with the rest of the new cast, assembled for the first time on the new stage – *The Orchid* was in rehearsal. A newspaper photographer recorded the occasion and Doris left a cutting showing herself and her fellow 'debutantes' as a reminder to herself and her family[16]. And on 26th October the curtain rose for the first time at the New Gaiety in the presence of King Edward and Queen Alexandra. Edward had returned to the theatre he had so often frequented in earlier, perhaps more carefree, days, a gesture that added to the glamorous success of the first night, and the extensive run that followed.

Doris had entered a remarkable new world. As Macqueen Pope described it in his evocative book, *Gaiety: Theatre of Enchantment*:

> 'The town was rich, so rich, that it seems incredible today. There was leisure and time for appreciation of quality and beauty . . . And a surprising number of young men about town found their leisure permitted them the privilege of spending a great deal of it at the Gaiety. This period, from *The Orchid* up to the outbreak of "World War the first", was perhaps the peak of the glory of the Gaiety Girl. Never had she been more beautiful or more adorable . . . The Gaiety stage door was, indeed, the gateway to romance. To know a Gaiety Girl, to take her out to supper, that was a cachet about town. The girls adorned the restaurants to which they were taken'[17].

It was all a marked contrast to the life Doris's mother Harriet was leading in Kilburn. How far Doris was able to help out with the family budget is difficult to discern. The trouble was that the Gaiety Girls, while adequately paid, were hardly overpaid in cash. George Edwardes took great care of their welfare. As he said, he helped them to pick up their aitches, clean their fingernails, dye their hair, inspect their teeth, remove their appendix and he dressed them from their underclothes to their boots[18]. But he was never well known for excessive generosity to his employees. Mink, diamonds, supper at Romano's or the Savoy were hardly unknown to the Gaiety Girls, but they were not the direct outcome of their pay packets. Their escorts helped them bridge the gap. Penny-pinching and high living went hand in hand.

Given Doris's example, it is hardly surprising that Cecile, Evelyn and eventually Iris should follow her on to the stage. They all shared her good looks and by the time they needed introductions, Doris could help. But with hindsight it hardly ensured the financial security they all needed. Over the next few years, Harriet moved closer to Doris, eventually settling down in the same street in Richmond, as the younger girls began to make their own way on the stage. Yet none of them were able to shake off the financial insecurity that their father had interposed between Wilkie's intentions and the cruel outcome.

Doris alone had the opportunity to escape from this general insecurity but, for reasons of her own, allowed it to pass. George Edwardes' policy of recruiting girls with poise and presence, as well as a pretty face and figure, had begun to attract a higher class of girl, from middle class families. And it was a short step from this shift of emphasis to the thought in the minds of the suitors who thronged the stage door of the Gaiety and of the blue-blooded escorts at Romano's, that matrimony might be a growing possibility. Their mothers had other views, but the growing number of liaisons between Gaiety girls and titled men soon demonstrated the eligibility of George Edwardes' girls.

One of the first matches was the marriage of Connie Gilchrist to the Earl of Orkney. Then came Rosie Boote, one of the stars of Doris's first Gaiety productions, *The Messenger Boy*, who married the Marquess of Headfort. Olive May, who was in several of Doris's productions, married Lord Victor Paget (heir presumptive to the Marquess of Anglesey) and eventually became the Countess of Drogheda. Soon George Edwardes was boasting, 'The King creates the peers, but *I* choose the peeresses'. It was a reasonable boast. In a decade and a half, no less than twenty-three Gaiety girls married titled men.

Doris too had her moment when a titled suitor offered her marriage, but to the disbelief of all her family she turned him down. Her Gaiety friends were convinced she was mad. The trouble was that she had already met Louis Bishop, one of the actors with her original touring company, and had lost her heart rather too soon. They were still together when her mother died in Richmond in 1905, Louis witnessing the death certificate as Harriet's son-in-law, but their ways were soon to part[19].

The disappointment of similar theatrical liaisons and marriages were to dog the other girls too. All three were attracted to musical comedy. Evelyn Beatrice became Eve Bevington on the stage, taking on Marie Tempest's roles on tour, and married Geoffrey Wontner, a cousin of Arthur Wontner, the well-known actor-manager, a few months after her mother's death. Cecile Marguerite, who was a couple of years younger than Doris, eventually married George Gregson, a fellow actor, when they were both in digs in Doncaster. The youngest, Iris, probably the most talented as an actress, dancer and singer, married Martin Iredale when they were touring in *The Dollar Princess*.

Glamour and money, however, did not go hand in hand. Theatrical touring companies were neither lucrative nor stable; and all the girls and their eventual families suffered accordingly. Their marriages collapsed and their children were constantly passed from one to the other. Not long after Evelyn's marriage, Geoffrey Wontner went off to Australia, leaving her on her own. For a time she was comforted in remarkable luxury by Percy Gordon Arthur, the manager of the King's Theatre, Hammersmith, who had earlier consolidated a fortune in the Alaskan gold rush. But the respite did not last. Percy Arthur died. Then Evelyn met an attractive Frenchman, had two children and was again deserted.

Shortly afterwards, she startled Arthur Wontner, who was on the Committee of the Actor's Orphanage, by applying for support in the name of Mrs Wontner. Arthur quickly got his son Hugh (now Sir Hugh Wontner, until recently Chairman of the Savoy Hotel), to find out about Evelyn's children. He found that both children were registered as Geoffrey's at Somerset House, but some quick letters to cousins in South Africa and Australia soon confirmed that Geoffrey could not have been responsible. 'They were certainly her children,' Sir Hugh recalls, 'but not his, and the use in both their names of Marcel suggests that this was the father's name, possibly a Frenchman'. He was right.

Cecile fared little better. She and George Gregson had a boy and a girl before she too was left on her own. Geoffrey, the boy, was soon touring the provinces with his mother, sleeping in a 'geisha basket', and getting to know the other members of Seymour Hicks' touring company. But once again tragedy struck. Cecile died young from cancer and her children were to spend the rest of their childhood moving between the other sisters. Iris, the youngest, suffered a similar desertion, shortly after the birth of her son, Ronald[20].

Doris's fortunes too were eventually blighted, though in her case it took rather longer for the underlying difficulties to emerge. Once *The Orchid* had been successfully launched at the New Gaiety, and her face had become widely familiar, she was constantly in demand as a photographic model, posing for the galleries and for the growing commercial advertisements. One of her reviewers described her as 'one of the most eagerly sought after photograph beauties' and went on: 'In one photographic gallery that I know of there will be found a collection of "studies" of this most lovely young lady that would tempt St Anthony himself'. Her face still turns up regularly in all the London shops selling Victoriana.

She followed *The Orchid* with three further successes at the Gaiety, *Spring Chicken*, *The New Aladdin* and *The Girls of Gottenberg*, adding the occasional special dance to the normal presence of a Gaiety girl. Seymour Hicks eventually tempted her away with *The Gay Gordons* and her next appearance was in *The Belle of Brittany* at the Queen's. The following year she married a mining engineer, Ivo Locke.

She had just turned thirty, but like her grandmother she had a cavalier attitude to marriage certificates and put herself down as twenty-six. The marriage, however, did not buy her the stability she still craved for and in the succeeding years (including the years of the First World War which she spent in Paris) her fortunes ebbed and flowed, until she was eventually provided with a little comfort in rent-free accommodation from the Bartley family, or rather her favourite uncle Frank.

Thus all the girls eventually suffered the impact of their father's aberrations. The Bartley family had felt some obligation to them from the outset and even after the death of Henry's mother his younger brother, Richard, continued to offer a sympathetic hand from time to time. The trouble was that once this sympathy was transformed into monetary help as it was when one of the girls called on his Blandford Street office, he found himself faced with similar demands as, in turn, each sister fell on hard times. He soon felt obliged to call a halt. Wilkie's legacy and Henry's misdeeds continued to strain relations continuously over the years.

CHAPTER SIXTEEN

Aftermath

THUS, WITHIN fifteen years of his death, Wilkie's closest dependants were all in difficulties; Martha's children suffering from the stigma of their background, Harriet's children reflecting the lack of parental stability, and all of them deprived of the financial cushion he had planned.

It is tempting to see the causes in circumstances beyond his control, but his own character too must be weighed in the balance. What his friends mainly recalled was a pleasant, stimulating companion. He was 'gentlemanly, patient and good-tempered' according to Wybert Reeve. 'Consideration and courtesy to old and young' and 'a keen love of fun' were recalled by Nathaniel Beard. He was 'as delightful in private as in public,' according to William Frith, 'an admirable raconteur' with an 'imperturbably good temper'. In Hall Caine's eyes 'he was a man to set you at your ease'.

'To be in his company was to be charmed, stimulated and refreshed,' confirmed William Winter. But he at least noticed something else too. 'His views,' he went on, 'were unconventional – the views of a man who had observed human nature and society widely and closely and who thought for himself. . . . His temperament was mercurial – his words alternating between exuberant glee and pensive gloom; but in society he was remarkable for the buoyancy of a youthful spirit, and at all times he dominated himself and his circumstances with a calm, resolute will'.

In short, humanity, humour and companionship went hand in hand with a clear appraisal of what was going on in the world. He had a closer grasp of public affairs than he has been given credit for. Nathaniel Beard left an impression that he was no great reader of newspapers, stressing that Wilkie would often remark 'I hear' or 'I am told', never 'I see' or 'I read'. It seems a flimsy basis for ignoring Collins's clear views of American and European politics, his professional writings in *The Leader*, as well as his continual interest in political issues of all kinds from his early days[1] onwards. He may have been considerate; he was also dogged and determined. His publishers, literary agent and reviewers felt the lash of his tongue or the harshness of a quickly-dashed note when they touched what he felt was a sensitive spot. Pirates of his work, innocent or otherwise, were quickly chastised and rarely ignored. Pretentiousness was put down wherever he met it, in a young over-serious politician[2] or elsewhere. Yet, when faced with a remark that his words were read 'in every back-kitchen in England', he showed no sign of irritation[3].

In literature and the arts his tastes were both catholic and clear cut. He appreciated Tennyson's shorter poems, read Walter Scott's poetry 'with admiration and delight', and believed Byron to be 'beyond comparison the greatest poet that has sung since Milton'[4]. Walter Scott he regarded as 'the Prince, King, Emperor, God Almighty of novelists', and pressed his friends to read *The Antiquary* 'over and over again'[5]. In his estimation Fenimore Cooper, Walter Scott and Balzac were the three Kings of Fiction. In English letters he regarded Boswell's *Life of Johnson* as 'the greatest biographical work that has ever been written'[6]. He read French novels by the dozen. He thought many to be 'dull and dirty' and *Le Nabab* by Daudet 'such realistic rubbish' that he rushed out to get something to take the taste out of his mouth. Prosper Mérimée's delicious *Columba* 'appeared providentially in a shop window'[7]. He adored Italian opera (Verdi, Donizetti, Bellini), but found it difficult to appreciate Wagner[8].

His knowledge of the art world may have bored Dickens; it was rarely overlooked by those who knew him well. As Holman Hunt later averred, 'Wilkie Collins had knowledge of the interest of art for more than one past generation; he spoke with authority on the matter'.

This then was a man who knew his mind, who had learned to keep his counsel while his father was alive (though still living his own life in the way he wished) and who continued to run his affairs with only a casual glance at contemporary *mores*. He took drugs, had a casual approach to liaisons, kept two mistresses and a morganatic family in an era when rigid codes of conduct existed uneasily alongside loose morals. But he did these things not to make a point, not to be ahead of his time, but simply because he was always at ease with his own decisions.

His attitude to women was in much the same mould. His writings suggest that he accepted women for what they really were, individuals in their own right, not Victorian appendages to a male-dominated society. As Dr Sue Lonoff has rightly concluded, 'the pattern young lady of Victorian fiction plays, at best, a minor rôle within his stories. His heroines are characters of substance and complexity; his harridans are forces to be reckoned with'[9]. But as she also acknowledges, there is more to it than that. His female characters often combine patent sexuality with strong personalities. And both she and Natalie Schroeder[10] have stressed the candid, even daring, exploration of female psychology undertaken by Collins in his major novels. As he himself put it in his preface to *Armadale*: 'Estimated by the claptrap morality of the present day, this may be a very daring book. Judged by the Christian morality which is of all time, it is only a book that is daring enough to speak the truth'.

He was at ease in most kinds of female company. The women he cultivated, and counted as his close friends, were women of talent and personality – from the artistic, literary and theatrical worlds. He carried on a teasing correspondence with many of them over the years. Casual companions at dinner parties were just as easily entertained with relaxed tales of his early days. He invariably had their measure. On one occasion he was trying unsuccessfully to fob off an actress in his study in Gloucester Place with any old photograph of himself. She was clearly determined to take his latest Sarony photograph and, sensing she was close to discovery in his desk, he seized her hand and said, 'For God's sake, don't look at that; it's *something indecent!*' He knew what would happen. She instantly answered, 'Then I must certainly look at it!' and got the portrait[11].

He was hardly the person to have indecent pictures in his desk. When Sarony sent him a crateful of his latest nude studies he spent hours poring over them writing ecstatic appraisals back to New York ('Bravo, bravo, carissimo Sarony!'), inviting his friends to take copies and placing his choice nude firmly on top of his desk for all the world to see.

His three favourites were a girl with closed eyes floating past the moon, a girl reclining with transparent lace over part of her body and more lace on her head, and, his clear favourite, a girl entering her bath. As he wrote back to Sarony, *his* Venus more than rivalled Titian's. 'Titian's Venus has just come *out* of her bath – and Sarony's Venus is just going *into* her bath and is by far the most charming woman of the two. She is now in her beautiful frame, exhibited in the best light in my front study. Everybody who sees her, admires her'.

It was with this same candid openness that he worked out his intricate relations with Caroline and Martha. Both knew of the other. Their families (one's grandchildren and the other's children) were thrown together at an early age. Only Caroline and Martha seemed to be kept apart. In their different ways they represented different sides of Wilkie's character.

His life with Caroline was, from the beginning, romantic, lively and shameless, running counter to everything his father and his own contemporaries regarded as 'proper'. He did not hide, nor even apologise for, his unorthodox behaviour, allowing his friends, and their wives, to come to terms with it as best they could. He did not flout current sensitivities, but rather ignored them. His relations with Caroline, and the atmosphere they both created for Harriet and her children, were a natural extension of his candid reaction to contemporary morality.

Martha, on the other hand, was different from the outset. She was never exposed to the openness Caroline thrived on. He took every precaution to see that she was protected by an aura of respectability. From the birth of their first child, he clothed them with a 'morganatic marriage' and called on them under a deliberate, assumed name, whether in London or Ramsgate. In a word, he conformed, in Martha's interests, to some of the conventions of the day. Martha too brought up their children, and later their grandchildren, under the strictest supervision. Both of her grandchildren remembered her with some awe, dressed invariably in black dress and cap, watching their behaviour at mealtimes, rapping their knuckles on the table, acting like any rigid Victorian grandparent. 'She was the last person in the world one would have expected to have lived in sin,' they recalled.

Wilkie's love and concern for her and her children have never been in doubt. Why, with his continual emphasis on these surface proprieties, he never married Martha is worth considering. In an identical situation in *Basil* (a young man from a well to do family in love with the daughter of a tradesman), his hero had no hesitation:

'. . . the base thought never occurred to me, which might have occurred to some other men, in my position: why marry the girl, because I love her? Why, with my money, my station, my opportunities, obstinately connect love and marriage as one idea, and make a dilemma and a danger where neither need exist? Had such a thought as this, in the faintest, the most shadowy form, crossed my mind, I should have shrunk from it, have shrunk from myself, with horror.'

What was a clear line of action to Basil was far from clear to Wilkie. He had grown to despise marriage, and the effect marriage had on his closest friends[12]. Having escaped the condition with Caroline, he was unlikely to rush into a legal liaison with Martha, with all the social upheaval it would have brought with it in Gloucester Place. Martha always insisted to her family that she could have married Wilkie, any time she wished. If so, only the wide gulf in their social backgrounds prevented him from behaving in reality as he continued to pretend to parts of the outside world, with the results we can now see.

The tight control exercised by Wilkie Collins over his plots was hardly paralleled in his private life. He meant well. His openness, candour and strength of will enabled him to choose a lifestyle at variance with the habits of his time. But it was a strength that was difficult to pass on to his dependents. Henry Bartley let him down; Martha's children, particularly Marian and Hettie, found it difficult to cope with the circumstances he had produced; and Harriet and *her* children ultimately suffered from the environment he and Caroline had created in Gloucester Place and Wimpole Street.

APPENDIX A

Sources of Letters

1 I have consulted and used excerpts from the letters of William Wilkie Collins in the following collections, which I gratefully acknowledge:

Pierpont Morgan Library, New York (plus letters of his mother, father and brother).

New York Public Library (Berg Collection; de Coursey Tales Collection; Vattemore Collection and Montague Collection).

Humanities Research Center, University of Texas at Austin.

Houghton Library, Harvard University, Harvard.

Department of Special Collections, University Research Library, University of California, Los Angeles.

Morris L. Parrish Collection, Princeton University Library, Princeton, New Jersey.

Lilly Library, Indiana University, Bloomington, Indiana.

Beinecke Rare Book and Manuscript Library, Yale University, Connecticut.

University Library, University of Illinois, Urbana, Illinois.

Huntington Library, San Marino, California.

Boston Public Library, Boston, Massachusetts.

Bodleian Library, Oxford.

Stanford University Libraries, Stanford University, California.

Folger Shakespeare Library, Washington D.C.

British Museum, London.

Mitchell Library, Glasgow.

Columbia University, New York.

University of Iowa Libraries, Iowa City, Iowa.

Brotherton Library, University of Leeds.

Robert Lee Wolff Collection, New York.

Andrew Gasson, London.

Faith Elizabeth Clarke (née Dawson), London.

Sir John Lawrence, London.

2 In addition, I have consulted and used original letters or other original sources, relating to Wilkie Collins's family and acquaintances in the possession of the following individuals or institutions:

Victoria and Albert Museum, London. (The diaries of Harriet Collins for the years 1835–37; notes of William Collins.)

Pierpont Morgan Library, New York.

Phillips Exeter Academy.

Marion E. Wade Collection, Wheaton College, Illinois.

APPENDIX B

Notes to Chapters

Preface

1 See note 28 to Chapter Ten.

2 Quoted in Hesketh Pearson, *Dickens*, London 1949 (p. 217). See also Dorothy
   Sayers, *Wilkie Collins, A Critical and Biographical Study* (Ed., Professor E. R.
   Gregory), the Friends of the University of Toledo Libraries, 1977. Some of
   Dorothy Sayers' notes, now in the library of the Humanities Research Center
   of the University of Texas, show that she had some successes (in tracing
   Caroline's family to Toddington, for example), but that she had some
   frustrations too (in chasing Caroline's first husband as a 'Captain in the Army',
   in searching in Lancashire for an early marriage of Collins's and in chasing
   others with a similar name eg in Oregon).

3 AMS Press, New York, 1982.

4 *Sunday Express*, November 24th 1974.

5 *Financial Times*, December 19th 1974.

6 Sue Lonoff refers to it briefly in her *Wilkie Collins and his Victorian Readers* (AMS
   Press, New York, 1982), p. 158.

Chapter One

1 Letter from Mrs Bartley (Harriet Graves) to *Reynolds News*. Cutting,
   undated, in possession of R. Iredale, Mitcham, London.

2 *The Times*, July 15th 1889.

3 Frederick and Nina Lehmann. Nina was the daughter of Robert Chambers
   (of Chambers's *Edinburgh Journal*). Her aunt Janet (Robert's sister) married
   W. H. Wills, Dickens's sub-editor on the *Daily News, Household Words* and
   All the Year Round. (Sources: John Lehmann, *Ancestors and Friends* (London
   1962) and R. C. Lehmann, *Charles Dickens as Editor* (London 1912).)

4 The sequence of events described here is different from that given in

Kenneth Robinson's *Wilkie Collins* and in Nuel Pharr Davis's *Life of Wilkie Collins*. Their description seems to be based on the account given by Frank Beard's son, Nathaniel Beard, in *Some Recollections of Yesterday* (*Temple Bar*, 1894). The original notes, and envelope, written by Wilkie to Frank Beard are dated September 21st, two days before his death, and can be seen in the Princeton University Parrish Collection. Nathaniel Beard's version has also changed the wording of the original notes.

5 The death certificate confirms that Dr Beard and Mrs Caroline Graves were present at death.

6 *Considerations on the Copyright Question Addressed to an American Friend* (London: Trubner 1880).

7 Lady Brassey was author of *Voyage of the Sunbeam*, a book which, according to her husband, had been 'translated into the language of nearly every civilised nation'.

8 Letter to W. Tindall, August 8th 1871, Mitchell Library, Glasgow.

Chapter Two

1 He wrote *The Memoirs of a Picture* (H. D. Symonds, London, 1805), which includes *The Life of George Morland*.

2 Captain Geddes rented Shute End House and gardens, and two other small pieces of ground (just over four acres in all) in the second half of 1798 and his family remained there for over forty years. (Sources: Wiltshire County Archivist and Donald C. Whitton *The Grays of Salisbury*.)

3 Donald C. Whitton, *The Grays of Salisbury*, San Francisco 1976.

4 *Memoirs of the Life of William Collins, R.A.* by W. Wilkie Collins, London, 1848.

5 Purchased for 150 guineas on July 10th 1818. It now hangs in York House, London, along with *Prawn Fishers at Hastings*.

6 His annual income was £399 in 1818, £845 in 1819, and £367 in 1820. See his diary of commissions in the Victoria & Albert Museum, London.

7 There are at least three such sketches, one owned by Douglas Ewing in New York, one by Donald Whitton in San Francisco and one by my wife. (See picture section.)

8 Finally purchased for 300 guineas on January 6th 1826. It now hangs in York House, London.

9 *Memoirs of the Life of William Collins, R.A.* by W. Wilkie Collins, London, 1848. Vol. I, Part II, Ch. 4.

10 Princeton Collection (June 27th 1874).

11 William first met Washington Allston in 1814. They went to Paris together with another friend in 1817, where Allston made a copy of Veronese's *Marriage of Cana*. (See letter from William to R. H. Dana, September 6th 1843, Massachusetts Historical Society.)

12 Pierpont Morgan Library, New York.

13 William Collins's commission diary. Victoria & Albert Museum, London.

14 His income dropped to £346 in 1833; he naturally sold little while he and his family were in Italy between 1836 and 1838; then his income picked up again to £850 in 1841 and 1842 and even reached £1,022 in 1845 and 1846.

15 *Memoirs of the Life of William Collins, R.A.* by W. Wilkie Collins, London, 1848. Vol. I, Part II, Ch. 1.

16 Pierpont Morgan Library, New York.

17 Two, of William and of Harriet, are in my wife's possession. (See picture section.)

18 Alfred T. Story, *The Life of John Linnell.* 1892. Vol. I.

19 *The Times,* June 8th and 9th, 1843. Also *The History of* The Times, Vol. I, pp. 405–8.

20 I am indebted to an unpublished thesis of Verlyn Klinkenberg, at Princeton University, for several of these points. I refer in more detail to his thesis and his contribution in Chapter Six.

21 Maurice Grant: *A Dictionary of British Landscape Painters.* 1952.

22 *John Constable and The Fishers.* R. B. Beckett, London 1952.

23 S. C. Hall, *Memories of Great Men and Women of the Age,* London 1871 and 1877. Hall founded the *Art Union* (which subsequently became the *Art Journal*) in 1839 and edited it for over forty years.

Chapter Three

1 Interview in *Men and Women*, February 5th 1887.

2 Memorandum quoted in *Wilkie Collins and Charles Reade* by M. L. Parrish and E. V. Miller (1940) and now in Parrish Collection at Princeton University.

3 I have adopted the family's nickname 'Willy' in this chapter and revert to 'Wilkie', as appropriate, later.

4 *Men and Women* Op. Cit.

5 *Henry Crabbe Robinson: Diary, Reminiscences and Correspondence.* (Ed. T. Sadler.) London 1869.

6 The first registered bathing establishment at Ramsgate is put at August 22nd 1764, when James Hawkesley was charted a rate of £3.00 for the privilege. Individual charges remained high, a single bather being charged 2s. 6d. at the end of the 18th century. (See *Fragments of History*, C. T. Richardson, Ramsgate 1885.)

7 They had moved for health reasons. William Blake in a letter to Linnell had pronounced that Hampstead, Highgate, Hornsey, Muswell Hill etc., 'even Islington and all places North of London, always laid me up the day after, and sometimes two or three days, with precisely the same complaint and the same torment of the stomach'. (February 1st 1826.)

8 E. von Wolzogen, *Wilkie Collins: Ein biographisch – Kritisch Versuch*, Leipzig, 1885.

9 See Miniature in oil of Mrs Linnell, 1818–20 in *Life of John Linnell*, Alfred T. Story, 1892.

10 Letter to William Winter, July 30th 1887, Princeton Collection.

11 Her handwritten daily diaries for 1835, 1836 and 1837 (*Poole's Elegant Pocket Album*) have been preserved in their original form and are in the Victoria & Albert Museum.

12 Margaret Carpenter, her sister.

13 In his library at his death were *Southey's Essays* with the inscription 'To Master Collins. 1st Prize. Maida Hill Academy. Xmas 1835' and Ritson's *Robin Hood* with the inscription 'William Collins aged 8 years, 1832'. (Catalogue of Messrs Puttick and Simpson, Auctioneers, January 20th 1890.)

14 See individual entries in Harriet's diary.

15 Written with Charles Dickens, in *Household Words*, 1857, and later republished by Chapman & Hall in 1890.

Chapter Four

1 A man who lived a full life. He had an illegitimate daughter by a Florentine girl of nineteen and then, at the age of eighty-seven, married the twenty-two year old daughter of the English vice-consul in Rome.

2 Joseph Severn was a close friend of John Keats. He is now buried in Testaccio cemetery beside Keats. He arrived in Naples and Rome in 1820 and took lodgings at 26, Piazza di Spagna (now the Keats–Shelley Memorial House). He made a drawing of Keats on his death bed (January 28th 1821). A portrait of Keats by Severn is now in the National Portrait Gallery. He became British Consul in Rome from 1861–72. Died 1879.

3 Via Felice. Some of the streets in Rome have changed their name. The maps in the Library of the British School in Rome (dated 1864) and in the Museum of Rome Print Office (1829) have helped to establish their locations. Via Felice, where the Collins stayed, ran from Via Porta Pinciana to the Piazza Barberini.

4 John Gibson had arrived as a virtually penniless sculptor in Rome in 1817. He was a pupil of Canova. His statues of Huskisson and Sir Robert Peel are in Westminster Abbey. His remaining works were bequeathed to the Royal Academy. He died, a millionaire, in Rome in 1866.

5 Henry Crabbe Robinson: *Diary, Reminiscences and Correspondence* (Ed. T. Sadler, 1869.)

6 'All my thoughts are fixed upon home' he later wrote to his wife Mary. 'There are (as must be the case with all companions of travel) so many things in habit and inclination in which Mr Robinson and I differ'.

7 Letter to R. H. Dana, June 17th 1850. *Nineteenth Century Fiction*, a bibliographical catalogue compiled by Robert Lee Wolff, Volume I. New York, 1981.

8 Harriet's diary, Victoria & Albert Museum, London.

9 *Gatherings from an Artist's Portfolio in Rome*, James E. Freeman, Boston, 1883.

10 In a burst of sudden inspiration, just as *Antonina*, his first novel, was going through the press, Wilkie suddenly realised that its title should be *The Mount of Gardens*. But he was too late.

11 Appendix, Book II, *Antonina*, 1850.

12 Letter to Georgina Hogarth, November 25th 1853. Berg Collection, New York Public Library.

13 Kathryn Sedgwick, *Letters from Abroad to Kindred at Home*, New York, 1841.

14 Mrs Frances Trollope, *A Visit to Italy*, London 1842.

15 *Madame Stark's Handbook* (1835): 'The Caves of Ulysses in Sorrento delved in a cliff beneath the Cocumella'. Wilkie Collins in *Memoirs of the Life of William Collins R.A.*: 'He could descend to the beach from the cliff on which his house stood, through the winding caverns consecrated by Ulysses to the Syrens'.

16 Son of Iggulden, the Neapolitan banker.

17 Son of Captain Thomas Galway RN, UK Consul Naples.

Chapter Five

1 Census, Highbury Place, 1841.

2 *History of London Transport*. T. C. Barlow and Michael Robbins. Vol. I, 1963.

3 The sort of use of foreign languages he seemed to approve of both in himself ('I can only write and speak the curious dialect which my countrymen in general have invented for their own use on the Continent') and in others. Source of letters: Pierpont Morgan Library.

4 *Reminiscences of a Story-Teller*, *The Universal Review*, 1888. Manuscript referred to in Appendix of Dorothy L. Sayers' *Wilkie Collins: A Critical and Biographical Study*. (Ed. Professor E. R. Gregory. University of Toledo 1977) pp. 119–20.

5 *The Universal Review*, 1888, pp. 183–4.

6 L. B. Walford, *Memories of Victorian London*, London, 1912, p. 62.

7 L. B. Walford, *Memories of Victorian London*, London, 1912.

8 William Winter, *Old Friends*, New York, 1909, p. 218.

9 *Men & Women*, February 5th 1887. *Our Portrait Gallery*.

10 *Men & Women*, February 5th 1887.

11 Edmund Yates, *Men of Mark*, *The Train*. ('All the facts of which I supplied' says Collins in letter to James Lowe, April 13th 1888(?): Humanities Research Center, Texas.)

12 The story, *The Last Stage Coachman*, is the first signed by 'W. Wilkie Collins'.

13 *Memoirs of the Life of William Collins, R.A.*, W. Wilkie Collins, 1848, Vol. II, p. 223.

14 *Memoirs of the Life of William Collins, R.A.*, W. Wilkie Collins, 1848, Vol. II, p. 217.

15 *Appleton's Journal*, September 3rd 1870. The article is clearly based on an interview with Collins. The topic and the episodes in the Polynesian novel clearly owed much to William Ellis's *Polynesian Researches during a residence of nearly six years in the South Sea Islands*, first published in 1829 and a copy of which Collins had in his library. It is easy to see what attracted him in the first place. 'No place in the world,' wrote Ellis, 'in ancient and modern times, appears to have been more superstitious than the South Sea Islanders, or to have been more entirely under the influence of dread from imaginary demons or supernatural beings'.

16 *Men & Women*, February 5th 1887.

17 The archives of the British Museum show that Collins was introduced by his father and issued with his first reader's ticket on March 26th 1846 and was renewed yearly until July 13th 1850. He entered Lincoln's Inn on May 18th 1846 and was called to the Bar on November 21st 1851.

18 See his own inscription on the original manuscripts of *Antonina*, University of Texas, Austin.

19 Pierpont Morgan Library.

20 Pierpont Morgan Library.

21 Pierpont Morgan Library.

22 Pierpont Morgan Library.

23 *Memoirs of the Life of William Collins, R.A.*, W. Wilkie Collins, 1848, Vol. II, pp. 281–2.

24 See original manuscript of *Antonina* in University of Texas, Austin.

Chapter Six

1 It was around this time that 'Willy' became 'Wilkie' to his closest friends, and, more formally, that 'William Wilkie Collins' became 'W. Wilkie Collins'. I shall use 'Wilkie' from now on.

2 *Memoirs of the Life of William Collins, R.A.*, W. Wilkie Collins, London, 1848. Chapter One, p. 2.

3 Private dissertation at the Department of English, Princeton University 1979. I am indebted to the author for these extracts.

4 Dorothy Sayers: *Wilkie Collins: A Critical and Biographical Study*, Toledo, 1977, p. 66.

5 *The Atheneum* in 1850: 'Another instance of perversion to be regretted is *Berengaria's Alarm for the Safety of her Husband* by Charles Collins'.

6 Hunt, Vol. I, p. 298.

7 Hunt, Vol. I, p. 309.

8 Millais, Vol. I, pp. 88–90.

9   Mrs E. M. Ward, *Memories of Ninety Years*, pp. 38–9.

10 S. M. Ellis, *Wilkie Collins, Le Fanu and Others*, 1931, pp. 11–12.

11 S. M. Ellis, pp. 59–60; Lona Mosk Packer, *Christina Rossetti*, Cambridge University Press, 1963.

12 *The Unpublished letters of Charles Dickens to Mark Lemon*, (Ed. Walter Dexter) Halton and Truscott Smith, London, 1927.

13 *Charles Dickens*, Mamie Dickens. Cassell & Co., 1885, pp. 95–6.

14 Nickname of Dickens's youngest son.

15 J. W. T. Ley, *The Dickens Circle*, 1918, p. 97.

16 Kenneth Robinson, *Wilkie Collins*, 1951, 1974, pp. 85–6.

17 He only just made it. By the date of the second edition, a year later, the railways were already encroaching on Cornwall. Wilkie decided that the title at least should remain unchanged.

18 Westaway Books, London, 1948.

19 Letters between Edward Piggott and Collins in Huntington Library, San Marino, California.

20 Kirk H. Beetz, in his detailed analysis of the Piggott letters and Collins's work for *The Leader*, comes to the same conclusion. He has successfully identified several of Collins's contributions. (See 'Wilkie Collins and *The Leader*' by Kirk H. Beetz, *Victorian Periodicals Review*, Vol. XV, Number 1, Spring, 1982, University of Toronto.)

21 See Nuel Pharr Davis, *The Life of Wilkie Collins*, Urbana, 1956, pp. 115–22; Kenneth Robinson, *Wilkie Collins*, London, 1951, pp. 64–8; Dorothy L. Sayers, *Wilkie Collins: A Critical and Biographical Study*, (Ed. E. R. Gregory) Toledo Libraries, 1977, pp. 85–94; Robert Ashley, 'Within my Experience', *The Wilkie Collins Society Journal*, Vol. I, 1981.

22 Letter to Sarony, March 19th 1887, University of Iowa.

Chapter Seven

1   In a letter to Collins, dated September 1862, following the publication of *No Name*.

2   R. C. Lehmann: *Charles Dickens as Editor*, 1912.

3   *Letters of Charles Dickens to Wilkie Collins*, (Ed. Laurence Hutton, 1892) p. 12.

4   *Edmund Yates: His Recollections and Experiences*, 1885, Vol. I, p. 266.

5   James A. Davies, 'Forster & Dickens', *The Dickensian*, September 1974, pp. 145–58.

6   *Letters of Charles Dickens*, London, 1903, p. 295.

7   J. W. T. Ley, *The Dickens Circle*, 1918, p. 242.

8   *The Dickensian*.

9   Pierpont Morgan Library. October 16th 1853.

10 *Letters of Charles Dickens*, 1903, p. 303.

11 Fred Kaplan, *Dickens and Mesmerism*, Princeton University Press, 1975, pp. 74–105; Michael Slater, *Dickens and Women*, J. M. Dent & Sons, London, 1983, pp. 122–5.

12 *Letters of Charles Dickens*, Vol. I, Nonesuch Press, 1938.

13 I am indebted to Mr Jeremy Maas, of the Maas Gallery in London, for the discovery of this series of articles. See my article 'The Mystery of Collins's Articles on Italian Art' in *The Wilkie Collins Society Journal*, Vol. IV, 1984.

Chapter Eight

1 Pierpont Morgan Library, September 1854.

2 Letter dated September 2nd 1855, Pierpont Morgan Library. This letter answers several of the questions raised by Kirk Beetz in his article 'Plots Within Plots' (*Wilkie Collins Society Journal*, 1984).

3 In the preface to *After Dark* he wrote '. . . these stories are entirely of my own constructing and writing'. (First edition, 1856.)

4 Huntington Collection.

5 'Cruise of the Tomtit', *Household Words*, December 22nd 1855.

6 *Galignani's New Paris Guide*, Paris 1856; *Parisian Sights*, Harper & Brothers, New York, 1852.

7 Pierpont Morgan Library, February 14th 1855.

8 Letter dated August 14th 1885. In possession of Mrs F. E. Clarke.

9 May 22nd 1857, *The Letters of Charles Dickens*, Nonesuch Press, 1938.

10 J. Ashby-Sterry, 'English Notes', October 5th 1889, *The Book Buyer*.

11 'The Lazy Tour of Two Idle Apprentices', *Household Words*, October 1857. Dickens's letters to John Forster, Henry Austin, W. H. Wills, Georgina Hogarth (September 1857). *The Letters of Charles Dickens*, Nonesuch Press, 1938.

12 John Britton and Edward Brayley. Vol. III, *Cumberland, Isle of Man and Derbyshire*.

13 Tungsten was later discovered and in 1980 the National Carbonising Company convinced itself that Carrock Fell had tungsten reserves stretching at least ten years ahead (*Daily Mail*, July 7th 1980).

14 John Forster, *The Life of Charles Dickens*, Vol. II, 1872–1874.

15 Letter to Georgina Hogarth, September 9th 1857, *Letters of Charles Dickens*, Nonesuch Press, 1938.

16 Thomas Penrice and Sons. Donald Penrice's late aunt owned the King's Arms until 1941 and he confirmed that she discovered Charles Dickens's pencilled signature on the wall when the hotel was being decorated. It was inadvertently covered up by paper and paste before it could be preserved. (Letter to author dated 2nd September 1980.) See also *History of Wigton* by T. W. Carrick (1949), p. 104.

17 Letter to Georgina Hogarth, September 12th 1857. *Letters of Charles Dickens*, Nonesuch Press, 1938.

18   Chapter V, *The Lazy Tour of Two Idle Apprentices.*

19   John Forster, *The Life of Charles Dickens*, Vol. II, Book VIII, Ch. I.

Chapter Nine

1   John G. Millais, *The Life and Letters of Sir John Everett Millais*, London, 1895, Vol. I, pp. 278–281.

2   S. M. Ellis, *Wilkie Collins, Le Fanu and Others*, London, 1931.

3   Gladys Storey, *Dickens and Daughter*, 1939.

4   Mary Lutyens, *Millais and the Ruskins*, p. 245 and Nuel Pharr Davis, *The Life of Wilkie Collins*, pp. 321–22.

5   The latter date is rather earlier than that suggested by Nuel Pharr Davis (*The Life of Wilkie Collins*) because of Millais' departure from London.

6   The basic facts about Caroline (Elizabeth) are contained in the censuses of 1841 (Toddington New Town), 1851 (Clerkenwell, London), 1861 (Marylebone, London), 1871 (Marylebone, London) 1881 (Marylebone, London) and in her first marriage certificate (1850), her daughter's birth certificate (1851), her second marriage certificate (1868), her daughter's marriage certificate (1878) and her death certificate (1895). The first two censuses establish her year of birth as 1830 (or the second half of 1829). Later ones and the other certificates deduct four or five years from her age. She was certainly in Toddington in 1841 aged eleven, with her mother (Sarah) one sister (Martha) and three brothers (Methuselah Sison, George Mathias, and William). Her other sister (Teresa Mary) and her father (John) are not recorded on the census form and were presumably away from Toddington that day. Elizabeth Compton's birth or baptism certificate has not come to light in the area.

7   Mentioned in her birth certificate (May 6th 1832), her marriage certificate (March 30th 1850) and Harriet's birth certificate (February 3rd 1851). Sarah Compton, in the Census of 1841, is described as 'Carpenter's wife'.

8   See census return of 1851.

9   They are still there.

10   In her daughter Harriet's marriage certificate.

11   In Caroline's death certificate.

12   In the certificate of her later marriage to Joseph Clow.

13   See letter dated March 19th 1856, to his mother (Pierpont Morgan Library). The rate books of Marylebone show Mrs Collins paying half the normal rates for Hanover Terrace in 1856 and paying a half year's rates in Harley Street.

14   April 30th 1856, *Letters of Charles Dickens to Wilkie Collins*, 1892, p. 60.

15   February 12th 1856, *Letters of Charles Dickens*, Nonesuch Press, 1938.

16   April 13th 1856, *Letters of Charles Dickens*, Nonesuch Press, 1938.

17 Pierpont Morgan Library, July 30th 1845.

18 'Laid up in Two Lodgings', *Household Words*. June 14th 1856, p. 521.

19 Pierpont Morgan Library, July 30th 1845.

20 The rate books (Marylebone) put this between February and September, 1858. 'Mrs Graves was the rate-payer'.

21 Census return of 1861 for 12 Harley Street.

22 April 7th 1861.

23 *The Life and Letters of John Everett Millais* by J. G. Millais and *Wilkie Collins, Le Fanu and Others* by S. M. Ellis.

24 Gladys Storey, *Dickens and Daughter*, 1939, p. 105.

25 Pierpont Morgan Library, December 20th 1860.

26 Pierpont Morgan Library, December 3rd 1860.

27 'Charles A. Collins' is recorded in Albany Street in 1858. This was a surgeon.

28 Charles opened an account at Coutts Bank on July 18th 1860, and Wilkie on August 22nd 1860. (Source: Coutts Bank.)

29 Pierpont Morgan Library, December 30th 1860.

30 Pierpont morgan Library, December 3rd 1860.

31 See Census for 1861.

32 Letter to Esther Elton, daughter of a member of Macready's theatrical company. March 5th 1861.

33 Elkin Mathews catalogue. No. 124.

34 Pierpont Morgan Library, June 1860.

35 Princeton Collection, December 24th 1862.

36 *Ancestors and Friends*, John F. Lehmann. London 1962, p. 175.

37 September 16th 1859, *The Letters of Charles Dickens*, Nonesuch Press, 1938.

38 July 12th 1861, *The Letters of Charles Dickens*, Nonesuch Press, 1938.

39 Source: Coutts Bank.

40 The policy had a reducing premium and was duly paid out, following his death, on Friday, October 18th 1889. (Sources: Coutts Bank and National Provident.)

41 Pierpont Morgan Library, August 18th 1859.

42 Serialisation began on November 26th 1859 (*Harper's Weekly* began at the same time in the US). See the full chronology of publication in 'The Woman in White: A Chronological Study' by Andrew Gasson, *Wilkie Collins Society Journal* Vol. II, 1982, pp. 12–13.

43 Letter to 'my dear Collaborateur' dated March 15th 1886, Princeton Collection.

44 Edmund Yates, *Celebrities at Home*, 1879, p. 150.

45 Op. Cit., p. 150.

46 See Clyde K. Hyder, *Wilkie Collins and The Woman in White*, Publications of the Modern Language Association of America, 1939.

47 Wybert Reeve, 'Recollections of Wilkie Collins', *Chambers's Journal*, June 1906.

48 Edmund H. Yates, *Celebrities at Home*, 1879, p. 154.

49 Walter M. Kendrick: 'The Sensationalism of The Woman in White', *Nineteenth Century Fiction*, June 1977, Andrew Gasson, Op. Cit.

50 *Saturday Review*, August 25th 1860. (See also *Wilkie Collins, The Critical Heritage*. (Ed. Norman Page) London, 1974.)

51 Hall Caine, *My Story*, London 1908.

52 Princeton Collection, October 10th 1862.

53 Pierpont Morgan Library, June 2nd 1863.

54 Letter to Rev. Dr Deems, October 5th 1865. Humanities Research Center, University of Texas, Austin.

55 Pierpont Morgan Library. August 12th 1862. Letter to his mother.

Chapter Ten

1 Pierpont Morgan Library.

2 Several paintings along the Norfolk coast were exhibited by William Collins at the Royal Academy in 1816. *A scene on the coast of Norfolk*, exhibited two years later, was bought by the Prince Regent, for 150 guineas (on July 10th 1818). It now hangs in York House. The Prince Regent later bought another Collins picture *Prawn Fishers at Hastings* for 300 guineas (on January 6th 1826). This, too, is in York House.

3 The copy was still in his library when he died in Wimpole Street.

4 See Daniel Defoe, *A Tour Through the Whole Island of Great Britain, 1724–27*.

5 I am obliged to Peter Carracciolo for drawing my attention to this point. See his article 'Wilkie Collins's 'Divine Comedy': The Use of Dante in '*The Woman in White*', *Nineteenth-Century Fiction*, 1971 (footnote on p. 385).

6 *Life and Letters of Sir John Everett Millais* by J. G. Millais, 1889, Vol. 1, pp. 288–89.

7 She was born on January 10th 1845 and was fifteen years younger than Caroline and twenty-one years younger than Wilkie.

8 The Census for 1861 no longer recorded Martha at Brick Street in Winterton. She was there in 1851.

9 Richard Monckton-Milne, who had become Lord Houghton in 1863, had a well known collection of French pornographic writings, particularly by de Sade. (See *The Other Victorians*, Steven Marcus, 1966 and *Monckton-Milnes, The Flight of Youth*, James Pope-Hennessy, 1951).

10 The sum of £51.17s.10d. was paid from his bank account to the Victoria Hotel,

Yarmouth on August 23rd 1864. (Coutts Bank.) It naturally does not reveal the dates he stayed at the hotel.

11 If they met in Norfolk as seems most likely, Wilkie visited both Yarmouth and the Broads in 1864 and was back for a brief visit in 1865. He did not apparently go back later.

12 Mrs Graves is recorded in the rate book from the Christmas quarter of 1864 to the Michaelmas quarter of 1867.

13 March, 1869, Coutts Bank.

14 Huntington Collection, July 2nd 1855.

15 S. M. Ellis, *Wilkie Collins, Le Fanu and Others*, p. 12.

16 Sue Lonoff (*Wilkie Collins and his Victorian Readers*), has confirmed that this section of the original manuscript is *not* in his hand, (p. 171).

17 Mary Anderson, *A Few Memories*, London 1896.

18 *The Globe*, September 25th 1889.

19 See Census of 1871. I can find no evidence that he was a plumber (Nuel Pharr Davis, *The Life of Wilkie Collins*, Urbana, p. 259).

20 *The Letters of Charles Dickens*, Nonesuch Press, 1938, p. 676.

21 The diary is in the Berg Collection in the New York Public Library.

22 Mrs F. E. Clarke.

23 They were resumed again on February 19th 1872.

24 His bank accounts have regular payments marked 'house' for this purpose.

25 See Census of 1871. Joseph Clow, senior, died in 1878. Frances Clow, his widow, died in 1902, leaving £2,114. Joseph Charles Clow (Caroline's husband) received £1,000 and his father's gold watch.

26 Gladys Storey, *Dickens and Daughter*, p. 214.

27 The notion that Martha's first child was born exactly nine months to the day from Caroline's wedding day, thus partly supporting Nuel Pharr Davis's further idea that he had gone round from Caroline's wedding to Martha's bed, seems to be based on an incorrect date for Caroline's wedding in both Kenneth Robinson's *Wilkie Collins* and Nuel Pharr Davis's *Life of Wilkie Collins*. They both put the date at October 4th 1868. The marriage certificate is actually dated October 29th 1868. Martha's first child, Marian, was born on July 4th 1869.

28 T. S. Eliot described it as 'the first, the longest and the best of modern English detective novels', though some purists give the accolade of the first detective novel to *The Notting Hill Mystery*, which appeared in the magazine *Once a Week* in 1862–63, and in book form in 1865. (See Julian Symons, *The Times*, London, July 12th 1975.) Wilkie Collins, however, has received further backing for his *The Monkstons of Wincot Abbey* written in 1852 and published in 1855. (See R. P. Ashley, 'Wilkie Collins and the Detective Story', *Nineteenth Century Fiction*, June, 1951, and Andrew Gasson: 'Wilkie Collins: A Collector's and Bibliographer's Challenge', *The Private Library*, summer 1980.)

29 Benham & Co. were probably his solicitors. There had also been a payment of £321 to Bonham & Sons, the auctioneers, in May 1868. (Source: Coutts Bank.)

30 Mrs Wells paid the rates between 1869 and 1871, and, in the Census of 1871, is shown as occupying 33 Bolsover Street, with (in separate 'dwellings') Mrs Dawson and her daughter Marian, and another lodger, Charles Lepage, an unemployed hairdresser from Paris.

31 The entertainment consisted of a one-act operetta, a three-act comedy drama and a 'new operatic extravaganza' or burlesque. Wilkie and his friends went on February 3rd. The first night had been on December 21st.

32 He also had the Consols he had inherited from his mother.

33 The letter, which is the only one relating to Wilkie Collins in the possession of the Marylebone Public Library, is mainly written in French but, has, in Wilkie's own handwriting at the top, the comment: 'C. Fechter, relating to the looking glasses in the drawing room at 90, Gloucester Place'.

34 *Wilkie Collins's Recollection of Charles Fechter*, January 18th 1882. (Extract from Kate Field, *Charles Albert Fechter*, New York 1882.)

35 Letter dated April 29th 1868, plus other correspondence in Ouvrey Collection (in possession of Farrer & Co., Solicitors, London).

36 W. Teignmouth Shore, *Charles Dickens and His Friends*, (quoting John Hollingshead) p. 276.

37 Letter from Georgina Hogarth, July 1st 1870.

38 Letter to Mr Benzon, February 26th 1869. (Letter in possession of Andrew Gasson).

39 This was not necessary until the Births & Deaths Registration Act of 1874. Thereafter Wilkie's son, William Charles, was registered.

40 Presumably from Mr Dawson, the doctor at Blackwater Park, in *The Woman in White*.

41 'Mrs Dawson' received £20 on December 28th 1869 and almost monthly until 1871 when it was raised to £25 monthly. (Coutts Bank.)

Chapter Eleven

1 Letter to Shirley Brooks, May 29th 1869 (de Coursey Fales Collection, New York Public Library).

2 Berg Collection, New York Public Library.

3 *The Globe*, September 25th 1889. She was actually seventeen in 1868.

4 *Daily Express*, April 3rd 1934; *Thomas Wright of Olney*, London, 1936; *Dickens Incognito*, Felix Aylmer, 1959; *Dickens and Ellen Ternan*, Ada Nisbet, California, 1952; 'Mr Tringham of Slough', *The Dickensian*, September 1968.

5 'Dickens's Forgotten Retreat in France', *The Dickensian*, May 1966.

6 Gladys Storey, *Dickens and Daughter*, 1939.

7   Letter of May 15th 1869, Massachusetts Historical Society Library, Boston.

8   See letter from Charles to Wilkie, June 16th 1865. Pierpont Morgan Library.

9   Coutts Bank.

10 Letter to W. F. de Cerjat, October 25th 1864. *Letters of Charles Dickens*, Nonesuch Press, 1938.

11 'A Note on the Dickens-Collins Friendship', Arthur Adrian, *Huntington Library Quarterly*, No. 16, 1953; Arthur Adrian, *Georgina Hogarth and the Dickens Circle*, London, 1957; Sue Lonoff, 'Charles Dickens and Wilkie Collins', *Nineteenth Century Fiction*, 1982.

12 See Note 41, Chapter 8.

13 Letter from Walter Dexter to Comte Alain de Suzannet, February 22nd 1939 (Dickens House, London), quoting a conversation with Gladys Storey, *Dickens and Women*, Michael Slater, London, p. 420.

14 John Lehmann, *Ancestors and Friends*, London 1962, p. 210.

15 January 27th 1870, *Letters of Charles Dickens to Wilkie Collins*, London 1892, p. 185.

16 Letter to W. F. Tindall, Mitchell Library, Glasgow.

17 June 20th and 22nd 1870, Humanities Research Center, University of Texas, Austin.

18 A presentation copy of *Man and Wife*, Robert Lee Wolff's collection, has the inscription 'To Mrs George Graves from Wilkie Collins, October 1870'. It implies that Caroline had left Joseph Clow and was probably back in Gloucester Place. (*Nineteenth Century Fiction*, R. L. Wolff, 1981, p. 264.)

19 The domestic staff were still three in number five years later, comprising a cook, housemaid and parlourmaid. Letter to Kate Field, September 25th 1875. (Boston Collection.)

20 Death certificate, February 21st 1927.

21 Birth certificate dated 22nd June, 1869 and death certificate 25th July, 1870.

22 Letter to K. Field, April 22nd 1876, Boston Public Library.

23 Letter to W. F. Tindall, April 27th 1875. Mitchell Library, Glasgow.

24 Yale University Library, March 13th 1878.

25 *Charles Reade: A Memoir*, by Charles L. Reade and the Rev. Compton Reade. (London 1887.)

26 Malcolm Elwin, *Charles Reade. A Biography*, London 1931. Julian Hawthorne, *Shapes That Pass*, London 1928.

27 Thomas D. Clareson, 'Wilkie Collins to Charles Reade: Some Unpublished Letters', *Victorian Essays: A symposium*, 1967.

28 August 29th 1871. Nuel Pharr Davis, *The Life of Wilkie Collins*, Urbana 1956, p. 268. Mr Davis wrongly assumes that Caroline had not returned to Gloucester Place by this date.

29 Wybert Reeve, 'Recollections of Wilkie Collins', *Chambers's Journal*, June 1906.

30   Wybert Reeve, 'Recollections of Wilkie Collins', *Chambers's Journal*, June 1906.

31   October 10th 1871. Letter to George Smith, Berg Collection, New York Public Library.

32   Caroline and her daughter Harriet (see chapter 9).

33   *On and Off the Stage*, Mr and Mrs Bancroft. London 1889. He read the play to the company on December 21st 1872. (Pierpont Morgan Library.)

34   The receipted bill dated February 4th 1873 and the devotional chair are now in the possession of Mrs Faith Clarke (née Dawson), their great grand-daughter.

35   Wybert Reeve, 'Recollections of Wilkie Collins', *Chambers's Journal*, June 1906.

36   Georgina Hogarth to Annie Fields, May 12th 1873, Huntington Library.

37   Wybert Reeve, *Chambers's Journal*, June 1906; letters dated April 10th 1873 (Berg Collection, New York Public Library; and University of California).

38   Letter to John Millais, April 17th 1873. (Pierpont Morgan Library.)

39   May 8th 1873 (Berg Collection, New York Public Library).

40   Monday, May 19th 1873. Two farces were in the same bill.

41   Letter to George Bentley, May 1873, Berg Collection, New York Public Library.

42   Frank Archer, *An Actor's Notebooks*, London, p. 147.

Chapter Twelve

1   Letter dated March 14th 1873, Berg Collection, New York Public Library.

2   Percy Fitzgerald, *Memories of Charles Dickens*, 1913.

3   *The Illustrated Review*, July 10th 1873.

4   Letter to William Tindall, September 12th 1873. Mitchell Library, Glasgow.

5   *Boston Evening Transcript*, January 9th 1874.

6   Gladys Storey, *Dickens and Daughter*, 1939, p. 119.

7   *Men and Women*, February 5th 1887.

8   Kate Field, *Charles Albert Fechter*, New York 1882, p. 172.

9   J. Henry Harper, *The House of Harper*, New York 1912.

10   Correspondence with Collins's solicitor, W. F. Tindall, 1867–77, Mitchell Library, Glasgow.

11   The contact culminated in a joint production two years later, entitled *Lotos Leaves, Original Stories, essays and poems by Wilkie Collins, Mark Twain and other members of the Lotos Club* (Chatto and Windus, London 1875). It contained Collins's story *A Fatal Fortune*.

12   *The Daily Graphic*, New York, October 3rd 1873.

13   See Clyde K. Hyder, *Wilkie Collins in America*, University of Kansas Humanistic Studies.

14   *Philadelphia Press*, October 18th 1873.

15 *Public Ledger*, Philadelphia, October 18th 1873.

16 Schlesinger worked as the agent of Naylor Vickers in Boston. Fred Lehmann's sister Elizabeth had married Ernst Benzon who was in partnership with the Vickers family (*Ancestors and Friends*, John Lehmann, 1963).

17 Huntington Library. October 10th 1871.

18 Huntington Library. August 30th 1873.

19 Letter dated January 1st 1873.

20 Passage in handwritten diary of Annie Adam Fields, dated Saturday, November 1st, 1873. Massachusetts Historical Society, Boston.

21 *Boston Transcript*, October 31st 1873.

22 *Boston Advertiser*, October 31st 1873.

23 Letter to Mrs Bigelow, January 2nd 1882, New York Public Library.

24 L. B. Walford, *Memories of Victorian London*, 1912, pp. 208–9.

25 R. C. Lehmann, *Memories of Half a Century*, p. 65.

26 L. B. Walford, *Memories of Victorian London*, 1912, p. 209.

27 R. C. Lehmann, *Memories of Half a Century*, p. 65.

28 *The World*, New York, November 11th 1873.

29 *New York Daily Tribune*, November 11th 1873.

30 November 12th 1873.

31 *New York Daily Tribune*, November 12th 1873.

32 *The World*, New York, November 12th 1873.

33 *New York Herald*, November 12th 1873.

34 *New York Herald*, September 27th 1873.

35 R. C. Lehmann, *Memories of Half a Century*, p. 66.

36 During Wilkie's visit the stock market 'panic' of 1873 was being compared to earlier stock market slumps in 1837 and 1857.

37 Wybert Reeve, 'Recollections of Wilkie Collins', *Chambers's Journal*, June 1906.

38 Letter to Sebastian Schlesinger, December 25th 1873, Harvard University.

39 Letter to Schlesinger, January 17th 1874, Harvard University.

40 Letter to Alexander Gray, Wilkie's cousin, in San Francisco, May 26th 1888 (letter in possession of Alexander Gray's great-grandson, Donald C. Whitton, in San Francisco).

41 'Our Portrait Gallery: Mr Wilkie Collins', *Men and Women*, February 5th 1887.

42 His mother's sister, Catherine, had married John Westcott Gray. Their son, Alexander, had grown up in Salisbury but left England in the early 1850s, originally to go to Australia, but later to California. (*The Grays of Salisbury*, Donald Whitton, San Francisco, 1976, pp. 14–15.)

43 *Lost Chicago*, by David Lowe (Houghton Mifflin Co. Boston, 1978).

44 *Chicago Daily Tribune*, January 17th 1874.

45 Letter to Mr and Mrs Bigelow, New York Public Library, January 17th 1874.

46 Letter to Ward. Boston, February 27th 1874.

47 With the Boston offices of the Manhattan Life Insurance Co. and the New England Mutual Insurance Co.

48 Letter to Schlesinger, March 4th 1876. Harvard University.

49 *Boston Evening Transcript*, March 9th 1874.

50 L. B. Walford, *Memories of Victorian London*, Edward Arnold, London, 1912, p. 209.

51 Source: *Lloyd's List*, March 19th 1874, Column 7.

52 L. B. Walford, *Memories of Victorian London*, London, 1912.

53 Frank Archer, *An Actor's Notebooks*, London, p. 158.

Chapter Thirteen

1 Dominique Borges, the existing rate-payer at 55 Marylebone Road, paid the last instalment at the end of December, 1873 and the new rate-payer began on Lady Day 1874. At the same time the first instalment in Taunton Place seems to have been paid by Caroline around Lady Day 1874. The actual date is unfortunately indecipherable in the Marylebone rate-book. Since Martha had to be given three months notice before leaving Marylebone Road, it seems likely that this expired around Lady Day (March 25th).

2 Source: Rate-books, Marylebone Public Library, Marylebone Road, London.

3 Letter to George Bentley, May 16th 1874, Berg Collection, New York Public Library.

4 Letter to Miss Bigelow, December 31st 1874, New York Public Library.

5 Coutts Bank.

6 Letter to Tindall, his solicitor, December 29th 1874, Mitchell Library, Glasgow.

7 Birth certificate, dated February 1st 1875, in Marylebone, London.

8 See the directions in *The Moonstone: A dramatic story in three acts*, 'privately printed for the convenience of the author', by Charles Dickens and Evans, Crystal Palace Press, 1877.

9 Coutts Bank.

10 Letter to George Bentley, December 31st 1877, Berg Collection, New York Public Library.

11 Letter to Charles Kent, 20th June 1881, Princeton Collection.

12 Wybert Reeve, 'Recollections of Wilkie Collins', *Chambers's Journal*, June 1906.

13 William Winter, *Old Friends*, New York, 1909.

14 Rudolf Lehmann, *An Artist's Reminiscences*, London, 1894.

15 'Some Recollections of Yesterday', Nathaniel Beard, *Temple Bar*, July 1894.

16 Frank Archer, *An Actor's Notebooks*, London, 1912, p. 303.

17 See *Memoirs of the Life of William Collins, R.A.*, Volume III, Part IV, Chapter 1.

18 When he was writing *Armadale* (see Chapter Nine).

19 British Library, 4th January 1812.

20 Letter to Miss Field, 13th January 1883, Boston Public Library.

21 Letter to Paul H. Hayne, 16th July 1884, Berg Collection, New York Public Library.

22 Letter dated 2nd February 1887, Princeton Collection.

23 See Chapter Ten.

24 See Chapter Three.

25 *Memoirs of the Life of William Collins, R.A.*, Volume II, pp. 284–91.

26 William Winter, *Old Friends*, New York, 1909.

27 Hall Caine, *My Story*, London, 1908.

28 Marie and Squire Bancroft, *The Bancrofts*, London, 1909.

29 *Ibid.*

30 Percy Fitzgerald, *Memoirs of an Author*, London, 1895.

31 Extract from newspaper cutting, signed 'Family Doctor', found in album of Doris Beresford, the Gaiety Girl, who was one of Harriet's daughters. I have been unable to trace the source or date of the cutting. But it was probably prompted by his death and the subsequent obituaries.

32 Letter to Charles Kent, August 17th 1884, Princeton Collection.

33 Alethea Hayter, *Opium and the Romantic Imagination*, London 1968.

34 Letter to solicitor, Tindall, 18th June 1872. Mitchell Library, Glasgow.

35 I am indebted to Mrs Edith Muriel Upton (née Bartley) in Eastbourne for the material relating to the Bartleys in this and the subsequent chapters.

36 Source: The Law Society, Chancery Lane, London WC2.

37 Mrs Upton still has the wedding gown in Eastbourne.

38 The wedding menu was kept by Doris Beresford, Harriet's eldest daughter, and is now in the possession of Mr Iredale in Mitcham.

39 129 Alexandra Road, London NW8.

Chapter Fourteen

1 Source: Coutts & Co.

2 The nicknames are still remembered by descendants of Martha and Caroline and several recur in Collins's correspondence.

3 Source: Collins's bank account at Coutts and the rate-books at Ramsgate.

4 Julian Hawthorne, *Shapes That Pass*, 1928.

5 William Winter, *Old Friends*, New York, 1909.

6 *Household Words*, 'The Cruise of the Tomtit', 22nd December 1855.

7   Wybert Reeves, *Chambers's Journal*, June 1906.

8   *Memoirs of the Life of William Collins, R.A.*, Wilkie Collins, 1848, Vol. II, p. 166.

9   Pierpont Morgan Library, 4th August 1863.

10 Letter to Paul H. Hayne, 28th January 1885.

11 Princeton Collection, 31st March 1880.

12 Princeton Collection. 'Dah' was the nickname of Doris, who became a Gaiety Girl.

13 Princeton Collection, 16th July 1886.

14 Princeton Collection, 13th November 1885. See also letter to Piggott, dated 23rd October 1885, from Ramsgate indicating Caroline's and Charley's presence at 14 Nelson Crescent. (Huntington Collection.)

15 Martha's youngest was then aged eleven.

16 Source: 'Bobbie' West, (née Dawson), Wilkie's grand-daughter.

17 Official Census, 1881.

18 Now in the possession of Mrs F. E. Clarke (née Dawson).

19 Mary Anderson, *A Few Memories*, London 1896.

20 Anthony Trollope, *An Autobiography*, Vol. II, 1883.

21 Letter to Rev. Dr Deems, 5th October 1865, Humanities Research Center, University of Texas.

22 Letter to Mrs Bigelow, 11th January 1883, New York Public Library.

23 Walter de la Mare, 'The Early Novels of Wilkie Collins', *The Eighteen Sixties* (Edited John Drinkwater) Cambridge University Press, 1932, p. 69.

24 Letter dated 3rd April 1881, Huntington Library.

25 Frank Archer, *An Actor's Notebooks*, p. 303.

26 12th January 1886. Humanities Research Center, University of Texas, Austin.

27 Census return, 10 Taunton Place, 1881.

28 New York Public Library, 6th September 1881.

29 Mrs 'Bobbie' West.

30 Princeton Collection, 31st August 1885.

31 Coutts Bank, 15th December 1885.

32 Revised and republished, *Harper's Weekly*, October, 1885.

33 Sir John Lawrence has some forty letters written to his mother (Nannie) and grandmother.

34 Birth certificate.

35 Death certificate.

36 Princeton Collection, 14th March 1888.

37 Princeton Collection, 12th July 1888.

38 Huntington Library, 11th April 1888.

39 23rd April 1888, Humanities Research Center, University of Texas (signed 'MD').

40 Mrs Upton.

41 Coutts Bank.

42 Harvard Collection, 26th August 1888.

43 Harvard Collection, 24th January 1889.

44 See letter to Schlesinger, 27th March 1889; catalogue of George Macmanus & Co. Philadelphia, January 1979; Berg Collection, New York Public Library (Manuscript drafts of *Iris* and *The Lord Harry*); references on pp. 257–8, Robert Lee Wolff, *Nineteenth Century Fiction*, Garland Publishing Co., New York, 1981; letter from Collins to Horace Pym dated December 5th 1887 (heirs of Horace Pym).

45 Letter to Sir Hall Caine, from Mrs H. E. Bartley, 1st July 1889. Berg Collection, New York Public Library.

46 25th September 1889. Letter from George Redford to Mrs Bartley (Harriet), Princeton Collection.

Chapter Fifteen

1 The payment may have been made direct to Wilkie's estate, though Schlesinger at least of the two executors would know that it was meant for Marian and Hettie.

2 Source: Lionel Dawson.

3 See Jack Adams, *South Wales Borderers*, Hamish Hamilton, London, 1968.

4 They moved from Brondesbury to St Julian's Road, Kilburn, in 1897.

5 Military records, Public Record Office, London; and *The Chauffeur*, 8th March 1913.

6 *Catalogue of the sale of the furniture and effects of the late Wilkie Collins*, Walter Holcombe, 24th October 1889; *Catalogue of the interesting library of modern books of the late Wilkie Collins*, Messrs Puttick and Simpson, 20th January 1890; *Catalogue of the collection of modern pictures, water-colour drawings and engravings of Wilkie Collins*, Christie Manson and Woods. 22nd February 1890; *Catalogue of original manuscripts by Charles Dickens and Wilkie Collins*, Sotheby, Wilkinson and Hodge, 18th June 1890. (All in possession of Mrs F. E. Clarke.)

7 Source: Christie's, London. The Millais portrait is now in the National Portrait Gallery. Two portraits of Wilkie's father and mother, formerly owned by the Pym family, are in the possession of Mrs F. E. Clarke (née Dawson).

8 *London Gazette*, 6th June 1893.

9 Source: The Law Society, London.

10 Letter in possession of National Portrait Gallery, London. Millais no doubt gained this impression from a report in *The World* (2nd October 1889).

11 In a letter from 24 Newman Street, 18th October 1894, now in the possession of the National Portrait Gallery. She owned pictures of Wilkie's mother and father by Mrs Carpenter and Charles Collins respectively.

12 Will of Mrs Margaret Bartley, 5th February 1900.

13 Death certificate. He died on 9th August 1897 at 11 Pewley Hill, Guildford. He was not shown in the rate book and was presumably a lodger.

14 Guy Degly, *Paradise in the Strand*, The Richards Press, London.

15 *Photo Bits*. Review of *The Girls of Gottenberg*, 1907.

16 It remains in the family album of Mr Ronald Iredale in Mitcham.

17 W. Macqueen-Pope, *Gaiety: Theatre of Enchantment*, London, 1949.

18 Alan Hyman, *The Gaiety Years*, London, 1975.

19 Death certificate, Richmond, 26th February 1905. No marriage certificate in the names of Doris Beresford (or Bartley) and Louis Bishop has been traced. In her later marriage certificate (when she married Ivo King Hervey Locke in 1910) Doris is described as 'spinster'.

20 Sources: Ronald Iredale and the late Geoffrey Ivo Gregson.

Chapter Sixteen

1 See his interesting assessment of 'the absence of any leading Great Man in England' in letter to R. H. Dana, 17th June 1850, just after the publication of his first novel. (*Nineteenth Century Fiction*, Robert Lee Wolff, Garland Publishing, New York, 1981.)

2 Sir Charles Dilke, L. B. Walford, *Memories of Victorian London*, 1912, pp. 132–3.

3 W. P. Frith, *My Autobiography and Reminiscences*, Vol. II, 1887.

4 Berg Collection, New York Public Library.

5 Frank Archer, *An Actor's Notebooks*, London, 1912 (p. 281).

6 Princeton Collection, July 14th 1887.

7 Letter to Fred Lehmann, 28th December 1877. Princeton Collection.

8 Nathaniel Beard, 'Some Recollections of Yesterday', *Temple Bar*, July 1894 (p. 324).

9 Sue Lonoff, *Wilkie Collins and His Victorian Readers*, New York, 1982, p. 138.

10 Natalie Schroeder, '*Armadale*: A Book that is Daring Enough to Speak the Truth', *Wilkie Collins Society Journal*, Vol. III, 1983.

11 Letter to Sarony in New York, 19th March 1887, University of Iowa.

12 'Bold Words by a Bachelor', *My Miscellanies*, Vol. II, London, 1863.

APPENDIX C

Wilkie Collins's Bank Account

Wilkie Collins and Charles Collins, his brother, opened bank accounts at Coutts and Co., 59 Strand, London, in the summer of 1860. Wilkie's account began on August 22nd 1860 and Charles's on July 18th 1860. Coutts and Co. are still in the Strand and are now part of the National Westminster Bank Group. I am indebted to the Chairman and Directors of Coutts and to Faith Clarke, my wife, (as a Collins descendant), for permission to use and quote from the Collins accounts. I am particularly indebted to Miss Veronica Stokes, the Chief Archivist at Coutts, not only for her help in examining and assessing the accounts but for her own earlier assessment of Charles Dickens's accounts at Coutts (*The Dickensian*, Vol. 68, 1972) which I found essential reading.

Wilkie Collins's father, William John Thomas Collins, opened an account at Coutts in 1844. It is clear that by that time William had already accumulated a welcome cushion of investments, as his account shows the regular dividend payments from government stocks and railway stocks. Wilkie is shown as the recipient of sums ranging from £5 to £20 in a period when he was in the tea trade and preparing for the bar.

On William's death in 1847, the account was closed and transferred to a new account 'Exors. of William John Thomas Collins' under the names of Mrs Harriet Collins, Rev. Dodsworth and John Bullar. From then until Harriet's death in 1868, the income remained fairly steady, consisting almost entirely of the return on investments. In the period up to 1860 both Wilkie and Charles were recipients of regular sums, but thereafter only Charles seemed to benefit.

These bank accounts are contained in large yearly ledgers written up in a strong, legible hand. Few details are given, apart from a brief line indicating the source or recipient of individual payments. The yearly totals and some knowledge of the individuals' names, however, enables one to build up a picture of Collins's financial situation and his pattern of income and expenditure.

While his mother's income remained between £600 and £700 and that of his brother between £600 and £1,000 throughout most of the 1860s, Wilkie's never dropped below £1,000 and in his peak year of 1868–69 (the accounts run from June to June) topped the £6,000 mark. (Both Wilkie's and Charles's accounts reflect the receipt of part of Harriet's capital in that year.)

The total income flowing through his account in the 1860s (the period of publication of *The Woman in White, No Name, Armadale* and *The Moonstone*) rose from £1,223 and £1,160 in 1860–61 and 1861–62, respectively, to £2,533 in 1863–64 and £3,823 in 1867–68, only dropping back temporarily, in 1866–67 to £1,931 (a year in which there appears to have been no income from writing). The largest individual payments into his account are quarterly items of £1,000 from Sampson Low in 1863–64, presumably for *Armadale*.

Apart from the peak year of 1868–69 which was affected by capital items, the peak income years were between 1867–68 and 1877–78. In two of those years his income was above £4,000 and in only two others did it drop below £3,000. From 1879–80 until his death in 1889, his annual income was around an average of £2,500 (dropping, exceptionally, to £1,472 in 1886–87). It is worth noting that Collins's peak income of £6,000 in 1868–69 would be worth about £160,000 in 1988.

His payments to Caroline Graves and Martha Rudd (always identified as 'Mrs Dawson' in his accounts) span a period between 1864 and 1889 in the case of Caroline and between 1869 and 1889 in the case of Martha. The first payment to Caroline (of £20) is recorded on August 23rd 1864; the first to Martha (also £20) is on December 28th 1869.

Payments to Caroline varied considerably both in amount and timing, no doubt reflecting her role within the house, since he clearly drew individual sums out himself (identified in the accounts as 'Him') and passed some of the balance to her. Harriet, Caroline's daughter, also received significant sums, particularly in the period following Caroline's marriage to Charles Clow when she was clearly running part of the household.

The payments to Martha (Rudd) Dawson were more regular, starting at a sum of £20 monthly and rising to £25 monthly in 1871. On his return from the United States, in 1874, the payments to Martha became more frequent, often weekly, and bigger, no doubt reflecting the growing needs of three children. Both Caroline and Martha received similar sums of £200 each from the 'Exors. Account' after his death.

Collins's pattern of life emerges naturally from the accounts. His expenditure on travel, hotels, wine, club subscriptions (Garrick, Atheneum and Royal Victoria Yacht Club), rental payments, insurance, school bills, furnishing – all flow through the accounts, alongside personal cash withdrawals under 'him' or 'house'. His own travel was clearly financed through cash withdrawals itemised as 'travelling expenditure' or 'circular notes' (the latter could be cashed at several places abroad listed on an accompanying Letter of Indication, presumably agreed before departure). He also paid cheques to recognised travel agents or bankers such as Fenzie and Co., Fribourg & Co., Iggulden & Co., Negra Frères, etc. Other, more domestic payments are revealed through payments to Heal & Sons (bed manufacturers and furnishers), Maple & Co. (furnishers), Benham & Co. (ironmongers and silversmiths), Justerini (wine-merchants), Dremel (wine-merchants), Grondona (Italian and French cook), Klumpp (bakers), Stechelback (tailor) and Bonham & Co. (auctioneers). Several still remain in business.

His friends' names also flow through the accounts; Edward Piggott, Charles Dickens, Charles Fechter, Frank Beard, Ada Cavendish.

BIBLIOGRAPHY

Books

Wilkie Collins to the Forefront, Ed. Nelson Smith & R. C. Terry, New York, 1995
The King of Inventors: A Life of Wilkie Collins, Catherine Peters, London, 1991
Wilkie Collins. A Biography, Kenneth Robinson, London, 1951 & 1974
The Life of Wilkie Collins, Noel Pharr Davis, University of Illinois, 1956
Wilkie Collins, Robert Ashley, London, 1952
The Life of William Collins, Wilkie Collins, London, 1848
Celebrities at Home, Edmund H. Yates, 1879 (Reprinted from *The World*)
Edmund Yates: His Recollections and Experiences, London & Leipzig, 1865
The House of Harper, J. Henry Harper, New York, 1912
On and Off the Stage, Mr & Mrs Bancroft, London, 1889
Recollections of Sixty Years, The Bancrofts, London, 1909
Victorian Wallflowers, Malcolm Elwin, London, 1934
Dickens & Daughter, Gladys Storey, London, 1939
Memories of Great Men and Women of the Age, S. C. Hall, London 1871 & 1877
Memoirs of an Author, Percy Fitzgerald, London, 1895
Memories of Half a Century, R. C. Lehmann, London, 1908
An Actor's Notebooks, Frank Archer, London
A Few Memories, Mary Anderson, London, 1896
The Eighteen Sixties, Ed. Drinkwater, London, 1932
Selected Essays, T. S. Eliot, 1907–1932
Wilkie Collins & Charles Reade, Parrish & Miller, London, 1940
Life and Letters of Sir John Millais, John G. Millais, London, 1897
Wilkie Collins, Le Fanu and Others, S. M. Ellis, London, 1931
The Letters of Charles Dickens: 1833–1870, Mamie Dickens & Georgina Hogarth, London, 1903
Excursions in Victorian Bibliography, Michael Sadleir, London, 1922
Recollections of Sir Henry Dickens, London, 1934
New Cambridge Bibliography, 1800–1900, Watson
Wilkie Collins: The Critical Heritage, Ed. Norman Page, London & Boston, 1974
Dickens and Mesmerism, Fred Kaplan, Princeton, 1975
Wilkie Collins, William H. Marshall, New York, 1975
The Flint and the Flame, Earle Davies, Missouri, 1963
Dickens Incognito, Felix Aylmer, London, 1959
Dickens, Hesketh Pearson, London, 1949
Letters of Charles Dickens to Wilkie Collins, Ed. Georgina Hogarth & Lawrence Hutton, London, 1892

BOOKS

The Life of Charles Dickens, John Forster, London, 1872–74

Charles Dickens as Editor, R. C. Lehmann, London, 1912

Mr & Mrs Charles Dickens: His Letters to Her, Walter Dexter, London, 1935

My Story, Hall Caine, London, 1908

Old Friends, William Winter, New York, 1909

Dickens to His Oldest Friend (Letters to Thomas Beard), Walter Dexter, London, 1932

Victorian Fiction, Harvard 1966 & New York 1978

Under the Management of Mr Charles Dickens, Robert Louis Brannan, Ithaca, New York, 1966

Gaiety Theatre of Enchantment, W. MacQuen Pope, London, 1949

Christina Rossetti, Lona Mosk Packer, California, 1963

Millais & the Ruskins, Mary Lutyens, New York, 1967

Dickens & Women, Michael Slater, London, 1983

Wilkie Collins & his Victorian Readers, Sue Lonoff, New York, 1982

Opium and the Romantic Imagination, Aletha Hayter, London, 1968

The Grays of Salisbury, Donald C. Whitton, San Francisco, 1976

Nineteenth Century Fiction Vol. I, Robert Lee Wolff, New York, 1981

The Unpublished Letters of Charles Dickens to Mark Lemon, Ed. W. Dexter, London, 1927

Charles Albert Fechter, Kate Field, New York, 1882

Charles Dickens, Mamie Dickens, London, 1885

Wilkie Collins, A Critical and Biographical Study by Dorothy Sayers, Ed. Professor E. R. Gregory, University of Toledo, 1977

Shapes That Pass, Julian Hawthorn, London, 1928

An Artist's Reminiscences, Rudolf Lehmann, London, 1894

Memories of Victorian London, L. B. Walford, London, 1912

Wilkie Collins: Ein Biographisch – Kritisch Versuch, E. Von Wolzogen, Leipzig, 1885

Henry Crabbe Robinson: Diary, Reminiscences & Correspondence, Ed. T. Sadler, London, 1869

The Life of John Linnell, Alfred T. Story, London, 1892

Ancestors & Friends, John F. Lehmann, London, 1962

Wilkie Collins: A Critical Survey of his Prose Fiction, R. V. Andrew, 1979

Wilkie Collins: An Annotated Bibliography 1889–1976, Kirk Bectz, New Jersey & London, 1978

Letters of Charles Dickens, W. Dexter, Nonesuch Press, London, 1938

The Letters of Charles Dickens, Pilgrim Edition Vols I–IV, Oxford, 1965–1977

Articles

'How I Wrote my Books', Wilkie Collins, *The Globe*, 1887

'Recollections of Wilkie Collins', Wybert Reeve, *Chambers's Journal*, 1906

'The Novels of Wilkie Collins', Edmund Yates, *Temple Bar*, August 1890

'Mr Wilkie Collins's Novels', Andrew Lang, *Contemporary Review*, January 1890

'Wilkie Collins', A. C. Swinburne, *Fortnightly Review*, November 1889

'Wilkie Collins in America', Clyde K. Hyder, University of Kansas Humanistic
  Studies, 1940

'Wilkie Collins & *The Woman in White*', Clyde K. Hyder, Publications of the Modern
  Language Association (University of Kansas), 1939

'A Wilkie Collins Check List', *English Studies in Africa*, R. V. Andrew, 1960

Obituary, *The Spectator*, 1889

'A Living Story-Teller', Harry Quilter, *Contemporary Review*, 1888

'Some Recollections of Yesterday', Nathaniel Beard, *Temple Bar*, July 1894

'The Wilkie Collins Collection', Robert Ashley, *Princeton University Literary Chronicle*,
  No. 17, 1956

'Wilkie Collins', Arthur Compton-Rickett, *The Bookman*, 1912

'From Mystery to Mission', J. I. M. Stewart, *Times Literary Supplement*, September 6,
  1974

'Seeker of Sensation', C. P. Snow, *Financial Times*, December 19, 1974

Appleton's Journal, September 3, 1870

Wilkie Collins Society Journal Vols I–VI, California & London, 1981–86

'Our Portrait Gallery: Mr Wilkie Collins', *Men and Women*, February 5, 1882

'Wilkie Collins and *The Leader*', Kirk Beetz, *Victorian Periodicals Review*, Toronto,
  1982

'Men of Mark', Edmund Yates, *The Train*

'Wilkie Collins to Charles Reade: Some Unpublished Letters', Thomas D. Clareson,
  Victorian Essays: A Symposium, 1967

'Wilkie Collins: A Collector's and Bibliographer's Challenge', Andrew Gasson, *The
  Private Library*, Summer 1980

INDEX